Anthropomorphism in Christian Theology

Explorations in Philosophy and Theology

**Series Editors: Kevin Hart (University of Virginia, USA) and
Jeffrey Bloechl (Boston College, USA)**

This series promotes philosophical and theological works committed to drawing on both disciplines, without either holding them strictly apart or overlooking important differences between them. The series favours philosophical approaches covered under the umbrella of 'continental European,' by which is meant a general commitment to developments sharpened since the work of Kant, German idealism, and Nietzsche. It provides a space for theological approaches historically informed and actively engaged via modern thought and culture. The series will focus on Christian theology in the first instance, but not to the exclusion of work in dialogue with multiple religions. Expanding the historical and cultural origins of both continental European philosophy and Christian theology, the series will embrace a global outlook. The series thus provides a platform for work from Africa, Asia, Australia, North and South America. Featuring edited collections, single-authored works, and translations managed by an active and global editorial board, the series is one of the main destinations for scholarship in the continental philosophy of religion today.

Editorial Board

Sarah Coakley, University of Cambridge, UK
Werner Jeanrond, University of Oslo, Norway
Jean-Yves Lacoste, Paris
Adriaan Peperzak, Loyola University of Chicago, USA
Pheme Perkins, Boston College, USA
David Tracy, University of Chicago, USA
Claudia Welz, Aarhus University, Denmark
Olivier Boulnois, École Pratique des Hautes Etudes, France
Nythamar de Oliveira, Pontifical Catholic University of Rio Grande do Sul, Brazil
James Heisig, Nanzan Institute for Religion and Culture, Japan
Robyn Horner, Australian Catholic University, Australia
Leonard Katchekpele, University of Strasbourg, France
Judith Wolfe, Durham University, UK

Available Titles

By Faith Alone, by Lev Shestov and translated by Stephen P. Van Trees
The Book of Experience, by Emmanuel Falque and translated by George Hughes

Forthcoming Titles

The Poetics of the Sensible, by Stanislas Breton and translated by Sarah Horton

Anthropomorphism in Christian Theology

The Apophatics of the Sensible

William C. Hackett

BLOOMSBURY ACADEMIC
LONDON • NEW YORK • OXFORD • NEW DELHI • SYDNEY

BLOOMSBURY ACADEMIC
Bloomsbury Publishing Plc, 50 Bedford Square, London, WC1B 3DP, UK
Bloomsbury Publishing Inc, 1385 Broadway, New York, NY 10018, USA
Bloomsbury Publishing Ireland, 29 Earlsfort Terrace, Dublin 2, D02 AY28, Ireland

BLOOMSBURY, BLOOMSBURY ACADEMIC and the Diana logo are trademarks
of Bloomsbury Publishing Plc

First published in Great Britain 2024
This paperback edition published 2025

Copyright © William C. Hackett, 2024

William C. Hackett has asserted his right under the Copyright, Designs and
Patents Act, 1988, to be identified as Author of this work.

Series design: Ben Anslow
Photography © Sashanna Hart

All rights reserved. No part of this publication may be: i) reproduced or
transmitted in any form, electronic or mechanical, including photocopying,
recording or by means of any information storage or retrieval system without
prior permission in writing from the publishers; or ii) used or reproduced in
any way for the training, development or operation of artificial intelligence
(AI) technologies, including generative AI technologies. The rights holders
expressly reserve this publication from the text and data mining exception
as per Article 4(3) of the Digital Single Market Directive (EU) 2019/790.

Bloomsbury Publishing Inc does not have any control over, or responsibility for,
any third-party websites referred to or in this book. All internet addresses given
in this book were correct at the time of going to press. The author and publisher
regret any inconvenience caused if addresses have changed or sites have
ceased to exist, but can accept no responsibility for any such changes.

A catalogue record for this book is available from the British Library.

A catalog record for this book is available from the Library of Congress.

ISBN: HB: 978-1-3503-5911-6
PB: 978-1-3503-5915-4
ePDF: 978-1-3503-5912-3
eBook: 978-1-3503-5913-0

Series: Explorations in Philosophy and Theology

Typeset by Deanta Global Publishing Services, Chennai, India

For product safety related questions contact productsafety@bloomsbury.com.

To find out more about our authors and books visit www.bloomsbury.com
and sign up for our newsletters.

Contents

Preface	vi
Introduction: "To Make Tangible the Inexpressible"	1

First

1	A Religious Question (Balthasar)	13
2	Anthropomorphism and the Angel: The Anthropic Principle	29

Second

3	Between Contemplation and Concepts (Bultmann)	55
4	Anthropomorphism and Some Aspects of Modern Thought	74

Third

5	Symbolical Apophatics (Pseudo-Dionysius the Areopagite)	117
6	Anthropomorphism and Realism	142

Fourth

7	The Priority of the Image in Christology (Cyril of Alexandria)	163
8	Anthropomorphism and Transcendence	176

Fifth

9	Concluding Sign	197

Appendix: Annotations to a Few *Loci Classici*	211
Notes	220
Bibliography	241
Index	248

Preface

The paradox, the glory, and perhaps often the tragedy of the human experience are that in the two basic dimensions of human pertinence, knowledge and action, utility is primary. For knowledge to arise or for action to make its crease *in the world*, there must be purpose. In all intelligible human knowledge and action, the observer can discern an end, a goal, a *telos*. If you see me placing an inordinate amount of pickles and mustard on my hamburger, it is not for nothing. There is a reason. Like every other human event, whether one of knowledge or action, however banal or profound, utility is involved. But that is not all: there is also enjoyment. Realizing the algorithm or set of algorithms that mimic a range of human emotional responses to set stimuli elicits a certain degree of pleasure as does squeezing the mustard tube onto a crisp pile of sliced, pickled cucumbers. In both instances, utility is aimed, the activity has purpose, and when the end is realized, an amount of pleasure is involved. In the case of AI as well as in condiment usage, the primary end transcends the proximate one just described. In the first case, it is supremely technological: if we can imitate human emotions more transparently then, say, doing the deed with a sex robot may become as pleasurable as doing it with a real person (Or more? Ah, the beguiling enchantment of modern science . . .). Programmatically, sex robots may become a viable cure to pervasive male loneliness and alienation. No doubt, such a technologization of "emotion" would only exacerbate, dangerously, modern male loneliness, but that is neither here nor there. In the second case, the pleasure of squeezing the mustard tube (always shake first!) is only an anticipation of the real pleasure of biting into a warm beef patty topped with cold pickles sauced to dripping with yellow American mustard set between halves of a sesame crusted bun.

In the know-how of condiment usage and algorithm technologization, just as in every other kind of human knowledge-action, there is, then, a mixture of use and enjoyment. We have an ancient philosopher, Augustine of Hippo, to thank for the distinction. For him, both use and enjoyment are instances of a higher thing, which he calls "love." You can love something for its own sake, and that is enjoyment. The thing you purpose is the end you desire to accomplish. Enjoyment knocks on the door of "happiness." You can also love something as a means to something else and that is use. The whole human problem, thought Augustine, involves a confusion of the usable and enjoyable: God is the supremely lovable and hence the true source of happiness; the world is the supremely usable and can only be loved when used as a means to discovering the enjoyable behind and beyond it. Let us take one certain thing from Augustine here: God and the world are wholly distinct, and it is right to treat them wholly differently. The paradox, the glory, and, no doubt, the source of the tragedy of the human experience are found in the intellectual and moral manners of confusing this distinction. We are tangled up with the world and can only know God, wholly beyond the intelligible order of the world, through that intelligible order itself.

God's distinction from the world is wholly distinct from the intelligibility we discover by making distinctions within the world. One reason for our limitation is that our distinctions arise for us through the use we want to make of the world. Take modern science for example. The symbol-systems that make up the tools of modern science conform our intelligence to the world in a narrowly utilitarian way. With modern science and its technologically oriented symbols, we are presented with a face of the world that only speaks the language we are using to address it. One thing this points out to us already is that our world-tangled sort of knowledge is symbolical: we represent to ourselves things of the world in their patterns and differences through constructions aimed at specific ends, constructions that do not coincide with the things themselves but which validly bring them to mind, making them present in their absence.[1]

Another kind of human knowledge in regard to the world is found in religion. It is no exception to the utilitarian rule, although through its symbols, experienced in ritual and explained in myth, our utilitarian attunement to the world is perhaps as broad as humanly possible. In religion, humans "use" the world to make contact with its source and its end, its foundation and basis. We rearrange the furniture of the world, so to speak, in order to cause it to signify what is in excess of it that makes it ultimately meaningful for us. The symbols of religious intelligence are sacred to us not only because they bring us into contact with the source of life and being itself ("God") but also, more profoundly, because we believe them to be enactments of our knowledge and action of God that coincide with divine knowledge and action of and upon us. We are interfacing with God through the world. In religious knowledge and action then, our utility of the world becomes one with the divine purpose. This use of the world would be eo ipso the highest possible enjoyment attainable within it.

The present study wants to articulate an initial response to the question of the *divine* purpose in and with the world precisely where and how our human purposes become transparent to it. A line in Christos Yannaras's *Elements of Faith* I take as a clear description of what is sought. Belief about the world is predicated on its valuation through "use": if the world, on the Christian account, is "used," through "ascetical apprenticeship" to Christ, as a "gift of love," then the Christian community's belief about the world can be exegeted through an investigation into "the principle of the uniqueness of things, such as the possibility for matter to incarnate the relationship of man with God, to share in the life of the uncreated."[2] That Christian "principle of the uniqueness of things" I attempt to understand a little better through the following pages. The concept of "anthropomorphism" I use as a diagnostic problem-concept allowing the principle to be expressed at least to a certain pitch of its difficulty, that is, to be wondered at. The thesis is that figurative symbolization is more capable of signifying such a principle than is the conceptual-theoretical approach, which turns out to be a moment or stage in a wider process: the initiation into the apophatic truth that (determines human life and) requires a verification of empirical participation before concepts are born and beyond their extinguishment: an apophatics of the sensible. I can only leave this to you but perhaps this work might be read with a share of the "ascetical attitude" at the heart of cosmological ecclesiality, namely, an act of human freedom seeking to *use* it as a gift of love, not as a data-object to be exploited for egotistical ends. That is the spirit, at least in aspiration, with which it was composed: an attitude, I would like to think, making more likely anyone's understanding of the very principle of the uniqueness of things that is its reason.

W. C. H.

Introduction

"To Make Tangible the Inexpressible"

"Justice and Mercy," said Léon Bloy, "are *identical* and consubstantial in their absolutes." He continued:

> Here is what neither the sentimentalist nor the fanatic is willing to understand. A teaching that proposes the Love of God as its supreme end above all needs to be virile, under pain of avowing all the illusions of self-love or of carnal love. It is all too easy to emasculate souls by teaching them nothing but the precept of loving one's brothers, to the hurt of all the other precepts which you seek to hide from them. What one gets in this way is a flabby and sticky religion, more fearful in its effects than even Nihilism itself.[1]

Because of what is given it to think, Christian intelligence, or so said Florensky, is an intelligence that makes a virtue out of contradiction. His disciple, Bulgakov, virtually defined dogma by its contradictory nature, making a principle out of what for Kant was evidence of failure: antinomy. For these Russian thinkers, the task of dogmatic theology is to disclose and follow the intensification of the logic of reason's basic antinomies in order to evince the capacity of this world of earth to signify, through its terminating breakup into contradictory conclusions, the speech of heaven. The hieroglyphs of heavenly speech, scattered throughout the world and holding within themselves the truth about our human condition and about the final meaning of our world, are indecipherable without a key furnished from above. The key to the decipherment of the enigmas of the world and of our humanity flowering on the thousand hills of human culture is the Incarnation of the Son of God, which joins the irreconcilable absolutes of the heavenly and earthly worlds: the Absolute, revealed as a tri-hypostitic Personality, on the one hand, and the absolute of creaturely nature in humanity, revealed as the image of God, impossibly set over against him through the fall, on the other hand. I say "impossibly" because God's creation partakes of his goodness and therefore cannot be evil but through contradiction in excess of our capacity to comprehend. Says Bloy, with precision: "The evil of this world is of angelic origin and cannot be expressed in any language."[2] Evil is incomprehensible, like a parodic inversion of the Absolute incomprehensibility of God (and, for that matter, the relatively absolute incomprehensibility of humanity). Because they exist, in themselves, in God, that is, in eclipse of world, we cannot think divine justice and divine mercy together in their complete identity in God. And yet, we have been given the controlling and paradigmatic image of the crucified Christ, which manifests this unity in the world, beyond our understanding.

A major task of theological thinking—whether, like Bulgakov, an exercise of dogmatic theology, or like Bloy (how to put it?), literary or spiritual authorship—is to do the work of holding both ends of the antinomy (whichever antinomy one chooses: the Hypostatic Union, the Triune Nature, divine foreknowledge and predestination, creaturely freedom and divine omnipotence, law and grace, the coexistence of good and evil . . .) as long as one can. In this task, the theological thinker is like a rodeo rider, a skinny cowboy holding on to the back of a 1700-pound bull seething with virile power: in only a few seconds, he will be thrown to the ground and potentially trampled or kicked in the teeth. He rides the longest who hands himself over completely to the vital energy of the bull, whose rolling red eyes and stomping flanks quiver with a violent beauty that impatiently wants to shake the world.

Bloy called himself a "pilgrim of the Absolute": I would like to think any serious theological thinker, when thinking about his theological thinking in any adequate way, would have to take on the same mantle. In his introduction to the 1947 introduction to Raisa Maritain's selection from Bloy's writings, Jacques Maritain said of Bloy that "his natural habitat was *dissatisfaction*, in the intellectual order as in all the others."[3] By this, Maritain meant to signify the source of Bloy's genius. Bloy felt the human tragedy to a unique degree: he was "disconsolate at not possessing now on earth the vision of the divine glory."[4] Imagine, for a moment, that this feeling of disconsolation—and I invite you to compare Schleiermacher's strangely compelling, relatively valid, but finally inadequate stand-in (*das schlechthinnige Abhängigkeitgefühle*)—is the authentic Christian religious feeling, sine qua non, which gives Christianity its unique character—at least, at the level of emotion, which (later studies mentioned in the text are meant to help you understand) cannot be separated from intellectual activity inasmuch as it is human, an activity on earth before heaven.[5] Perhaps we would be on to something in that thought experiment after Léon Bloy. Despite a perennial temptation to misunderstand, to simplify, to escape the *weight* of the difficulty, the heart of the Christian longing, if we were to tear our own flesh and lay it bare, ragged, insatiable and beating hungrily before us, is *not* to leave this world of trial for a heavenly homeland, but rather to see *and to be* the transparency of this world to divine glory.

The controlling or paradigmatic biblical image is "a New Heavens and a New Earth," a new (i.e., "renewed") creation, a lived, conscious and fully awoken experience of self and world no longer alienated from the divine presence, from (same thing) the source of purpose of its Life, no longer ruled by, defeated by, death, but "liberated from bondage to decay," in a union of perfect love with the Uncreated Good through an undying bond and ever-deepening bliss-joy-beatitude wherein an ecstasy of ached longing and a slaked plunging into the Desired are one—unto eternity. Bloy was inconsolable in the face of the tragic distance of this world from that divine glory, a glory that is the key that alone unlocks an infinity of goods and an eternity of wonders hidden in the world but that remain locked away behind a screen of injustice, banality and suffering. His inconsolability matched the depth of the tragedy, just as the pathos of the tragedy matched, in an inverse way, the bliss of our original human intimacy with God:

> The basis of Paradise, or the idea of Paradise is union with God starting in the present life, which is to say the infinite Distress of man's heart, and union with God in the future Life, which is to say Beatitude.[6]

We can learn a lot from Bloy, but we cannot feel what he felt, to the degree that he felt it, unless (I think) given such by God. And this is a gift of great suffering, if also a strange suffering that secretly bears an abyss of bliss beneath its wildly toiling waves: the pathos of ached longing ("infinite Distress") is an anticipation of the very beatitude that Scripture calls the vision of the face of God, or (in another controlling or paradigmatic metaphor) the marriage of heaven and earth. Both images are eschatological, and that is significant: Christianity is an eschatological religion, if I can risk the expression, by which I only mean to say that Christianity is the practice of the mystery hidden in God but disclosed in Jesus Christ, the *apocalypsis tou mysteriou*, the revealed mystery of God's original purpose for creation "hidden from the foundation of the world," a singular purpose drawn up into a deeper and deeper enigma from the time of Abraham's election, through the exodus, wilderness wanderings, giving of the Law, inheritance of the Land, the gift of a king and the exile and restoration of the people and finally unfurled, established, and made manifest at the climax of the covenant in the death and resurrection of the *Messiach Yisrael*, wherein the problem of the universality of the reign of Israel's covenant God is overcome, and in whom the union of heaven and earth is achieved, the new creation project launched.

This *apocalypsis tou mysteriou*, "revelation of the mystery," bleeds backward, from the end, coloring the entire age-long witness of Sacred History, making of it a single story pointing to this very purpose revealed and brought about in Jesus Christ. Bloy's Christianity, strange, visceral, and wild ("foolish" in the Pauline sense), is the activity of a mad flowering of that deep longing for eschatological union in the fruit of faith, hope and love here below, ahead of the end, and his constructive expressions are redistributions of what is given in the earthly scene (in its personal, social, political, economic, and all other domains) in order to forge symbols that signify the hidden things, to *show* that the world is made for God, a vast cosmic temple built for his infinitely Just, infinitely Good, infinitely Living and Holy Presence and stewarded by his creatures, *humanity*—that strange union of matter and spirit—in pride of place. Humanity possesses in Christ "that into which angels long to look" and Bloy wants to remind us of the wonder, the terrible wonder of such a "weight of glory" borne *now* by humanity. Such signification is accomplished in Bloy's stories by *intensifying the chiaroscuro* of inanity and wonder, the repugnant and the beautiful, injustice and justice, through the harshest means possible, referring to excrement one moment, and the tears of a mother for her newborn child in the next.

We want to know and experience the definitive in itself and as such. We want to behold God. And so we *need* the world to become replete with the limitless goodness of the infinite. The definitive alone will make sense of our greatest, undying enigmas that not only problematize our existence but also inspire our greatness: love, freedom, evil, goodness, justice. The definitive must be something real, something alive, with flesh, something worthy of our humanity, which, on the one hand, can only absolutely exceed our temporal boundedness, our limitations and our failures, but which also, at the same time, must not *eclipse our world* of meanings and values in such a way as to shake them off like dust. Rather it must draw them up, somehow, into their full stature, which we know, feel, and demand is signified already in their very shadow-forms that we now taste so obscurely through the bleeding chiaroscuro of the human experience. Theological thinking, thought reblended with prayer and praise, intelligence reblended with feeling, metaphysics and theology reblended with mystic or spiritual writing,[7] every stop must be pulled in order to signify *something* even partially worthy of the world of human experience, longing and anticipation, of the goodness or holiness or justice or benevolence or beauty or terror of God who at once infinitely *is*, infinitely *aware* and infinitely *enjoyment* of this infinitely being-known, who is, in short, super-abundantly alive and free, and who addresses his creature at the final end toward which he steers all things, the

Last Judgment where there is no longer any creaturely support but only a face to face before this All-Consuming Life. Anyone presuming to think and write about Christian things must endeavor to something worthy of the chiaroscuro of our humanity, of the goodness and tragedy of the world and of the glory, the all-surpassing glory of God—and of a common destiny of these.

In his description of Bloy's work, Maritain makes a far-reaching distinction that places Bloy in the total universe of Christian thought and its traditional disciplinary division of labor erected through its rich, millennia-long history. In his dissatisfied disconsolation at the alienation of humanity from God, of earth from heaven, at our paradoxical disenfranchisement from our home, the very earth upon which we spring up, rove, and die along a fragile crust, and also at the repulsive sin, injustice and ignorance that marks our distance from the divine glory that is our only good and true inheritance, Bloy, says Maritain, "did not use human language, as do metaphysicians and theologians in their formulas, to try to express, according to the imperfect mode of our concepts, whatever we are able to know of transcendent reality." Do not let the compounding of phrases in this sentence obfuscate for you the elegance of its insight: metaphysics and theology (at least when articulated *in their distinction from* "spiritual writing," the authorship of "mystics," even disconsolate ones like Bloy) are marked, sine qua non, by the dominance of concepts and formulas (or theory) in order to express that about ultimate things of which human knowledge is capable. Fine. But this is not Bloy's enterprise. He aims to reach deeper, somehow, into the heart of the theological and metaphysical than concept and theory (on their own) allow. "[B]ut on the contrary," Maritain continues, "he used it [i.e., human language] to try to evoke that which in this reality goes beyond the mode of our concepts, and remains unknown to us."[8] The pilgrim of the Absolute, unsatisfied and perpetually restless, toiling in a spiritual peregrination that is goaded ever on by a painful disaffection with the imperfection of reality rooted in a soul-rending vision of and (same thing) aching for total and complete justice in the world, turns to that through which this vision is promised and this longing is imparted: the Scriptures. "The study of the sacred page is, as it were, the soul of sacred theology."[9]

Scripture, a library of Jewish meditation literature composed over millennia, is the perpetual sustaining source, the life force of theological activity. For theological thinking to be theological—in the Christian sense—Scripture, its images, metaphors, symbols, stories, categories, and (yes) concepts must seep into one's soul and transmute the feelings, joys, hopes and longings, and intelligence of a human being, *making them Christian*. This occurs through a lifetime of meditative reading. There are no shortcuts. The third study with which you will join me, taking a distinction of Bultmann's as starting point, is meant to be a reflection on the necessary passage of conceptual articulation from contemplative meditation.

We can reach into the truth of the final all-encompassing beatific vision, "which precisely no sign will ever be able to express," says Maritain, where our concepts are undone, becoming dark and going silent, by means of "parables and hyperboles." These are called upon by Bloy as by the mystics in their kind of discourse. Concept and theory articulate what we can say, "whatever we are able to know," and to move beyond that, *to proceed any further into the mystery*, looming ever virgin and anew before us, we must inevitably return, at the far end of our exhausted conceptual articulations, to the figurative and hyperbolic. Like the mystics, then, Bloy used words "less to state truths directly then to procure . . . the feeling of mystery and of its actual presence," closer to us and more intensely vibrant than our expressions can signify through the normal process of purification that takes up a distance from the particular through generalization. Instead, Bloy "used reason and intellectual speculation according to a mode more experimental than demonstrative" with the purpose of expressing "reality in the very darkness that joins it to this feeling [of the immanent *and* imminent presencing of the divine glory]," in imitation of and complete creative debt to (as noted earlier) Holy Scripture, which, in the Pseudo-Dionysian perspective (Study 5) authorizes such a return to the images, metaphors, hyperboles, and stories in order to speak more adequately of divine things than our metaphysical and theological concepts (which really are themselves umbilically bound to the earth *through* the figures, images, and narratives that give rise to them in the first place and which they can only exegete and never exhaust, though they are ever-forgetful of this harsh fact of their anthropomorphic character). For Bloy, "a word is used primarily *to make tangible the inexpressible*," not to articulate what we can say, in order then to signify, by negation, what cannot be said, through the dialectical process of negative theology.[10] Such a dialectic is *only a beginning*, once reason reaches its end, in *sigē*, silence before the divine mystery that, from out of this presence *speaks* and calls forth the creature to an undying adventure. This perspective is also that of St. Cyril of Alexandria, in his approach to the union of divinity and humanity in the one Jesus Christ, explored in the seventh study.

Making tangible the inexpressible through the redundance of the figurative that shakes and topples our conceptual towers that reach into the clouds, on the one hand, and the conceptual work of climbing these towers into the dark and dizzying clouds above, on the other, alas, are two distinct enterprises, but two which cannot and must not be separated. The Church has named a Mystical Doctor, and the wisdom of such a title points to the entire game the present work has the ambition to call to the attention of any theological thinker. St. John of the Cross used the Scholastic conceptual apparatus to exegete his poems, at least partially, but only to give us our bearings, to help us enter into the cloud, where a fully human language of figuration, of delight, awe, terror, wonder and joy reigns, through which we may worship the Almighty with every ounce of strength and gift, and for which the great mystery of language is such a treasure. St. John of the Cross says somewhere that a single human idea is of greater value than the universe, since we can *form a concept* of the world in its totality. Even more, we can contrast the whole with the God who exceeds it beyond the entire order of contrasts that makes up our human kind of signification *within the world*. This is noteworthy, but perhaps even more so is what the present text is devoted to: the recognition that such a valuable thought is only the beginning, only the new beginning of signification, where idea dissolves into cloudy abstraction, located at the farthest outer limits of a reality effusive in unbearable intensities and unfathomable excesses. Hegel pointed out long ago that our idea of being, at its point of perfection, and our idea of nothing, at its own, converge in a *coincidentia oppositorum* (the ideas, note, not the *res* they signify). It is this convergence, where our greatest ideas erupt in a puff of smoke that may become the moment of awakening, in a pseudo-Dionysian, Juan de la Cruzian, and Léon Bloyian approach, to the higher way, to a signifying of transcendence that is as rich and glorious as a mountain scramble with sudden panoramas, dangerous overhangs, and breathtaking, vertiginous heights looming around every turn, but that appears to the "scholar and the learned of this age" (this *aeon*, or present, fallen ordering of the *kosmos*, with its own spiritual economy ruled by *thanatos*, death) as a lower and lesser way appropriate for (say) the unthinking Joe Schmoe with his loud, snotty children in the pew, or the pursed-lip church lady with her mantilla and beads, for unenlightened minds, that is, of marginal talent and weakness ("foolishness," again, in the Pauline sense).

"Hyperbole," said Bloy, "is a microscope for discriminating between insects, and a telescope for drawing near to stars."[11] Without a microscope or telescope, we are restrained to the natural limitations of our vision, so profoundly restricted to the slight dynamic range of a certain set of wavelengths on the electromagnetic spectrum called visible light and, under the right conditions, between .1 millimeters at the small scale and several hundred miles on the scale of distance. We are delimited to the patch of earth upon which we live and move. For us the vast, profound, and idiosyncratic eclipses of our normative intellectual-physical laws uncovered within the movement and relation of energy and time at the subatomic and metacosmic levels suggest that reality is much denser, more profound and peculiar than the little circle of our physicality would at first evince—but not to modern science or the world's classical religions or the intellectual traditions correlate with these. The deeper we look, even from within the scientific reduction (when its power comes around to a religious, mortal, sensibility and awe), and the more we ponder from within this circle of limitation, our frayed outer limit of the real, the more difficult, profound, and full of wonder does the world show itself to be. We penetrate more deeply into the depths of reality when we are made capable of sensing more acutely the ultimate mystery in its actual presence and its actual absence, its (as it were) "already" and "not yet." The apophatics of the sensible that seeks (and partially shows, through anticipation from within the chiaroscuro of human history, whether by the darkness of distance or the brightness of proximity) the ultimate vision of repletion of the earth with the divine glory ("as the waters cover the sea") is practiced, intellectually, through devotion to a kenotic kind of rationality that returns to the sensible sphere in devotion to the Creator fully descended into the world, identifying himself with a piece of the world and a fragment of history. It acclaims (so to speak) the capacity of the lower to reach the higher more immediately and directly than the spiritual procedure of abstraction. It devotes itself (intellectually as much as affectively or spiritually) to the hyperbolic significations of literary art shown capable of making tangible the inexpressible. Paired with the four studies noted earlier, the second part of each division attempts to identify the issue, giving it a traditional name, "anthropomorphism," and erects a distance from the phenomenon in order to provide a conceptual, theoretical handle on it from the vantage of four domains, within negative theology (Study 6), in relation to the concept of transcendence (Study 8), in modern thought, indebted to a revolutionary breakdown in the concept of transcendence and also, implicitly, to negative theology, within which it may profitably be considered inscribed (Study 4). The second half of the first pair of the text (Study 2) introduces the distinction much involved through the remainder of the text, between angelic and anthropic kinds of knowing.

Generally speaking, the text, from the starting point of this introduction, wades in and then immerses itself through a kind of deepening progression into the apophatics of the sensible that is—I would like to think—a distinctive feature of theological thinking in the peculiar living religion, part-madness, part shrewd sanity, Christianity. Two modern theologians (Balthasar, then Bultmann), therefore, are followed by two of the greatest theological thinkers of Christian antiquity, the Pseudo-Dionysius (*c.* sixth century) and Cyril of Alexandria (fifth century). With these latter thinkers, the apophatics of the sensible is, I think, on full display. To it we may yet backtrack.

A tiny phrase appears in the annals of western letters: "and a different kind of failure."[12] I would like it to serve as a kind of exergue to the present exercise. It does not—humor me, for a moment—come from Bloy but from Eliot. The poem is justly famous. And if copyright restrictions prohibit me from quoting more than the slightest splinter of "East Coker," let the reader recall that it comes from section five of the great poem, which begins, presumably, with an allusion to the first line of the first part Dante's *Comedia*, begun *nel mezzo del cammin di nostra vita*, halfway through a human lifespan, lost in the woods. This section of "East Coker" may serve as a meta-reflection on the poet's self-appointed task to say something true and definitive, something transcendent, something even worthy of God, yet always failing. He calls it making a "raid on the inarticulate" with equipment (human language) not up snuff. Eliot, well more than Dante, it seems, knows the task is impossible. His only business is to make the attempt. I suspect that Bloy would not have liked that phrase, "raid on the inarticulate,"[13] not because it was not a phrase worthy of art or because it was (merely) not his own invention but for another reason. For him, signification of the divine was less a raid of human creativity into the domain of transcendence than an impassioned, awoken response to the raid of the divine into a realm (the human) that would consider it an inconvenience and that truly has the power (at least temporarily) to ignore it, to live as if it is of no import to earthly affairs. Writing was only an expression of the truly human discontent that drives Christian "hunger and thirst for righteousness," a response to the raid of the divine into the realm of human affairs, which, before healing it—or precisely as the means of its healing—must reveal to it the depths of its sickness. And that requires a harsh, burning light. The following attempt to sketch some aspects of the apophatics of the sensible partakes (in aspiration) of Bloy's sensibility if also looking with respectful admiration at Eliot's phrase and the entire poem within which it occurs.

First

1. A Religious Question (Balthasar)
2. Anthropomorphism and the Angel: The Anthropic Principle

1

A Religious Question (Balthasar)

[The Fathers] say that God and man are paradigms of each other: God is humanized to man through love for humankind to the degree that man, enabled through love, deifies himself to God; and man is caught up noetically by God to what is unknown to the extent that he manifests God, who is invisible by nature, through the virtues.

—Maximus the Confessor, *Ambigua* 10 (PG 91.1113 BC)

In the opening pages of the last part-volume of his *Theological Aesthetics*,[1] concerned with the biblical conception of the divine glory, Balthasar poses a religious question, that is, a question that serves as the deep motivation for believing reflection, for faith seeking understanding. I will quote him at length. He asks:

> How can revelation take place? How can the abyss and Ocean of all reality make itself knowable and perceivable to the "drop in the bucket" and the "speck of dust" (Is. 40.15) that is man? How can the "grass that withers" and the "flower that fades" be touched by the "word of our God, that will stand for ever" (Is. 40.8)? To have an inkling of the divine, to adore it from afar, to learn to be silent before it and to allow it to hold sway: this may be granted to creatures at their very limits. Such an intimation appears to creatures to be revelation enough: on the shore of their finitude they discover the Wholly Other, and buffeted all about by the surge of its breakers creatures learn something like piety—a sense of awe before the undecipherable Meaning that pervades and directs even the apparent meaninglessness of their existence. They can also invent gods for themselves, cosmic or supra-cosmic beings that exhibit themselves majestic and free at a level where men stand in the grip of fate. They can elaborate for their gods qualities which they themselves would like to have, or qualities that they do not have but would like to understand better. They put words in the mouths of their gods which correspond to their own dreams and longings; they ascribe to them deeds and powers that surpass their own, and they manifest their idea

of the absolute in concrete gestures, prayers and sacrifices by means of which they put themselves under the protection of their gods and participate in their praeternatural might.

But suppose that these pious attempts of humanity to penetrate into the region of the inscrutable are all pushed aside by a contrary movement whereby the Abyss and Ocean of all reality, on its own initiative, presses in upon humanity in order to disclose itself, in order to reveal itself as "what" it "is": if this *could* happen, how *would it have* to happen? Does not man immediately give to everything that approaches him as an infinite or absolute reality a limited form and a relativity which fixes it as the "other pole" of a finite relationship, which is the only thing of which he is capable? Or can the infinite—which, as Abyss and Ocean of all reality, must be fullness of omnipotence—bring about what is unthinkable for man and make itself known, in spite of everything, as what it "is"?[2]

Under the sign of this question ("dramatically" articulated and appropriately so), Balthasar begins his labyrinthine treatment of the biblical revelation as an account of the self-revelation of the divine glory, which culminates, many hundreds of pages later, in the composite and kaleidoscopic image of Jesus Christ portrayed in the Gospels—with all the startling simplicity and fragility that marks the face of Christ that gazes at us through the palimpsest of these sacred documents. But here, at the beginning, Balthasar's answer to this question, or rather his presentation of God's answer in the biblical revelation, is only the presentation of a deep problem, what he calls the "problematic situation that is posited by the *kabod-Yahweh* in the Old Testament."[3] This problem is articulated by Balthasar as the dialectic at the heart of God's sensory manifestation, that is, the *kabod* (glory). First, the *kabod* of God always, as far as the biblical revelation is concerned, involves the *sensory manifestation* of God (therefore making a "theological aesthetics," a doctrine of the perception, *aesthēsis*, of God, relevant in the first place), not only because the human being is not, like the angel, a purely spiritual being, but also because, simply, the Creator takes the world as it is when he reveals himself in it.[4] Hence, the sensory manifestation of the divine *kabod*, that is, the theophanies of God presented in Scripture (the burning bush, the glory cloud, quaking mountains, the whisper to Elijah, etc.), is *not* the divine *kabod* in itself but only, Balthasar says, its "indication" (*Anzeige*).[5] In a 2010 article, Greek Orthodox theologian John Manoussakis suggested that through the utilization of this term, Balthasar makes implicit appeal to Husserl's distinction in the *Logical Investigations* between the two types of signs (*Zerche*): expression (*Ausdrücke*) and indication (*Anzeichen*).[6]

Let us recall the basic elements of Husserl's distinction. For Husserl, an *expression* is a sign that mediates meaning, is primarily linguistic (but not exclusively), and is a material vehicle "animated" (*beseelt*) by the "meaning intention" of the speaker.[7] An *indication*, on the other hand, is a sign that establishes a "causal link" between two things: smoke is the sign that there is a fire. Expressions and indications are often "interwoven" (*verflochten*): all expressions, says Husserl, except expression in isolated mental life, are indications since an expressive sign always indicates the presence of the meaning intention itself, which is a fundamental part of the expressive signification. The reverse is not the case: indications cannot be expressions. The "indicative relation" is one in which a certain object or state of affairs "of whose reality someone has actual knowledge" indicates "the reality of certain other objects or states of affairs." The relation is one of constitutive judgment by which one's "belief in the reality of the one thing is experienced ... as motivating a belief or surmise in the reality of the other."[8] The existence, or rather, my perception of a thing—or even, as Husserl puts it—the "givenness" of some things (state of affairs A: canals on the surface of Mars) leads to the judgment that certain other things either may or must exist (state of affairs B: the existence of Martians).

Plugging Balthasar's distinction into the scheme, the sensory manifestation, or theophany, of God is the *indication* that God is present, "comparable" Balthasar says, "to the way a person catches his interlocutor's attention before he begins to speak with him." It is "*only*" an indication, which "calls the person addressed to 'attention' before the absolute Subject that is making itself present to him."[9] In using this term with its phenomenological sense in the background, Balthasar wants to protect the divine transcendence from any crass and idolatrous equation of God with the sensory theophany, all the while indicating that God, who is Lord of the sensory realm, is nevertheless truly capable of being present through it, in however a paradoxical manner this presence occurs: in this case, present as unavailably present, infinitely transcending his presence—*present in that way*. Yet, it is also true, as Manoussakis, following Merleau-Ponty, makes plain, that indication, by contrast to expressive signification, actually invokes and uniquely "entangles" that which is indicated in a sensible embodiment of presence, in this case, divine presence: because God infinitely transcends his own appearing, and appears as infinitely transcending himself, the sensible world is no impediment to the divine revelation as he is in himself, as who he really is.[10] The paradoxical situation of theophanic indication, as a unique kind, can therefore be articulated in the following manner: God is his theophany, but the theophany is not God. The divine presence, in other words, is a presence that infinitely transcends itself and it is fully present precisely in that way. Think, for example, of sacred representations, like icons, which make an unavailable, transcendent presence available by virtue of the mediation of sensible reality, which is only present, paradoxically, *through* transcending its presence. Icons, images of "divinized" persons, are images of those who share in God's kind of presencing. It is therefore illuminating to juxtapose the nature of theophanic presence with Eastern Christianity's theology of sacred images, of which the latter are extensions of theophanic events. Iconology turns on a distinction developed out of reflection on the relation of God to his own revelation in the world through the economy of salvation that culminates in Christ: the essence (οὐσία)/energies (ἐνέργεια) distinction, which emerges, arguably, as a more generalized expression of a prior distinction demanded by theological controversy, that between essence and person (ὑπόστασις). The first distinction expresses God's essential transcendence of his own revelation through his "energies"; the latter is a more specific distinction used to articulate the logic of the incarnation as well as the Trinitarian constitution of God, but it performs the same task of expressing the paradoxical nature of God's sacral self-presence. In sacred images, the *hypostasis*, not the essence is "circumscribed" through its incarnation in the sensible wood and paint. God, in the icon of Christ Pantokrator for example, is in this way truly present through the sacred image while simultaneously wholly transcending it. The principle I appeal to is expressed in the following apothegm often used in the onomatodoxy ("Name-worshiping") controversy of twentieth-century Russian theology: the energies/Name of God are God himself, but God is not his energies/Name.[11]

To understand this dialectic of sensory appearing at the heart of theophany, one must understand the *personal* nature of theophanies to which Balthasar has already alluded. It is tempting to allow again the dogmatic distinction between *hypostasis* and *ousia* to guide us here. Theophanies of the *kabod-Yahweh* are, simply, an event of personal self-manifestation: here the essence of God is present, for God himself is personally manifesting himself in a sensory manner, but the divine essence is present as paradoxically "distinct" from (i.e., irreducible to but fully present as infinitely transcending) the personal appearing. To penetrate this, Balthasar draws an analogy between the theophanies at the heart of the Old Testament revelation and the dialectic of veiling/unveiling that occurs in any encounter of persons in the flesh, which he calls the "primal phenomenon of potency": as persons appear before one another in the world, they manifest themselves in their "naked existence" (*this* person *right there* is present). At the same time, to use Balthasar's words, they "cast a spell around themselves" in the *freedom* of their personal presence. No other person can ever possess the inner sphere of personality that is one's own. Precisely in this way the *personal presence* of someone bears a power or force that calls for, even demands attention. One need only think of Levinas' phenomenology of the "face" in this regard. Or again, why is it, as Walker Percy asked in his *Lost in the Cosmos*, that looking into the eyes of another person is an arresting experience, which we usually cannot endure for long?[12] To describe this "primal potency" of personal presence, Balthasar himself refers to the strange but common experience of "feeling" another person's stare in your back or, similarly, the sharp look of the teacher that can hold a classroom in check. Personality "attracts and holds at a distance" simultaneously. In the same way, the *kabod-Yahweh* is the "external radiance" *and* "radiant center" of the divine "I" whose sensory manifestation discloses who he is, imposing the weight (*kabod*) of its presence though in no way trapping or containing God.[13] Theophany is a true manifestation that preserves the divine freedom (otherwise it would not be true . . .). The hypostatic presence of direct concern here, of course, is not opposed to the divine essence. Perhaps we can put it this way: the personal presence of God gives the divine essence in a wholly unknowable way, that is, as boundless, as infinitely transcending even itself (thereby being itself), and therefore as truly present as it is in itself: God is his energies; the energies are not God. Think of the paradigm example of the hypostatic union in Christology: the union is not of two essences smashed together and being held in place by a sort of hypostatic glue. Rather, the humanity of Jesus of Nazareth simply *is* the humanity of God, the humanity of the divine Person, the Son. God is therefore present in Jesus of Nazareth without reserve. There is no more God in the Father + the Spirit + the Son than in the Son alone, in whom the whole God is fully present, present, as Trinitarian theology demands, in absolute excess of himself.

In presenting this notion of indication into the discussion of the divine glory, Balthasar, though with no further reference to Husserl (if indeed there really be one in the first place), contrasts it with the revelation through *expressive signs*, that is, the divine address through speech, God's word to human beings.[14] This dialectic between theophany and signitive address is established from the beginning of the text, in the general introduction to the entire part-volume, though it is elaborated only subsequently to the discussion of the indicative theophany that I have taken up here. The (chronological) priority of indication over word is fitting, because, as Balthasar notes, the divine address, revelation through signitive meaning-intentions, *always* follows upon theophanic indication in Scripture. This is a striking but little-contemplated feature of the biblical revelation that Balthasar (perhaps in implicit conversation with Barth) brings out for us. The manifestation of the *kabod* occurs as a precursor, even preparation, for divine speech. Like any speaker, God first *gets our attention*. To demonstrate the distinction between indication and expression in divine revelation, Balthasar lists "the great epiphany of Sinai, the vision in the burning bush, the visions through which Isaiah and Ezekiel received their vocations, the visions on Tabor and at Damascus, and finally the apparition of the Son of Man at the beginning of the Apocalypse."[15]

Given this fundamental distinction between indication and expression at the heart of the "total phenomenon" of revelation, Balthasar observes: "the fact that God's glory at first appears without any words makes clear whence it is that it comes and the consequent paths that God's word will have to take."[16] God's glorious sensory manifestation sets the stage for, as it were, and forms the horizon by which the meaning of the words is bound and on which such meaning, as *divine* speech, depends. Theophany, in other words, frames or contextualizes, creates the conditions for, the divine word spoken to the human. Balthasar goes so far to suggest that this *pre-linguistic* apparition is the manifestation of God's absolute alterity "who must be perceived in his reality and truth before the address can be heard." Without theophanic indication, the divine speech cannot be heard for what it is, the word of the Living God.

What is its effect, then? And what are the conditions that it lays down for hearing the divine word? What, furthermore, is the intelligible content that it communicates pre-linguistically?[17] In the manifestation of the presence of God, theophanies bring the creature in the first place to the recognition of its limit, which Balthasar describes as a kind of death, a death from which *God* alone restores him, putting him back on his feet in order that he may hear and obey the divine word. The purpose of this theophanic overwhelming of the creaturely sphere is to undo any preconceived conditions that the creature puts forth by which it thinks it can anticipate or grasp in advance the word of God according to merely immanent norms, for such conditions would only delimit the creature's ability to hear and to respond to God, whose boundless immensity knows no limit. Without such "death," the creature would, in his weakness, conceive God according to his own lights and even constrain, as Balthasar puts it, the "abyss of free and sovereign lordliness" by some inner-worldly necessity. God would be conceived as something set over against the creature, something of this world, reduced to the creature's capacity to see and understand, therefore becoming what the tradition calls an "idol." The creature, in other words, must come to recognize anew the absolutely unnecessariness of his own existence vis-à-vis the absolute freedom and gratuity and limitlessness of the divine presence. Balthasar states without reserve: "Such encounter with God cannot take place on a dialogical plane which has been opened in advance; it can occur only by virtue of the *primary sense* of being overawed by the undialogical presupposition of the dialogue that has started, namely, the divinity or glory of God."[18] To put it simply: by contrast to the transcendental approach, the event of revelation gives the conditions for its own reception. The a priori can only be discerned as a posteriori to the theophanic event. The conditions and limits of the knowledge of God are given nowhere but in the event of revelation itself. What Balthasar is calling this "primary sense" of awe is the fundamental site of intelligibility of theophanic indication. It is, for Balthasar, one in which one's whole humanity is at stake, a perception of God through the material senses, indeed, as well as a sense of God's presence as divine and holy. As an indication, the sensory manifestation includes primarily a "feeling" or awareness of the unqualified character of God, present as paradoxical infinite presence, in excess of our intelligence, as I described earlier.[19]

Husserl himself already mentions the key role of feeling or what I am calling awareness or sense here in the action of signitive indication, which serves as the link within epistemic judgment joining the indication as sign to that which it brings to consciousness: Husserl says, "If A summons B into consciousness, we are not merely simultaneously or successively conscious of both A and B, but we usually *feel* their connection forcing itself upon us, a connection in which one points to the other and seems to belong to it."[20] This feeling, Husserl says, bears a "force" that is greater than that of what is typically considered an "index," that is, a sign that merely points to the existence of some other thing. Instead, he says, the indication "provides evidence" for that to which it refers by virtue of the "feeling" or "character" or sense of the latter. He notes that "the fact of indication ... in virtue whereof an object or state of affairs not merely recalls another, and so points to it, but also provides evidence for the latter, fosters the presumption that it likewise exists, and makes us immediately feel this."[21]

The "striking" and "shock" and "impact" of the indicative theophanic presence of God, what the tradition calls his *holiness*, will shape everything God says subsequently. It is the condition by which the conversation with creatures must take place if it is not to begin on a false foundation of untruth (which would presuppose, again, some kind of reduction of God to the limits of the creaturely sphere). Theophanic indication will establish the conditions by which a human can understand the unqualified uniqueness of God's word, and therefore its absolute character. Balthasar provides a litany of biblical instances to demonstrate this overwhelming of the creature with a sense of God's unqualified character, which are, again, instructive to list here:

> When confronted by the appearance of God's glory, "Moses falls to his knees and bows his face to the earth," Elijah veils his face, Isaiah considers himself lost, Ezekiel falls with his face toward the ground, Daniel is oppressed in spirit and sinks in a swoon with his face to the earth, the Apostles on Tabor are "beside themselves," "drowsy," in great fear at the sight of it; Paul is thrown to the ground and blinded, and John falls as if dead at the feet of the appearing Lord.[22]

Theophanic indication is, in Balthasar's language, the "opening" of a new realm to humanity, an elevation by which humanity is "transported" outside of himself by the shock of the *kabod*, and in which he finds himself anew. Hence, it would be a misunderstanding to render modern judgment over such theophanic display of terrifying splendor as unfitting for the God of love. This is not, says Balthasar, "a power that does violence but rather one which summons insistently: in the word [that follows the indication], the infinite 'I' summons the finite 'I' to be fully itself."[23] Humanity only hears the word of God, not in himself or through his natural capacities, but "in God and through God," says Balthasar, by being freely brought into a realm which is made accessible to humanity beyond any claim of his nature or the power of his capacities. How else can *God* be truly known? The knowledge pertaining to this "perception" of the divine presence is, however, the knowledge related to a fundamental human religious sense (but not from out of an a priori natural religious sense), emerging, simply, from the weighty force of God's presence, as a response to the divine indicative presence gifted to the creature by the latter. Before the weight of the divine presence, the human is rendered absolutely mute; *only* the word of address that follows gives to humanity the capacity to both hear and respond. Strangely, it seems that the conditions and limits of the knowledge of God are not found primarily in the structure of human finitude at all (considered in itself), which, of course, provides no obstruction to the divine self-revelation. Rather it is human infinitude that provides the only limits, that is, desire and therefore the will, the finite infinitude of human freedom to receive or reject the divine communication, which is brought fully into play. The revelation of God reveals to the human who he really is, what is really at stake in his humanity. Humanity's peculiar infinitude, therefore, even in its negative expression of elected freedom over against God, is a sign of his vocation to correspond to God, to become a god with God, to be God's partner in whatever the creation project will turn out to be.

It is here that we can become more precise about the nature of the theophanic dialectic. In the first place, it is the revelation of the holiness of God, on the one hand, and the unholiness of humanity, on the other. The *kabod-Yahweh* leaves humanity in a state of complete suspension. The weight of God's holiness renders total judgment on humanity. The dialectic of theophanic indication, by which the absolute ontological difference of God calls humanity into question, the human who fails to acknowledge his own finitude and fails to acknowledge the absolute freedom of the divine will that is his measure, must be struck down. "Woe is me!" exclaims Isaiah in his vision of the enthroned uncreated glory, "I am lost; for I am a man of unclean lips, and I have seen the Lord of hosts!" (Isa. 6:5). Yet, this complete suspension of the creature before the holiness of God in theophanic indication is not the end of humanity. The God who has made himself present speaks. The word of God, emerging from this context, the expression of divine meaning intention in personal address, is, in the all-encompassing horizon of indicative presence, given the conditions by which the word of God can be heard. "All sensory revelation of glory," observes Balthasar "is directly oriented to the word of God."[24] The dialectic of the signitive address of meaning-bearing speech becomes clear here: it is one of judgment and unmerited grace at once. The dialectic is implied already in the theophanic indication. But it is not only the case that the theophanic presence is one of judgment and mercy, of total suspension before the divine glory, as seen in the shock of the prophets who "see" the divine presence and yet live. The word of address brings this implicit dialectic into full term: God's word is truth; it is the word of the Lord who judges all, the Lord who sees the heart, before whom everything is "but a breath." This word is the word of God, and nothing less. It is a word—the word of the Creator—that is infinitely weighty and bears a force that requires total response, the gift of one's whole being. Within the dialectic, the gift of oneself to God as interlocuting collaborator is, precisely, the greatest gift of God to humanity, the elevation or liberation (as the Scholastic tradition had put it) of nature by grace. If I may put it this way, in the dialectic of divine revelation, human finitude is suspended in its own finitude, as a pure expression of that finitude, made receptive of the infinite. It becomes the site of pure reception of the word that gives all of God in the kenotic form of finitude. Because, finally, God's transcendence is in eclipse of any proportion with the finite sphere—even the proportion that restricts God's capacity to take on finitude, this kenotic form is capable of immediately expressing his fullness.

This rather Barthian dialectic of judgment-mercy will be shown to be the central theme of the New Testament, where God's self-disclosure in sensory manifestation and word reaches its highest realization. Here we can perhaps discern the paradoxical structure of revelation all the more clearly: if God reveals himself as absolutely transcending his revelation, and thereby gives himself as he is, then we can perhaps conclude not only with the paradoxical formulation that "God's revelation is God, but God is not his revelation," but also that God gives all of himself in revelation by infinitely transcending it. All is given, therefore, but not all is manifested. What is manifested then? That all is given. This all of God is manifested through the paradoxically inadequate adequacy of a human response to it: in a human's response there is always more to give. This infinite surplus of self-gift to God is found in Jesus Christ, who gives himself all the way, into the peculiar infinitude, the absoluticity, one could say, of death.

Emerging from out of the theophanic "foundation," the word, says Balthasar, "confiscates the whole existence of its hearers, the entirety of their relationship to God and the world." Quoting Sir. 17:13 ["Their eyes saw the glory of his majesty, and their ears heard the glory of his voice. And he said to them, 'Beware of all unrighteousness (service to idols).' And he gave commandment to each of them concerning his neighbour."], Balthasar observes that the revelation of theophanic indication and personal address refigures the entirety of one's life. The knowledge of God, at this level of personal encounter and address, in which God appears in his *Herr-lichkeit* ("Lordliness" or "Lordly glory") is one with doing his will. God appears as who he is: the Lord of all things. His word, simply by virtue of the divine presence and its suspension of the creature before the freedom of God, requires the response of pure obedience and *in this way* is the "absolute truth." Here the dialectic of theophany and speech is reconciled and the word of God is—Balthasar's phrase—"pure objectivity." Here we must once and for all eradicate from our conception of the "objectivity" that pertains to the knowledge of God all vestiges of the paradigm of the knowledge according to the object of modern science (for which some thing is *conceptually* grasped without reserve), for this has nothing to do with the knowledge of God, who *is* in infinite excess over his appearing and his word—an excess manifest as Lordly glory, the one who is free to judge and to give mercy—and *only* appears as such. Objectivity, in *this* realm of knowledge, is "pure subjectivity" the taking hold of the recipient in the entirety of his being, whose life as unlimited response (for which there is always more to give God), and to the degree of its response, manifests the truth of who God is. The knowledge of God in his revelation is in this way, again, as Balthasar now puts it, "perfect immediacy" (in the Kierkegaardian sense). In giving the conditions for its reception, the divine word to man also gives the means for a true response to the absolute truth of God's revelation.[25]

St. Bernard Clairvaux made the following observation in answer to the question how we are to love God: we are to love him *modus sine modo*, "in a way without a way," that is, without limit, with no conditions.[26] We *must* love God beyond what we are capable; this love is the absolute commitment to the word that gives itself without reserve, a sort of correspondence of absolutes—divine and human freedom. The knowledge of God therefore is nothing but one's awakening to oneself through the response to the boundless one whose judgment is one that gives one a response, the ability to say yes: "The more deeply the human self awakens in the answer it gives," says Balthasar "the more boundlessly do the heights and depths of the absolute 'I' open out before him in the glorious lordliness of the divine word."[27] If our response is an ever-abundant yes without limits to the divine address, then we know God as he is, for he *is* the ever-greater surplus of himself. Here, Balthasar can affirm, even more radically than Levinas, that "to be in the image of God does not mean to be an icon of God, but to find oneself in his trace. The revealed God of our Judeo-Christian spirituality maintains all the infinity of his absence, which is in the personal 'order' itself."[28]

The double dialectic of sensory indication and personal address of the divine word is, arguably, the structure of the manifestation or revelation of God in its historical fullness. It refigures entirely the meaning of knowledge as that which concerns the entirety of the self of the one who sees and hears, who tastes and touches, who *feels* the revelation of God in his entire being and responds unconditionally. Only this unconditional response can be both an "absolute" knowledge of the Absolute God and at the same time that of a finite creature whose finitude is not annihilated, but rather buoyed up precisely in its ever-greater opening to the God who is ever more than himself as Trinity. This dialectic of divine self-manifestation of indication and expression, therefore, unfolds into a new dialectic of dialogical relation between the God who gives himself and the creature who is shaken, elevated, addressed and responds. For the creature, further, it unveils a new subsidiary dialectic of self-manifestation which is the adventure of the self in *pursuit* of the God who makes himself present, and in *response* to the God who speaks and calls. The response is the adventure of self-appropriation according to the wholly new coordinates of the God beyond any searching out, not merely ever-greater than our capacity to know him, but, as it were, ever-greater than himself. Hyperbolic being. This is so to speak the positive expression of the negative concept of infinite. This divine ontological excess forms the conditions for being known as he is in his infinite excess over his self-revelation. The human self unfolds according to a new tension rooted entirely in the event of revelation. Around it is organized a historical existence. The life of faith is one of response to the word of absolute truth; the self is the arrival to itself in the passage from self (grounded in its own autonomy and set over against God who is therefore reduced to some *thing* being set over against the finite subject) to self (grounded now entirely in God for whom finitude is no limiting condition for his self-revelation). This passage from self to self is made manifest as corresponding in unconditional freedom to the unconditionality of the divinity through the act of obedient response to the word. Absolute—or hyperbolic—knowledge of the hyperbolic absolute is one with the passage by which one becomes more fully oneself in loving God ever more fully; it is a passing back from word to the one who speaks and has made himself present in the fullness of his mystery in the first place. This hyperbolic dialectic is, of course, eschatological. Its terminus is in the vision of God, which is, first, nothing but the knowledge God has of us in the knowledge of himself, and which is, in turn, nothing but the love of humanity with the love by which God loves himself. Knowledge of God in himself is therefore only *the beginning* of the knowledge of God. We only know God to the degree that we love him. To love God is to know him as he is. Here the flesh of humanity becomes the flesh of God, and the life of God becomes the life of humanity. The more we love him, the more we see him as he is. Remaining here one finds the answer to the question with which we began. This is only ever incomplete and yet ever being fulfilled, itself an experience of the fullness that God is, the infinite convergence of love and knowledge.

So the peculiar infinity of human finitude can be immortal (by an ever-greater correspondence to the call of divine absolute infinitude) or mortal. The engrossing epistemological paradox deriving from this ontological one that I want to mount a case for is that *indirect* knowledge of God, the passage or dragging of the intellect through the kabodic-sensible domain (therefore metaphor, symbol, myth, image, etc.), is *more direct* than the *direct approach* of speculative metaphysics, ascent by the purification of concepts. The hyperbolic being of God is ontologically "indirect," essentially superfluous, boundless—and only in that way direct. Direct as that way. This viewpoint, it must be said, follows, strictly enough anyway, from the equation of goodness with being, and of necessity and freedom in God, or, more simply said, God's simplicity itself *if* thought with intellectual rigor as the basis for contemplating the "biblical" awareness of God's personal transcendence, itself fully integrated (so to speak), in the final analysis, with his nature. Perhaps measured reflection will permit the acknowledgment that Aquinas already substantially indicated the viewpoint I have initiated in this analysis of Balthasar when he made a distinction between the knowledge of God as the prime subject of metaphysics, the study of being as such (the "theology," he says, intrinsic to philosophy, approaching God, in other words, within the logic of Neoplatonic causality), and that according to the "true theology" of *sacra pagina*, the knowledge of God *through* the investigation of his manifestation in sacred texts, which incorporates the apophatic rationality of the emanative Cause, but which, in the face of revelation, is and can only ever be openly revisable, unfinished, ever-tempered by the Living God's self-transcendence manifest immediately in the excess of the sacred page's content (image, metaphor, symbol, narrative) over the conceptual-theoretical apparatus.[29] Exposing the seam in the tradition where Greek rationality is interlaced with Semitic sources (witnessing divine, historical action, a priori impossible on the terms of that rationality, a rationality itself, however, utilized to witness the hyperbolic rationality of this one God) is, I think, a central enactment of the tradition itself, as is sometimes unraveling it, sometimes restitching it.[30]

Let me finish by articulating, the best I can, some conclusions that will serve as a basis for the studies undertaken in what follows.

(1) The a priori. The religious a priori, the conditions for experience and knowledge, is the body, which bears the *kabod Yhwh*. Who knew that it was *in the body* that God would reveal himself as humanity's absolute truth? Theology tells us, in its explication of revelation, that the mystery of matter is that it is a fitting "container" for the glory of God; human flesh is fitting flesh for God. The significance of this for intellectual inquiry is that the dull density of matter can become saturated with an intelligibility of signification that may bear the weight of the divine presence. The material domain can become an opening in infinite excess of itself, being capable of the divine glory precisely as absolutely contingent vis-à-vis God, who is Lord of it. And such is its eternal goal and purpose. Analogously, and as a precondition activated by divine descent, the body, inexhaustible in its pre-linguistic intelligibility, specifically the body's inexhaustible finitude of sense in its bare opening to the irreducible meaningfulness of sensible experience, is the already constituted world of meaning that we only strive to catch in our intellectual reflection. Our knowledge pertains to this world—and only in and through this pertinence, to the God in eclipse of it. Theophanic indication occurs here, as the sensory manifestation of God, as he is in himself, namely, in his defining self-excess.[31] The naturally supernatural character of humanity, our own defining self-excessivity, according to which we discover ourselves and accomplish our nature only by a transcending self-transgression, is an echo, or image, of the divinity of God.

(2) Intuition. Intuition is the immediate ("participatory") knowledge of God only ever-unfolded, and more generally, to use Bergson's way of putting it, the seemingly magical occurrence of knowing something from within, that is, in itself. Intuition is seeing, of seeing as, the mystical seeing with the (divine) eye

that sees oneself. It is, indeed, the perception of the transgression of duality into a unity that transgresses itself. If our account of revelation is correct then perhaps we have to say that intuition is possible, but not, in the first place, intellectually—that is, aside from the incarnate world. Revelation is historical action of the divine kind, an intentional crease made in the world with its Lord as agent. Its end is the glorification, the divinization of the creation, and that *as a setting for* the renewed beginning of the story of God's collaboration with vice-regental humanity. *Religious* intuition is first embodied, being sensory and practical (and therefore symbolic), not speculative (and conceptual). And the latter must return to it. Divinity as "vision"—or more fully, "as vision as knowing"—is a central element of the Axial Age accomplishment. Despite its epochal profundity, this insight, first found in Xenophanes, the sixth century BC wandering poet (according to the extant fragments we have from this era), for whom "there is one god, greatest among gods and men, similar to mortals neither in shape nor thought," who "wholly sees, wholly thinks, wholly hears," does not exhaust the meaning of divinity.[32] Nor, therefore, does his ground-breaking critique of poetic anthropomorphisms.[33] It is, for us (who continue to think in its wake), the beginning, a renewed beginning for the task that emerges beyond it. This kind of intuition is already implicit within religious ritual and especially its apogee, the act of sacrifice where the gift of being is returned to the source (through a surplus *material* offering) in recognition of the contingency and self-excess of all that is. Mediation is the site of immediacy, mediation is the most immediate (a conception already intuited by the Neoplatonic notion of causality), a sharing in God's self-mediation, θέωσις of the creaturely sphere. Sacrifice, for example, is understood primarily as the work of the divine and the return or "redundance" of the gift in which humanity shares, being elevated into the sphere of partnering collaborator with the Creator; its sacrifice is therefore itself the highest gift that the divine *gives*. By this "redundance" the sacrifice and the sacrificer are consecrated, receiving a share in the sacrality that is the divine's alone. Sacrifice is therefore a theophany and the apogee of theophany since the "return of the gift" manifests the giver most fully: this becomes absolute when the sacrifice becomes humanity's return of itself, one's entire self to God through, again, the vehicle of matter (as the Eucharist paradigmatically gives us).[34] This redundance of love manifests the divine self-surplus and *is* the gift of a share in it.

(3) Symbol and concept. The determination of intellectual knowledge of God by the conditions of embodied existence, the inexhaustible intelligibility of the sensory domain, means that symbols bear more intelligible capacity than concepts. Iniitally, let us say that symbols are the concentration of the

mind on the intelligible intensity of matter, the discernment of a greater depth of intelligibility in the appearances even through the free "redistribution of the sensible," as Lacoste put it, borrowing a phrase of Rancière,[35] according to the deeper pattern, the disclosed "form" of revelation (Balthasar), the manifestation of that which is given in interlocutory response to it, a response that makes visible its invisibility, its absolute transcendence over its appearing, its appearing as absolute transcendence. Does this priority of matter for divine intelligibility mean that symbols precede and wholly determine concepts? The symbol participates in the reality which it conveys, and, like images, symbols give the reality in a material way, which is paradoxical, since they give the reality they signify only by being wholly set apart, by eluding any conceptual grasp of the reality (which can only be had by taking apart the symbol, thereby losing or at least severely distancing the presence of the reality), and by giving its distinctness, its transcendent otherness through itself as symbol. This is why symbols can be sacred things and concepts cannot (even Divine Names, which inexhaustibly name the nameless are not mere concepts but fully symbolic indications, "images carried in the caused" of the Cause, "as much as they are capable").[36] Concepts never exceed the intelligible density that symbols provide, giving to thought what can be thought. The origin of all concepts is perhaps the dense material intelligibility that precedes them in symbols, and concepts receive their life-power from the symbols out of which they derive. It is therefore more profound (*pro-fundus*: to the bottom), that is, farther reaching, to use symbolic images to signify divine transcendence than conceptual abstraction. The conclusion is tentative and appears to conflict with the speculative, and, I think, non-dual impulse of the tradition for which Intellect and Being are one in the Absolute. I am, for one, enamored with this impulse. This enamorment is a major subtext for the subsequent analysis. My initial approach presumes one must not choose between metaphysics and history, between theory and myth, between concept and figure, between the man Jesus and the unfathomable Godhead "beyond being," between duality and unity. One must instead, persist in their dissonance and their antinomy. And we do this by apprenticing ourselves to revelation, according to our philosopher, "the loveliest standard of truth."[37]

(4) Apophasis. Does the preceding imply that we ought to rethink our tradition of apophasis, which has been typically understood as keyed to the priority of speculative ascent by conceptual purification to the negation of the symbol? Is it less apophatic to say (a) God is truth, (b) we only know finite instances of truth, (c) God is infinitely more truthful than any of these, than saying God dwells in blinding darkness, or sits on a throne surrounded by earthquakes, lightning,

peals of thunder, or is a "consuming fire?" The latter, if the origin of the former, also emerges at its terminus. Symbols, in their indirectness, give the eclipse-alterity of the reality they communicate *more directly* than concepts. It will take the remainder of this book to explain the significance, on a theological basis, of this which should rightly perceived as a commonplace. Meaning stands in excess of the conceptual grasp of the skill of theoretical intelligence. Figurative achievement, literary or musical, sculptural or architectural, for example, presence meaning (in such a way as to appear perhaps as excess or, its opposite, as absence) in relation to conceptual mastery of their contents. *Othello* cannot be reduced to the dictionary definition of jealousy. Bernini's "St. Teresa in Ecstasy" presences the carnality of mystical rapture beyond the limits of conceptual explication. And so on. Symbols give their reality by *not* giving it, that is, by *giving it as unapproachable*, by revealing the divine transcendence over itself in the immanence of the symbolic manifestation. I will attempt merely to elaborate on these initial conclusions as we continue. The greatest symbols are sacred names where God is present as absent, as more than present, as freely present, as infinitely transcending his presence, in excess of presence. He is present *in that way* for he *is* that way.

2

Anthropomorphism and the Angel
The Anthropic Principle

The difference between the angelic and anthropic modes of knowledge is total: humans are embodied. Setting to the side Aquinas' near-irresolvable paradox of the perfect beatitude of the disembodied blessed, I am here concerned with the "eschatological structure of theological finitude," which includes the destiny of the body. Balthasar's account of theophanic indication has given us a clue to the intelligible structure of divine self-presencing in the world and its relation to the self-presencing that God is. Have we put our finger on the principle of coherence between the "economic" and "immanent" Trinities that modern theology has flagged since Rahner's *The Trinity*? Whatever the case (I am not writing a systematic theology), this point of electric connection between God and world is an invitation to reflect on the relation, now, from the side of the elected partner. Let us now initiate a search to find a conception of revelation that takes into full account our contemporary heightened sensitivity to the fundamental conditions of finitude: historicity, materiality, and so forth. Following the discovery, articulated earlier, of the identity of the divine structure ad intra with his manifestation ad extra, his mode of presence, I want now to elaborate more fully the "site" or place of revelation, arguing that what Christians call eschatology—the *logos* of the last things—is the best sphere of intellectual coherence to use regarding these conditions since, inasmuch as it articulates the *eclipse of world*, relativizing and hence *uniquely* bringing to light its conditions, it offers them full scope.[1] The suspicion ultimately arises here that it is eschatology itself—the *logos* of the last things—that ultimately grounds them. This chapter accomplishes its course in three major steps: (a) *reflection* on the difference between angelic and anthropic contemplation; (b) *critique* of the dominant trend of the phenomenology of revelation for its sidestepping of the defining conditions of our finitude; (c) *proposal* of an eschatologically informed phenomenology of revelation. The second and third steps of this course bring into conversation Jean-Luc Marion and Jean-Yves Lacoste, who become, for our purposes, *types* of the dominant and proposed approaches, respectively.[2]

Duns Scotus said: "The angelic intellect directly knows the singular. Our intellect does not know it in this way."[3] It chose the quote, an author, almost at random. But the observation of a fundamental distinction between the angelic and human kinds of being is as old as the tradition of Abraham itself, and the religions that derive from this tradition all share a philosophical understanding of the human, at least to some degree, by counterpoint or juxtaposition with the angelic. For these traditions, it would be easy to argue that the essential difference between angels and humans is that angels are spiritual, or we could say, *disembodied*, pure intelligences, and humans are *embodied*: our intelligence is fundamentally tied to the material realm of the senses, if not essentially determined by its unity with it.[4] The magnitude of such a composite unity of intellect and flesh for the human kind of being is seen in Thomas Aquinas' conception of those *beati* who in the intermediate state "see" God before the general resurrection: the un-composite beatitude of a creature whose essential nature is composite implies the necessity of an immediate divine creative act to secure its perfect beatitude in what is according to its nature an imperfect, because disembodied, state.[5] In this intermediate state, the disembodied blessed are angel-like intelligences—this irregularity vis-à-vis their human nature will be normalized when they are endowed at the final judgment with glorified bodies. The possibility of this irregularity, at least in the case of the *beati*, points to an essential community between the angelic and human kinds of being: however great the distinction between them, both angels and humans are rational beings, persons, with an intellect and will, capable of relation with God. They are also both unlike God in the essential sense of being contingent *creatures* of God. The Scriptures call them, together, "sons of God" and both angels and humans play a central role in the divine economy, that is, the outworking of the divine will for the creation. For Christians, inasmuch as they follow the philosophy of St. Paul, the angelic economy of the first creation, reaching its apogee in the Law and Jerusalem Temple, is fulfilled and metamorphosized through the ascension of Christ to the divine throne, *above* the cherubim; the "new creation," therefore, is an anthropic (and, indeed, anthropomorphic) economy, where man, not the angel or "god," is first vice-regent.[6] Hence, the church will "judge angels" and so forth. To complicate things further, for Paul, the new creation and its economy has already begun in the resurrection of Christ, but it overlaps with and for the most part secretly dwells within the first creation which enigmatically continues on. Even this quasi-esoteric "competition" between the angelic and human economies, between the age presently "passing away" and the "age to come" that has broken into the world in advance, played out on the stage of history under the name of apocalypse, is a sign of the fundamental community between angels and humans. There is a similar "personal" freedom that humans and angels share, which unfortunately—at least from one part of our finite perspective—includes their "god-like" capacity to reject the divine will and to make their own will—at least to the extent of their own power and freedom—"divine." For Christians, this replacement of the divine will with a creaturely will, a pseudo-divine will, is an essential feature of sin and is something that corrupts the creation and traps the creature in the shadow side of the divine economy ("judgment") established as a basic feature of the covenant of creation.

It is good to remember, modern dwellers of the *saecular* that we invariably are, Horatio's lesson that there is more in heaven and earth than in our philosophies, but for our purpose, let us set this to the side, or rather, accept it simply as the greater context for our thought, without, however, forgetting it.[7] What is essential is the *embodied difference* of human perception and reason. Regarding this (at least), both Scotus (quoted earlier) and Aquinas agree. For Aquinas, all spiritual knowledge, that is, knowledge of intelligible realities, requires, for human beings, a passage through the realm of the senses and even a return to it (hence the famous *conversio ad phantasmata*, which is required for knowledge *after* the active intellect "abstracts" the universal from the particular object of experience). And together Aquinas and Scotus agree with that mysterious early theorist of the angelico-anthropic difference, Pseudo-Dionyius the Areopagite, for whom angels and humans "contemplate" God in fundamentally different manners. Already, Aquinas' stages of the process of knowledge—sense impression-abstraction-return—repeat on a smaller scale in every act of knowing the "triplex via" or threefold path of the knowledge of God that he inherits from the Pseudo-Areopagite.[8] It also exemplifies the triadic anagogic ascent implied, or rather, truly enacted, in every act of knowledge. The dialectic of ratiocination emerging from out of the recognition of distinction (whether in the sensible or purely intellective domains), the *sic et non*, leads finally albeit proximately to immersion, either in the sensible or the narrative orders from which it emerged, which it explicates and to which it returns. The eclipse of the angelic economy of "this age" by the anthropic economy of the "age to come" pre-established, precisely, at Easter, from within "this age" that is both "evil" (Gal. 1:4), that is, errant and under divine judgment, and, by virtue of the definitive nature of the eclipse realized by the resurrection "passing away" (cf. 1 Cor. 2:6-8), requires a concomitant revolution in thought, particularly, of course, in metaphysics and epistemology (if also ethics and politics, for example, but the revolution, in these domains, has been, historically, much more readily apparent, if only because of the immediate cultural responsive consciousness to these "fields"). To prioritize, frankly, a final separation of the speculative (the ontological a priori identification of being and knowing) from the historical, the intellectual from the material, the theoretical from the narrative, the conceptual from the mythic is to assume that the *end* of revelation is the awakening of one to one's own divinity. Humans are gods. If such was the great teaching of the Greek Mysteries (and, of course, of the so-called Presocratics), it is tempting to assert that such is only a metaphysical banality of the Christian tradition. God is *non-aliud*, not other. Such is the meaning of creation: its divinity. Created gods, however, gods in flesh and blood, the least, we should say, among the vast hierarchy of (created) gods that stretches forth, perhaps infinitely, through the spiritual worlds, are, it is discovered at the "end of the ages," elevated, in an unfathomable reversal, to the place of uncreated authority and rule—and such was the purpose of the creation from the beginning. Or so says the Pauline μυστήριον. In this narrative vision, the end of creation, its telos, is precisely this reversal. The incarnation of God is the establishment of a New Eden, the union of heaven and earth. It is the renewal of the beginning. The biblical narrative, from its first to last words, takes place wholly within its first phrase ("In the beginning"). The final image of the story is the *descent* of the New Jerusalem from heaven to earth, not its ascent from earth to heaven. The angelic economy implies, or rather, demands of us a piety of *escape* from the world-tomb (and a metaphysics and epistemology concomitant with it that terminates in the awakening to a mere non-dualism, the clearly beguiling and exotic supernaturality of nature). To luxuriate, intellectually, in the piety of escape or ascent as end is to persist exclusively in the logos of the first economy and to deny the apocalypse of the latter.

Human contemplation, therefore, for the Pseudo-Areopagite, requires images, symbols, figures, and narratives—and ritual above all—which lives in and enacts them, mediating an embodied knowledge (so to speak) of divine presence. In anticipation of further elaboration, it is enough to observe the following indications here: the (eschatological) human economy of divine knowledge requires prioritizing the images over the abstract and conceptual (the opposite is the case for angels, who know wholly intelligibly), and this for multiple reasons, which include (1) the makeup of human nature (corporeality), (2) the tendency toward making greater idols out of our concepts by equating them with realities they signify or even simply thinking that their purity and breadth somehow achieve a greater proximity to divine reality, and finally, (3) because revelation itself makes this prioritization, as Scripture and the liturgy demonstrate. Implicitly, for the Pseudo-Areopagite, we can also add (4) it is the divine nature that itself requires this prioritization, since (in the first place) images, symbols, narratives are more adequate to the living and personal nature of ultimate reality than abstract, frozen concepts, inevitably drained of the color, vibrancy, and intelligible density that the figurative dimension retains. The working law for the Areopagite, we could say, is: the greater that which the human being contemplates, the more symbolic, figurative, and imagistic must the means of his contemplation become. To ascend toward the metaphysically divine, the human must descend all the more into the depths of his materiality.[9] Aquinas' "conversio ad phantasmata" and the apophatic "way of excess" repeat and universalize this specific kind of priority of the image over the concept for all human knowledge. The ultimate object of angelic and human knowledge is of course the same, intelligible reality, indeed, hyper-intelligible reality, but the human requires the mediation of the material domain and in this way actually reaches, paradoxically, levels of transcendence that the "immediacy" of angelic knowledge cannot attain by virtue of the obscure fittingness of matter, in its distance from the noetic, to the hyper-noetic divine in its own absolute distance from the intelligible.[10]

Two comments will form a bridge to the next step. First, about the fallen will, in order both to give it its universal due and to then set it aside, though, again, without forgetting it, if we can; second, about the nature of critique, an intellectual mode that forms a substantial part of this chapter. (1) Fallen human nature and the limitations of finitude. Concerning the intellectual task we have given ourselves here, what is "fallenness" and what are its basic implications? Distinct from the essential components of our finitude, materiality, and historicity, though inseparable from them, fallenness is the peculiar darkness of our mind resulting from a self-interested will. It is the perennial wild card, throwing a wrench into our chains of reasoning and disrupting any progress of knowledge that we humans build. Fallenness is our finitude, good in itself, become tragic, precisely by closing in upon itself, attempting a radical self-justification and self-creation.[11] It means to be ruled by death. Augustine laments about humans that "what they love they want to be the truth."[12] Our primary attitude is to delight in the truth that shines and pleases (shining for us) but to revulse from the truth that accuses and calls to account (shining on us, exposing us).[13] Commenting on this passage in Augustine, the young Heidegger says that

> they love [the truth] when it encounters them as glitzy, in order to enjoy it aesthetically, in all convenience, just as they enjoy every glamour that, in

captivating, relaxes them. But they hate it when it presses them forcefully. When it concerns them themselves, and when it shakes them up and questions their own facticity and existence, then it is better to close one's eyes just in time, in order to be enthused by the choir's litanies which one has staged for oneself.[14]

Despite this wrench, the thorn thrust into our human nature, we must continue to think, and to labor, with the hope that what we build is not totally built in vain. For in this Augustinian vision, the truth always has two edges, one that indeed cuts us, and, in our revulsion from it, veils the truth. Even though "the truth remains concealed to us," says Heidegger, *we* "do not remain concealed before" the truth.[15] The acknowledgment of this double edge of truth requires a specific attitude that defines a truthful approach to the truth. Part of this attitude is an essential recognition of the vanity of what we say, that the truth is not my possession, a recognition that gives us a freedom for the truth, a freedom that leaves the judgment of what is good in our work to the future and ultimately to another who can and will judge absolutely. All our thinking must therefore be conscious of itself before the *eschaton* (*coram novissimos*: before the new things); its appropriate freedom is rooted in this recognition of itself in the light of an absolute judgment that is not its to give, which is a recognition born out of a love for the truth in itself, in its essential transcendence from us and our nakedness before it. Fallenness, our revulsion from the truth, can be transformed by an attitude of truthfulness that is oriented to the truth by acknowledging that what I possess is not *the* truth in itself and so I, in my open nakedness before the truth, stand before a final truth to come and that, indeed, *already* impinges in the present but in the first place on me, first as my judge. Finally, then, the truthful attitude acknowledges that the content of the truth as judgment and as shining has *not yet* completely arrived. This incompleteness of the truth and the concomitant commitment to its forthcoming character leads directly to my second transitional comment. (2) Critique. What is critique? Critique is essentially problematic, for it seems to require always a counter-critique, since it is not absolute, even though it tends to assert itself by its very critical nature as absolute, as a divine or quasi-divine ability to see the wrong in light of an intuition of the right. Every critique, every critical attitude, tends toward its own impossible realization as the truth.

Yet there are two degrees of critique. On the one hand, the enactment of critique itself enacts a veiling reduction of that which it examines, a thought, a system or a philosophy that names things and describes them, that seeks intelligibility, and seeks understanding, something living, becoming something that reifies, determines, and conceptualizes objects. Critique at this level requires a distance from its object of inquiry and freezes its object into a stasis. Critique, in order to discern the reifying nature of a system of thought, must already reify that system of thought. By its essentially distorting approach, the stance of critique therefore inevitably contains that which it accuses its object to be.

On the other hand, the second level of critique is much more reserved and cognizant of its own essential limitations. Critique, in this instance, is that mode of thought which brings to our attention the conceptual reduction of reality that any thought, system, or philosophy entails or at least to which it tends when it establishes itself as a workable thought, system, or philosophy. Not only do the words we write take on a life of their own, containing implications that we ourselves could never see, but they also tend to propose themselves, over time, through a *history* of their reception (*Wirkungsgeschichte*), itself ascertained within that *longue durée*, as equal with or sufficient to the realities that (ideally and probably often) in the moment of their first gestation they only refer to and, at best, vaguely talk about. All our thought, when it is written down, is only a chasing after intuitions that are much too large to fit into our words. But our words tend to crystallize and assert a substantiality and reality about themselves that their own nature as words does not and cannot possess in itself. Critique acknowledges this and refuses the rest that a narrative, system, theory, or idea proposes and attempts to break up our reifying language. Critique keeps us on pilgrimage. With this second definition of critique, we are far from some ultimately irrational "autonomy" and closer to that which we ought to retain, I suggest, from the "postmodern" philosophy of yesterday. Like deconstruction, this kind of critique recognizes itself before the eschatological, which is the end of critique, not only in the abstract but perfectly normative sense that the last word belongs to God alone, but, unlike deconstruction, it *confesses* that this last word can be spoken (being God's word, after all), and has truly taken on shape for us, even in the midst of history and its delimiting conditions.[16] In this latter case, however, let us not forget: this shape is precisely shapeless—the empty tomb. In the half-light of Easter morning, precisely, critique finds its meta-origin and an ever-greater counter-critique.[17] In the first place, Easter, the Victory of God, his definitive work in history, is a blank spot, a vacuum, a critique of all of our triumphalisms—as if to make sure we would learn the lesson of the Cross.[18] Only there, stepping forth in perplexity out of the darkness of the empty tomb, may we see the risen Lord, but not by our own power. Most importantly, this meta-critique, the origin of critique, finds its place within the logic of a *promise*, an eschatology, detached from which critique—as in deconstruction too, I would argue—becomes absolute, a god-like, autonomous reason, an iron law of historical reason to which even God must submit. (Of course, this is a historical reason that conceives itself in its assumptions, execution, and conclusions as trans-historical, as concepts beyond the scope of their anthropomorphic origin.) Eschatology is the two-edged sword of truth from which all critique comes; the dark gaping entrance to the tomb of Christ is the unsealable wound of history, of language, of our reason. And this sword is simply not in our hands, though in "every act of thought and will" we find ourselves wounded by it.

With this sense of critique, critique in its lesser mode, and the openness to truth obtained by the recognition of its dispossession of ourselves before it, *attempting to remain there*, let us first acknowledge the ambivalence of the phenomenology of revelation in its present state.

In order to establish a valid criticism of the phenomenology of revelation, we must first observe its challenge and in the second place, be challenged by it. The advance of contemporary phenomenology in its conception of revelation is found in its demolition of the a priori and its absolutization of the affirmation of absolute alterity, an alterity that has the power to make itself truly known. In this way, phenomenology has found a way to conceive of revelation that challenges us, before which we can only stand with open hands and see what it gives, even finding ourselves in its gift. The truth that shines first shines from itself and shines on us: from it, in the first place—and thus not from a preconceived sketch of ourselves, especially our conditions of experience and knowledge—we can come to see what we are. Here the phenomenon of revelation is allowed its fullest scope; its horizon of possibility is found nowhere but in it itself and from itself. If God is *God* then to acknowledge anything less, to require God, for example, to submit to specific limitations and requirements in advance, even those determined by the receiver, would be, or at least could be, idolatry of a pernicious sort. The "a priori" conditions of the phenomenon of revelation, that is, of its appearing and hence our experience of it, can only be articulated *after* the phenomenon is given and from the phenomenon itself, which, we may find, resets the entire field of experience in general in a completely new way. For this phenomenology, revelation articulates *itself*, it even articulates its conditions for its perception and its knowledge: it gives its own horizons.[19]

The alternative philosophy of revelation is the philosophy that determines the conditions of divine appearing in advance, for example, by reasoning from a conception of basic human structures, like reason, or from a preconceived sketch of the structures of human language. This view says "God *cannot* do this" or "God *cannot* manifest himself in that way" because the fundamental structure of human reason or language legislates against its possibility. This alternative that the phenomenology of revelation critiques is what Jean-Luc Marion calls "metaphysics," inscribing himself, thereby, in Heidegger's wake (from which, in the same moment, he subsequently seeks to extricate himself) by delimiting the historical scope of metaphysics, and therefore, too, of nihilism, to late decadent, mainly Iberian Scholasticism. For him, "metaphysics" is, in the first place, any legislation of the possible before we get to what appears and manifests its own possibility, and second, any definition of the human that is defined by this transcendental account of experience and reason. To think from the event of manifestation, the original givenness of the phenomenon, means that we arrive to the conditions for its appearing only a posteriori.

According to Marion, phenomenology discerns the common rationality shared by all phenomena. There is a phenomenality as such, which is normatively governed by the concept of the event, that is, the phenomenon as its own origin: it is simply what it gives itself to be. Its perceivability, thinkability, and possibility comes from itself, in its appearing. Revelation in particular is the paradigm case of the phenomenon—paradigm *because* it proposes itself as the most radical phenomenon possible and paradigm *in the sense that* it determines our concept of the phenomenon in general and becomes the reference point for our understanding of *any phenomenon whatsoever*. Revelation, therefore, is central to philosophy, because it is the absolute phenomenon, the phenomenon par excellence, by relation to which every possible and actual phenomenon is thought. The event of revelation, and the conception of the phenomenon that it provides, demands that we raise impossibility above possibility, for the impossible—that which undoes every preconception, every limit put in place to secure the rationality of what appears in advance, limits which are undone by the appearing—is determinative of the very meaning of humanity and of human reason itself.[20] Marion summarizes this challenge of the phenomenology of revelation when he declares in a 2012 debate with Jean-Luc Nancy that "there is no outside of the Christological question," a question which establishes itself with all concreteness in the question Jesus posed to his disciples, "But what about you? Who do you say that I am?" [Mk 8:29].[21] This is the question that the phenomenon of revelation, that is the person Jesus Christ, poses to us: in being the human revelation of God par excellence, in identifying himself, in history, with the God of Israel, the God who is coming, Jesus of Nazareth places before us God's definitive word, a question to which we must give an answer. The human question "Who is Jesus of Nazareth?" is one with God's question, "Who, O mortal, are you?"

The question we must raise, precisely by virtue of our acknowledgment of the advance of phenomenology in our conception of revelation, an advance beyond any a priori transcendentalism, any subjective, existential, or linguistic legislation of possibility that constrains and delimits the appearing of revelation, is the question of *whether this advance has overshot the mark*. Is the demolition of every a priori conception of the conditions or limits of the experience and rationality of revelation, even those determinative of our finitude—our historicity and our flesh, particularly—is this demolition the same as *disregarding the fact of these very conditions themselves*? Theology offers the philosophy of revelation a principle that could help here, and may be required: that of "nature and grace." Grace does not destroy nature, but judges, heals, and perfects it. However "paradoxically" related, grace and nature are not reducible to one another, and any understanding of their relation implies the eschatological situation of our thinking (grace is ever eschatological), a situation which precludes us from considering that the revelation of God in history would *not* be subject to historical conditions.

This introduction of the eschatological allows us therefore to reset the question: Is the reduction to givenness, the refusal or demolition of every a priori, the rejection of any analogy vis-à-vis the event of revelation, is this an *ideal* or a phenomenological *reality*? And we can ask more particularly: Is it enough to suggest that these conditioning elements of creaturely experience and knowledge are "saturated" and set spinning, even unhinged or deconstructed, by the event of revelation? Marion is ambivalent: for him the anthropological categories that revelation saturates are provided, generally, by Kant, yet, at the same time, revelation is said to give its own conditions; *l'adonné*, the receiver, akin to the Platonic "receptacle" (χώρα), is a "blank screen onto which the phenomenon crashes."[22] And his fundamental distinction between givenness and appearing, according to which givenness is invisible, and all that is given does not appear, though all that appears is given,[23] seems to me to require a *radical reserve* about the meaning of the appearances themselves, even if and especially because it establishes their truthfulness.[24] And finally, corollary to this "reserve," it seems to require an eschatology to resolve the tension between these two components of phenomenality, for the reserve of the given points to the *provisional* nature of manifestation.[25] Perhaps it is the case that, at the very least, "excess" or "reserve" is a hermeneutical decision with which we begin. Is an "endless hermeneutic" of response because of the inadequacy of our concepts before the given enough here? Does "saturation" tell the definitive story of Christian concept of revelation? Doubtful. I doubt it because in this context, the argument asserts itself that the *reserve of the given* is more prominent in Christianity, even *particularly* in Christ, in the κένωσις of God, and in the emptiness of the tomb, an emptiness which the post-resurrection appearances only make agonizingly more apparent [*noli me tangere*], an emptiness which corresponds, markedly, to the utter poverty intrinsic to faith, that is, the *absence* of the presence of faith's divine object, in the *radical lack* of any saturation at all in our normative, historical experience of God. All this is symbolized well, at the center and apex of Christian faith, in the unleavened, tasteless Eucharistic host, a flat, colorless circle, a blank placeholder for the glory of God and yet identified with its presence, albeit under the form of history.

To restate the problem: the phenomenology of revelation, though essentially challenging the a priori character that defines, at least relatively, our finitude, still thinks *as if* revelation were already completely given, *as if* it were not *given as to come*, in a kenotic, promissory, hidden way, *sub specie mundi*. Revelation is, of course, divine action. It is kabodic (and kenotic, kabodic as kenotic, and vice versa), or material, and ultimately fleshly, involving a personal identification, a "hypostatic union," theologians say, between God and man, as a premise (so to speak) of the unfolding and collaborative eschatological action. The challenge of revelation itself to the phenomenology of revelation (and to any approach to revelation) is precisely that revelation, at least in the context of human history and finite, material experience, *keeps in play* the normative conditions of finitude, even if it radicalizes them to the point of establishing them as if for the first time precisely in its very act of revelation. The better we understand these conditions—and particularly the way in which they are tied to revelation—the better we understand revelation itself, in its essential eschatological conditions, which do nothing less than take hold of our normative human conditions (albeit as their master), build upon them, and promise their perfection.

We must take with equal seriousness the challenge of phenomenology to our conception of revelation, inasmuch as it calls into question the transcendental, that is, static, a priori, account of the conditions of our finitude, and also the challenge that revelation proposes to the *phenomenology* of revelation inasmuch as it discloses and puts in play, seemingly by *magnifying*, the conditions of our finitude, our historicity, and materiality. In revealing the conditions of our finitude as if for the first time, revelation reveals that the conditions of our finitude are plastic, that our finitude itself is open-ended and a divine project. Part of this open-endedness of our finitude is found in the way that it can be the locus of the impossible, that the conditions that our finitude cannot help raising up vis-à-vis the divine self-manifestation can become the site of the divine appearing that remains divine, that reveals itself as divine, and all the more divine in appearing as divine within the sphere of creaturely expression and understanding. Yet we cannot stop there, and we cannot stop there because we cannot start just there. The phenomenology of revelation that deconstructs our transcendental accounts of revelation, specifically, the static, transcendental accounts of reason that constrain, in whatever manner, the phenomenality of revelation—any "metaphysics"—must itself be chastised, tempered: phenomenology does not contain the Absolute; revelation is not identified with our reception of it, or our descriptions of its phenomenal structure, just as no reality *is* the words by which we refer to it, approach it, or understand it. The eschatological imposes itself: our signification only signifies a "non-parousiac" presence.[26] We must acknowledge the reserve of the given. Refusing this reserve would collapse the eschatological tension that defines Christian revelation and we would have to call any phenomenological account that does not acknowledge this reserve an "over-realized phenomenology" of revelation. Here grace would swallow up nature; eternity, history and heaven, earth. Yet for Christianity, we are certainly not there yet, and further, eternal life is not disembodied bliss beyond the worlds, but the transfiguration of all things according to the standard of Christ's resurrected body, about which [witness the Gospels] we only know very little, and in relation to which all we know is by reference to *our present historical categories*, the integrity of which it somehow retains through their yet incomplete liberation.

The basic question concerns, then, *the way that revelation puts our finite conditions in play*. I propose that eschatology provides the answers to this question and what is needed is an *eschatological way* of thinking this question. Our finite conditions are plastic and ultimately given as to come; they are themselves provisional. How do we think this way?

To introduce the way of thinking eschatologically—the horizon within which the Christian revelation proposes itself—I turn to Jean-Yves Lacoste, particularly his critical elucidation of the phenomenality of givenness in the closing section of his essay "De la donation comme promesse," the seventh study of his 2008 volume, *La phénoménalité de Dieu*.[27] In a subtle investigation, Lacoste ruminates on the significance of the "linguistic ubiquity" of the language of givenness, the gift and the given (159). He asks the fundamental question whether saying "being" is "given" is not ruled by a "*naive* anthropomorphism" (159; emphasis added): to be given, does that imply a giver from whom being is a gift? Should reality be understood fundamentally according to the logic of a mundane human economy of exchange, even if eclipsed by the logic of a pure unilaterality? This *critical* starting point, one as old, perhaps, as philosophy itself, leads Lacoste to an understanding of phenomenological givenness according to the phenomenality of the event, a linkage which "separates the concept and event of donation from any anthropological measure" (159–60).[28] This journey leads, in the end, to a theological conclusion concerned with the given par excellence, the given that is given only as promised, and thus the definitive eradication of realized eschatology from our phenomenology of revelation. This theological conclusion is governed by the basic theological-philosophical question introduced in the previous study: To what extent can the Absolute be given to us? If God is infinite and completely unbounded personality and being, can he reveal, can he truly communicate himself to us, essentially finite and bounded creatures? Like Balthasar, Lacoste observes, in the first place, that to say that the finite creature like us is capable of the infinite (*finitum capax infiniti*) is to assert the theologically primitive thesis that the infinite can infinitely give itself, that is, give itself as it is. The gift of divine revelation to the finite creature "by definition" is itself boundless, an "infinite gift" (175). The precise Latin definition of eschatological bliss (formulated in the fourteenth century) as "face to face vision of the divine essence" suggests no more in reality than the vision's necessarily "inchoate" character: the absolute giving of the Absolute is itself tied to an infinitely non-given, even if this non-given is itself given as non-given: eschatology, in other words, the horizon of Christian revelation, is ruled by a certain logic, *the logic of promise* (175).[29] Here, we must affirm that the infinite can be truly given if ever only in a finite mode, or, more adequately, a trans-finite or hyperbolically finite mode (which is not merely finite and therefore alone fully finite) wherein, again, the finite is redundant on itself, more than itself, as itself, precisely in the self-gift of God. In Aquinas, for example, the beatific vision is given through the mediation of the light of glory (*lumen glorae*) which is a created light, a new, fundamentally paradoxical and trans-finite capacity that adapts the creature to the vision of the uncreated essence, a vision that is for the creature, inexhaustible, and endless like an adventure that never ends in its "overflow" to the body and its cosmos. This distinction runs roughly parallel with the Eastern one between essence and energies; the latter, though uncreated, are what the creature participates in by grace and not the former.

For Lacoste, the play of seeing and not seeing that constitutes the vision contains both the knowledge that there is always more to know of God in eternity *and* that God can be truly known by us. Together they make up the double source of human blessedness. Needless to say, the infinitely exhaustive givenness of God, even—*and especially*—in the beatific vision, is a "strict impossibility" and ought to be distinguished from a mere "practical impossibility" of adequate perception, as if it were potentially realizable (175). It is a "practical impossibility" for a created intelligence, in the human mode, to perceive all the sides of a cube at once by virtue of our embodied limitations, though not, it seems for created intelligence as such, since it could be possible for the angel, not conditioned by material limitations, to perceive the cube in its totality. Yet, it is a "strict impossibility" for the angel or the human to know God exhaustively, in this world or the next. The incomplete character of the divine givenness to a finite intuition is permanent and defining of the relation, and is as much a source of beatitude as the truthfulness of the infinite self-communication. Happiness is partly found in knowing that we cannot exhaust God, that there is infinitely more to know even when we know him truly. Indeed, true knowledge of God knows God as ever greater than our reception of him, *ad infinitum*.

The fundamental division between finitude and infinitude that remains central here for Lacoste highlights the essential continuity between the state of *viator* and *comprehensor*, between the state of pilgrimage within the horizon of the world and that of being installed in the homeland of eternal beatitude.[30] Yet, the difference between these two fundamental human states remains stark: God is given to human intuition in himself only on the other side of death. On this side, in the world, established, as it is, on reality's out rim, God is not "seen" at all. "If one still wants to utilize the language of vision," Lacoste states, "then the appearance of God in the world is conditioned by a fundamental lack of intuition" (175). And hence "donation," he says, "gives only in order to be believed" (176). The scope of human intuition in the world deals always with the visible domain. This visible, for example, the body of Jesus Christ, whether the Eucharistic or, for the original disciples, his historical body, is, "perceivable as God giving himself *only on the condition* that we make a distinction between what is given to sensible intuition and what is given to a believing intuition" (176, emphasis added). Yet, at the same time, if we separate these things in order to consider the visibly given only in itself, apart from faith, all we get is the visible and nothing more. Thus, in the concrete revelation of God in the body, "the gift that we perceive possesses only promissory value and ought not be taken as a final word [*dernier mot*]" (176). This difficult situation, definitive of eschatological faith, means, for Lacoste, that the gift that is given in divine revelation is perceived *only as a promise*, as yet to be given, but pledged to be given. Here we are permitted a further clarification of the results of the first study. The visible *kabod* is only ever not God—God's excess over himself in the mode of what he is not.

The formula that Lacoste derives from the eschatological situation of divine revelation is the following: *Dieu jamais donné* "God (n)ever given" (176). God, as Absolute, has the right and power to reveal himself as he is, that is, in truth:

to see Jesus *is* to see the Father (as the Scriptures teach). Yet the divine gift of revelation is therefore less one of "saturation" (*rassasiement*) than it is that of *anticipation*, of trust in that which is given as promise (176). Finally, the promise already includes within its logic that the promised, when it arrives, will not ever be exhaustible by the creaturely gaze, and thereby something which the infinite hunger of creaturely desire would move on from to disappointment. In this way, that which is given in historical revelation is truly given: This always-more character of divine revelation is shared in the present and future state. That which is given is still given in the mode of promised-to-come even when the conditions of historical finitude are absorbed and fully metamorphosized in the "world to come." We could express this historical knowledge *in Christ*, from a different source, Newman in the *Apologia*: "The visible world still remains without its divine interpretation; Holy Church in her sacraments and her hierarchical appointments will remain, even to the end of the world, after all but a symbol of those heavenly facts that fill eternity. Her mysteries are but the expressions in human language of truths to which the human mind is unequal."[31] All this amounts to saying is that there is, therefore, a properly anthropomorphic character to knowledge of God inasmuch as it is, really, *human* knowledge which is the matter. *Quidquid recipitur ad modum recipientis recipitur*, "Whatever is received is so according to the mode of the receiver." So goes a familiar scholastic axiom.[32] The axiom echoes a Neoplatonic conception famously utilized by Boethius in the fifth book of the *Consolation*. To demonstrate the absolute difference between human and divine modes of cognition (dialectical *ratio* and intuitive, all-grasping *intellectus*), and the natures that employ them (viz., temporal and finite versus eternal and infinite), Boethius claims that everything that is known is known not according to its native power to be known but rather that of the capacity of the knower itself.[33] The senses know the external shape of an object while the reason (through discerning its specific difference with what it is not) knows the kind of thing, the form it instantiates. The intellect, or rather, Intellect, sees the form as the content of its own mind insofar as it itself, albeit beyond form, is the form or archetype of that which it creates and, without interval, knows. In all of this, the "higher power of comprehension embraces the lower, while the lower does not at all raise itself to the higher."[34] The difference is then not between two discrete actors functioning on the same plane, or even on distinct planes, or even, finally, anywhere but in a relation that is, and can only be conceived as completely without proportion the one to another. The higher, all-comprehensive power embraces all, transcending the differences while willing to preserve everything in its relative, or proximate integrity. The difference holds and establishes the destiny and vocation of man to "become a god" by elevation into the divine eternal nature, although the *ratio* presupposes and is ordered to, functions, then, as an interval, one could say, within divine *intellectus*. There is, as it were, a causal echo of the above in the below, wherein all activity of the latter is pre-contained in an eternal and perfect way within the seeing-mind of God as divine providence and knowing. From below, it is understood to be limited and free, a truly human action caused by oneself and terminating in proximate knowledge, yet from above the below, activity is pre-grasped (although there is no time, no before and after, from this vantage) within the absolute coincidence of divine knowledge and being. The Platonic word for all this is μέθεξις, participation. Radicalized, though, by the conception of God as creator, the term inflects causal freedom, the freedom of God to give the creature its own causal freedom within the horizon of its own proximate capacities and desire that only ever (in the end) expresses God's eternal ordering will, that is, to create a partner with whom he collaborates, even through the disturbed and wayward order dominated by sin.

Sin, of course, is only grasping instead of receiving. Man can only ever do what is in his nature, that is, to seek what he is ordered to, and yet cannot accomplish his nature except by collaboration with his maker. Man seeks immortality, beatitude, and knowledge. That which God alone possesses in infinite measure, a threefold possession that, only at infinity brings man into his completion, his fullness. Man becomes *a* god, a divine actor, by the gift of *the* God. It is true, at least on one reading, that Marion only conceives of unilateral saturation of intuition and gives no elaborated gesture, at least to my knowledge, to the tradition's emphasis (recovered and advanced by the philosophical godfather of French *ressourcement*, Maurice Blondel) on the inexhaustible excess of human intention over every relative, proximate fullness given to him on the finite horizon.[35] He never theorizes, as a phenomenological desideratum, the excess of intention over intuition. Yet he does align himself with the acknowledgment of man's "naturally supernatural" character, the excess of man's desire over anything finite, a "patristic tradition," he says in a text that is surely meant to be his magnum opus, that is "incontestable and absolutely certain."[36] Here man is already a revelation to himself in an analogous way that the world is, by disclosing, in its manifestation, an excess of givenness, its absolute contingency, and the mysterious absent-presence of its absolute source. Marion claims the intentional horizon's suspension and upending, its eclipse by revelation, but even so, it is not erased or annihilated. He conceives it, precisely in its creaturehood, perhaps even a posteriori definitive thereof, as a starting point, an activation of man's intentional capacity for God (and therefore for himself) from within the revelation of Christ, the personal disclosure of God in human terms and the gift of a vocation that actualizes the freedom of human nature in its higher plane. One could even say that for Marion, the infinite striving at the root of the finite intention, present in every act, surely, is banal. It requires, calls out for its ground, which can only be given to it through an elevation of the creature. And this recognition is, of course, met in the mode of promise, even in mystics, perhaps especially there, wherein the transgression of every creaturely support, the awakening, if you would like to venture it, to the non-duality of nature (in the Christian sense, of course, wherein God is *more than merely* non-dual with world), is but the most radical setting for a personal address that never ceases to give not just divine nature (which is, given as not given, as an adventure) but also true personhood, which is never without a share in the nature, and therefore nothing but created god-hood.

The long-range importance of Marion's thought, if I may risk the prognostication, will be found in his critique of the "epistemological interpretation of revelation," an accomplishment limited, more or less strictly, to the phenomenological apparatus by which he accomplishes it.[37] It is aimed, exclusively, at an "overcoming" of "metaphysics," on the one hand, and at a fundamental surpassing of the propositional account of revelation, on the other. Of course, these are only two sides of the same coin. The former is but the philosophical expression of the latter, and vice versa. By "epistemological interpretation," he means the elaboration of revelation as knowledge, of man as possessing a nature that suffers an incompletion of knowledge only filled by a gratuitous elevation to a share in the supernatural knowledge of God. This supernatural knowledge is *ratio*, indeed, par excellence, *logos*, divine *intelligentia* overcoming the lack endemic to natural reason functioning on its own steam, but this conquest comes only at the high price, one must say, of its implicit subordination to the defining strictures of revelation as knowledge as (Aristotelian) *science*.[38] The co-arrival of noetic contemplation (θεωρία), as the highest and best cosmic excellence (ἀρετή), with the logical systematization of Aristotelian ἐπιστήμη (wherein knowledge appears or at least is secured in propositions) shows how close the *duplex ordo* of discrete natural and supernatural ends is with the collapse of the contemplative into the ecstatic and frankly masturbatory rigors of mere conceptuality that will appear in the decadent era of Thomas' proto- or early modern interpreters.[39] Yet surely one of the fundamental consistencies of the Neoplatonic frame of the intellectual tradition of Christianity is its epistemological, or let us say noetic or intellective, τέλος.[40] For it is a "blessed vision," a *knowing* that beatifies man, for God is, essentially, intellect without limitation, infinitely replete in the unfathomable fullness of the knowledge of himself. Here, essentially, *man* is knower, the seer of abstract or universal truth, who accomplishes his nature by participation in *God* who is—full stop—knowing itself. The "epistemological interpretation" in the narrow sense is found, most explicitly, in the scholastic appropriation of Aristotle, for whom the divine was, most essentially, knowing-as-seeing (νόησις νοήσεως).[41] Aristotle is, of course, only echoing his teacher, for whom knowledge is a central aspect of divinity and of man as, essentially divine himself, belonging to the noetic cosmos of undying realities dimly perceived in the midst of the visible world's travestied chaos by, first, awakening to oneself. And Plato himself is likely simply passing on the pre-Socratic revolutionary insight—only an extension of the core claim of the Greek Mysteries—that mortals are, really, immortals.[42] For Aristotle, man, whose dignity is tied to an essential contact with the divine seeing, realizes his essence in the contemplation of what is highest, partaking, as much as possible, in the divine self-seeing itself.[43] It is remarkable how thoroughly the tradition has been marked—in the Fathers as much as in St. Thomas himself, whose continuity with them is, in this aspect, seamless—by the Greek account of divinity-as-seeing. For Marion, surely, the "epistemological account" is limited to the elision of θεωρία by bare theory, a slide from contemplation to a content of arranged propositions, wherein the master concept, "being," calcifies into an a priori abstraction signifying no more than the illusion of graspable permanence in reality, "subsisting persistence in presence," a foothold for an illusory account of self as a permanent reality amidst the flux of finite passing.[44]

Husserl, it should be said, ties one as equally to vision as Aristotle, although phenomenology recovers, Marion would have us think, the conception of truth as noetic, as apocalyptic disclosive manifestation, and as such, precisely, as seeing, as a seeing, most radically, coincident with (Trinitarian) being itself. And I think he is right. Christ is the visibilization of the Son (in the Spirit, as power of visibilization) *as* the self-manifestation of the invisible Father to himself in the Spirit.[45] Marion (and, it must be said, his rather exemplary utilization of biblical material) works too from out of the particularly Greek axialization of God as transcendent ground of knowledge-as-vision coincident with itself, and the condition, thereby, of man's ultimate share in that divinity through vision. For the Greeks, beatitude is coincident with knowledge and immortality (or power, the greatest power being transcendence of death). These are divine possessions, or rather, the divine self-possession, everywhere that an enlightened monotheism gained traction. By the time of Plotinus, these are found in God or the One as infinite plenitude, in an abyss of fullness that is wholly without limitation.

We should marvel at how fully the Greek Enlightenment of the fifth and fourth centuries before Christ have come to inform our understanding of the Jewish and Christian revelation, and we should marvel, equally, at how distorted this revelation can become through the tradition's meandering historical course, in its reduction to science as an arrangement of revealed propositional truths. But we should also marvel at how completely such a recovery of the tradition, through a backtracking reform of our thinking, can permit a fresh encounter with other "axial" civilizational traditions, most especially in their varied and most-sophisticated monotheistic, knowledge-as-seeing forms. If it is the case that the axial revolution is predicated on an awareness of the capacity of reason to plumb the narrative sources of religion to their veiled source, to discern, through myth, the intelligible structures of permanence that frame our relation to reality, it is also the case that reason is irreparably tied to the forms of finitude by which its access to reality is first framed for it. These forms, as Plato apparently saw, are narrative and ritual, especially. Concepts forged through the discernment of embodied experience's most fundamental distinctions are as equally as anthropomorphic, tied to the potentials of this world to give us our vision, as are the apparently more aboriginal horizons of figuration in the myth-ritual complex. A religious fidelity to the Jewish and Christian revelation, precisely in its "western" form (i.e., biblical and Hellenistic, or, if you like, religious and philosophical, reciprocally interlaced and interpenetrating), means that the epistemological, and behind it, the noetic account of the divine has a setting, one now several millennia rich. Like anything in history, it has an origin (in the ten thousand year history of humanity since the Neolithic revolution) from which it can only detach itself at its own expense. And it has a lifespan, a *place* within the religious and cultural evolution of humanity. If there is a final consistency to this evolution, a meaning, then it has a direction, an end. And if Easter has the universal and definitive significance for humanity that Christians have discerned in it (if, indeed, it really and truly happened), then Easter is the (it must be said, inchoate) ἀποκάλυψις of that end, which happens to be the transcendence of (not from) mortality (and therefore including with it, presumably, a share in the infinite blessedness and knowledge that are equally God's self-possession). More stringently put, grace elevates and heals nature, it does not escape from it but, *by immersion in it*, takes it beyond (hyper-, super-) itself and thereby, alone giving it, through its own empowerment, its accomplishment. I would no doubt be testing your patience by noting the implicit and necessary role of narrative in the present paragraph's account, as in any theoretical account (analogous, of course, to the relation of figure to concept for the mind, of body to soul for humanity, of world to kingdom for eschatology).

So I am merely advocating, here, for a definitive contextualization of theoretical enlightenment for the sake of comprehending Christian revelation and its implications, as well as, I venture (however tentatively), for gesturing to what opens beyond the Axial accomplishment(s), without abandoning all that is definitive within it.[46] Setting Marion's thought with the eschatological distinction (à la Lacoste) has large implications. However foregrounded the theoretical enlightenment may be in our account of it, for this ἀποκάλυψις the flesh is primary. It is, as the ancients had it, the hinge of salvation, *caro salutis cardo*.[47] The epistemological-noetic account of human fullness turns on—and only functions by turning on—the embodied τέλος of revelation. The hinge metaphor is wholly apt. It turns on the narrative μῦθος, then, of the people Israel, as unique bearer of a revelation for the world, a revelation that reaches its fullness in Christ. According to this μῦθος, in the language of axial revolution, the opening into the eschatological future apocalyptically carved into the present, historical age. In it, the renewed human community constituted by πίστις ("fidelity" or "faithfulness") to Christ as the world's one, true, definitive judge and principal of its transfiguring renewal, is elevated to the dignity of collaborative partnership with God in accomplishing his πρόθεσις ("that which is set forth," "plan"), to refer to two Pauline concepts, and this, in a future that is open to be written in fully human speech, creased with fully human folds—fully human, but not merely. If the revelation—the divine action—is true, that is, trustworthy, something worth believing in, saying "Amen" to, in Christian liturgical idiom, then it demands the ever-renewed priority of the narrative order over the theoretical, though it will preserve the constructive tension between them inasmuch as the latter serves to sound, critically, to unblock the narrative intelligence and keep (as it were) the tradition moving in constructively unrestful ambition for the completion of all things. Narrative, I could say, is more worldly than theory, and the terminus of revelation (again, divine action) is a new world, the glorification of the embodied world, a descent of the kingdom into cosmos, not ascent as escape from world to kingdom.

I suppose it should be made plain that I follow a major gesture found in the thought of Vladimir Soloviev here, which is a remarkable transposition of biblical narrative into theoretical key, the latter intended precisely as an explication at the service of the former. It comes into focus most clearly, I think, in his concepts of "free theurgy" (where man collaborates with God to the accomplishment of divine purpose) and "all unity" (wherein there is a final coincidence of universal and particular in the created order as it receives, in a more and more explicit way, the divine descent through man's natural activity of unlocking the creation's "sophianic" potential).[48] And yet similar indications may be found in Thomas Aquinas. For example: "Intelligent creatures are ranked under divine Providence most excellently because they participate in Providence by their own providing for themselves and others. So they join in and make their own the Eternal Reason through which they have their natural aptitudes for their proper activity and purpose."[49] This τέλος is precisely where the critical edge emerges between Christian confession and its Greek sources, as well as, for the future, when Christian intellectual μάρτυρας ("witness") to the Easter confession will find its seam in future post-Axial developments on the far side of the, to us, still nearly unfathomable synthetic accomplishments with the world's great civilizational traditions already underway.

I am attempting to realize, in all that has been said, that it is of the nature of God to ever-transcend his self-giving and to give himself in that way is to give himself truly. And that this essential surplus forms an ultimate precondition for the anthropic mediation of divine glory in "the age to come" wherein God can re-establish the hierarchical τάξις and elevate humanity in its fullness of place, as μεταξύ, drawing the embodied milieu to the role of definitive economic mediator of the world to come.

God, in history, transcends his revelation, at least normatively, by way of eschatological reserve. The same applies to eternity, the difference between the pre-eternal and eternal modes being that partnership of God and humanity is perfected, that is, truly (finally) begun in the advent of the latter. This ever-greater character of revelation is a result of the fact that God is not an abstract concept or a logic of relations among concepts, but Living Person, and even personal in perfect, threefold excess of himself (as tri-hypostatic personality). When Christians articulate the truth of God within the conditions of finitude (e.g., reciting the Creed, or more abstractly, the formula of the Trinity), or better, when we address or invoke God, the Father, Son, and Holy Spirit, or better, when we, through the Spirit, make the sacred offering of Jesus' living flesh on the altar of the Father, there we are knowing God, *in the gifts*. Our knowledge is "participatory," beyond proposition and concept, coincident with the act of worship. Here the *concrete* particularity of the *bare words* (in the case of the formula), of the *prayer* (in the case of raising one's mind to God), of the *act* (in the case of the Eucharistic sacrifice), in degrees of *intensity*, express the unfathomable reality of God in a way more, and more, and most fitting for the divine as humanly possible, if also more, and more, and most provisionally and, finally, with more, and more, and most eschatological reserve. We acknowledge that our anthropomorphism is unavoidable, even at the far end of our critique of it, and we acknowledge that after all, when it is held within the reserve of an eschatological judgment, it becomes most properly signitive of the divine. Here, to quote Louis Bouyer, knowledge is "always renewing itself in the measure that it deepens itself."[50]

The divine gift infinitely transcends the gift itself, and the gift, in order to be truly given, can and must give to us the recognition that that which is given—in the case of Christ, God himself *in the flesh*—infinitely transcends the gift, and this, for the last time, precisely because *he is the gift*. Hence the gift of the Father in Christ is never past tense "given" but only given as to come. In this way is the gift truly given to us in the present without deceiving us. In the case of God, then, the gift is a "pledge." In anticipation of what is to come, I can now offer a proximate conclusion to bring this chapter to an end:

Apophasis is, first, a rhetorical device. One mentions something by saying that one will not say it in a typical ironic fashion: "I will not tell you that I prefer anchovies on the pizza: you decide!" In philosophical religion and theological practice, apophasis is a way of approaching God; one negates significations, saying what cannot be said, in order to reach the fundamentally unknowable God. Everything said about God is inscribed within the recognition that it does not reach the divine reality. To negate is to leap into the darkness of the unapproachable, to affirm that God exceeds even our greatest significations. Apophasis also involves a mode of knowledge. Knowing rests on the phenomenological experience of presence and absence. Apophasis names the *unknowing* implicit in the experience of divine presence, since God's presence uniquely oversupplies experience in a way that manifests as absence, in an otherness that is a presence (as I have said) in excess of presence. The fullness of divine presence is given in eschatological reserve; the transcendence of what is given to faith is given as to come, as an advance on what will be, which promises "resurrection," a transfiguration or metamorphosis, of what is, an eclipse of the way things are. The believer knows in Christ to whom he is pledged, and he therefore willingly pledges himself to him without reserve, that is, in direct proportion to the degree of Christ's pledge, first, to him (which is itself without reserve, in the Cross). But the absolute nature of this mutual self-giving is inseparable from a reserve that is not just historical—even if revelation only makes more evident and more drastic the lines that mark our finite historicity—a reserve that is founded on the recognition of the promissory nature of the gift, as well as a refusal to close the limits of the gift, particularly by reducing what is given to the scope of our present capacity to receive it—for we do not know what we are except from the starting point of grace, which, as (strictly) a renewal of the starting point of our cosmic nature, and nothing less, harbors a hyperbolic density within the reserve. After all, it is the *consummation* of a marriage that makes it valid, nothing less. The presence in excess of presence experienced as absence (cosmos) will be eclipsed by the presence in excess of presence experienced as presence (kingdom), as "seeing face to face," which requires an eschatological refiguration of the present cosmic order. In anticipation of that, the *factus est* of the enfleshment of God in Jesus immerses God (fully) in the human cultural, historical order. Already in the time of pre-parousiac absence, "non-naïve" anthropomorphic significations eclipse the angelic abstract verities of theoretical transcendence as (mere) escape, for those with eyes to see that which they cannot.

Second

3. Between Contemplation and Concepts (Bultmann)
4. Anthropomorphism and Some Aspects of Modern Thought

3

Between Contemplation and Concepts (Bultmann)

The question "What does it mean to speak of God?" once posed by Bultmann is something common enough, a theological question posed by a biblical scholar influenced by specific philosophical modes of reasoning (here, Heidegger). The immediate implication is that this question unravels any strict categorization of disciplines: as a basic human question at the heart of theology, philosophy, and biblical inquiry, the question of God, and of the possibility of speaking of God, demands nothing less than that we perpetually rethink what we are doing when we are thinking. With the help of Balthasar, we have begun to think about the relation between God's manifest non-otherness, his self-presencing in the world and his reality in itself, beyond-but-not-in-contrast-to the world and by introducing a contrast to the angelic, we have considered (with the toolset of phenomenology) the particularly eschatological meta-conditions of the world of our finitude in faith's constitutive awareness of its all-determining relation to the God who promises, the God who is coming. Now I will turn to Bultmann, and to the character of theological thought that grows, to my mind, like the garden of paradise in the presence of God, to continue the development of our inquiry.

"What does it mean to speak of God?" Rudolph Bultmann posed this question in a well-known essay from 1925. The manner in which Bultmann posed this question remains significant for it exposes, as I have said, the a priori link between biblical studies, theology, and philosophy: study of Scripture, conceived as an irreducibly religious enterprise, is already theological and philosophical; theology is, it could be said, philosophically trained reason applied to Scripture; and philosophy implicitly contains theological presuppositions and ends that are wholly determined by one's religious sensibility vis-à-vis the biblical data.

In the first place, therefore, what Bultmann asked in 1925 is not a question conceived as a "prolegomena" to thought, one that we can pose in order to secure an answer from which we can then pass to other questions and answers (which may or may not be true about it). It is already in Bultmann precisely a "postmodern" question: with this question, reason forcefully discovers its already religious and mystical character; it is not transparent to its own ground but discovers that it is awoken to itself by a primordial contact with the unsayable. Reason's perplexing question is one posed to itself in the face of reason's greatest and most fundamental question: Bultmann's "What does it mean to speak of God?" is a question that the thought or idea of God first and perpetually imposes on us as rational beings. It is a question that, like all the most important questions, is insoluble and permanent. Fundamentally, therefore, it is a question that is both philosophical and religious at once, allowing us no self-securing gap among disciplinary categorizations.

"What does it mean to speak of God?" is therefore a question without an "answer" with an almost Socratic-like character. Through (1) reflecting on Bultmann's proposal in the light of Trinitarian dogma, we will see that dogma itself, when believed and thought *through*, is a "liturgical" employment of concepts and not (contra Heidegger) a ready-made 'answer' to another question, the metaphysical question ("Why is there something rather than nothing?"): to "speak of God" through dogma only intensifies the essential character of the existential question of being, its insolubility. Exposing the essentially mystical and contemplative character of dogma will allow us then to (2) re-propose a Patristic commonplace by reference to a biblical locus classicus, St. Paul's address on the Areopagus in Acts 17: classical philosophical piety (which I call the "way of abstraction") is complementary with Christian theological piety (which, I hope—following a certain Areopagitical tradition, toward an explication of which I am straining—not too misleadingly call the "way of the symbol"). Finally, (3) the broadly conceived "liturgical condition" of religious thought, of theology, is made explicit, and I will suggest (perhaps not unsurprisingly at this stage of my argument) that eschatology is the key that unlocks the path of access to the right understanding of the relation of concepts and contemplation, of our speech "about" God and our existential "being before God": the ultimate unity-in-difference of sign and signified in the beatific vision allows us (a) to distinguish them here and now, under the conditions of history, without a bad conscience, (b) thus to embrace the ambiguity and insolubility that the question of God exposes as inherent to reason, which then also (c) urges us to bring contemplation and concepts into interplay through the way of the symbol. This interplay proposes itself as an ideal form of theological writing, of which the biblical corpus itself furnishes the incomparable archetypes but which is not absent from certain modern theological or philosophical authors (Rosenzweig, say, or Karl Barth) in whose writing the content is (so to speak) alive, in other words—this is difficult to express—the realities they seek peek at us through the very interrogations they elaborate.

First, to Bultmann, whom I read as a figure who scratches off the temporal surface of Christianity to find a rather classical conception of the divine. I do not need to argue that this is wrongheaded, at least as a pursuit of intellectual labor. The God of Abraham, Isaac, and Jacob is not (reducible to) the God of the philosophers. The seam that has joined them in the Christian tradition is real; it is more tightly woven in some places than others; sometimes it rips apart through wear. In asserting this, I acknowledge, we are approaching a commonplace (though one that is not enough understood). Nevertheless, the partial argument I want to make now, in simplest terms, is that far from being opposed, the classical, philosophical account of divinity still underlying Bultmann's picture of the theologian's task may itself be utilized as an appropriate, let me say, *preparation* for rightly understanding the specificities of the Christian account of God—dogma and all—which deepens, through a correcting transformation, the former's intellectual piety.

"What does it mean to speak of God?" is *not*, as a question conceived as a prolegomena to thought, one that we can pose in order to secure an answer from which we can then pass to other questions and answers (which may or may not be true about it). Rather it is a question that the thought or idea of God first and perpetually imposes on us. It is a question that, perhaps like all the most important questions, is insoluble and permanent, and, which is both philosophical and religious at once.[1]

If we *believe* in the reality of God, Bultmann observes right out of the gate, we can be sure that by this we have no *comprehension* of this reality. In fact, belief in God, a belief worthy of the God in whom one believes, contains as an element within it the defining assertion that God is greater than our thoughts, outside or beyond, other than that which we can distinguish through the operations of our thinking. "Whenever the idea, God, comes to mind," says Bultmann," it connotes that God is the Almighty; in other words, God is the reality determining *all else.*" It is worth marveling again at this divinity, for it is by and within this "all else" that our thought moves—for our thought is itself an item among the set of everything actual and possible that exists. This total set of things we call the world. God is beyond the world, but not in such a way as to be set over against it, for in this way God would be merely another item or thing added to the world, an expansion of the totality of things that are. On the contrary, God *determines* this "all else": this means that God is that by which this all else is and that upon which it, this totality of the world, has no *essential* effect or implication whatsoever. The existence of the world adds nothing at all to God, who alone "is" properly speaking. The world exists before God as *nothing* and is only *something* by virtue of God's freedom to give it to itself by giving it a wholly redundant (as far as the perfection of being goes) participation in himself.

Bultmann's essay explores the implications for the practice of theology of this unique "God" that is its object. Its clear but implicit debt to classical sources is mediated through a Kierkegaardian insistence on the dramatic fact of existence. The most important observation for Bultmann is that the divinity of God—a divinity that fundamentally exceeds the distinctions that compose worldly being and hence the context of our knowledge and experience—fundamentally calls into question theology, understood as our speech "about" God: "every 'speaking about,'" he says, "presupposes a standpoint external to that which is being talked about." But with this God, the God in whom we believe (and what other God is there?), there simply "cannot be any standpoint external." Our speech is historically conditioned, whereas God is not; if we try to make general statements of what Bultmann calls "scientific validity" about God—speech that on its own terms reaches to and secures for itself the universally true—then we are not only attempting to place ourselves beyond these historical conditions, which is impossible, but we are also asserting for ourselves a divine standpoint, beyond or outside of God, a point from which we can stand and refer to God as a signified to our signification, as an object that corresponds to our thought. This leads to a twofold error that expresses the absurdity and irrationality of this speech: here we are placing God *within* the horizon of the world, the horizon within which our speech makes sense, and placing ourselves *outside* of it in the position of God! A determining element of human thought and speech is that it must occur in a place; our kind of reason, human reason, is topological— it inheres in the world. The place, for Bultmann, that demarcates our speech about God is described as our "concrete, existential situation" that determines our humanity: this situation is paradoxically and therefore properly understood as inhering without grasping its own conditions for inhering, that is, as carrying within it the question of ourselves, unfolded as the question of the God that is our absolute condition, a *question* that most properly defines our human situation. But this situation, for Bultmann, makes speech "about" God meaningless. "It is impossible," he concludes, in a manner, I would think, that is quite consistent, "to speak meaningfully *about* God (*über Gott*)."

"God" has no possible meaning in the horizon of the world—nor then does our human situation which the (empty) concept of "God" singularly illumines as an irresolvable crisis. We *must* speak meaningfully about God. We must get a conceptual grasp on "God" in order to get a handle on our humanity. But we cannot do so. To elucidate this necessary impossibility that is the human situation, Bultmann, much like St. John of the Cross before him or Jean-Luc Marion after him, immediately observes an analogy in the phenomenon of love.[2] We cannot speak meaningfully *about* love from a standpoint external to love itself: "one cannot speak about love at all," he says, "unless the speaking about is itself an act of love." The same goes, he next observes, for the experience of parenthood, which bears an essential relation to childhood, or to be more concrete, of fatherhood and motherhood to the experience of being a daughter or son.[3] The relation that defines this experience is missed when it is spoken about extrinsically, that is, as a "special case of a natural process which operates between individuals of the same species." Merely to speak *about* love or of the relations of "sonship" and "fatherhood" is to miss the "essential relation" which can only be known as experienced from the inside. Our speech *about* the relation of fatherhood, of love, and eminently of God, is only negative, a "speaking about" that is "in the negative," a speaking "of" that only discloses what God is not, even as partaking of the joy of participatory encounter. In the erotic encounter, intimacy stirs up mystery.

To these examples provided by Bultmann, it seems a countless number of essential aspects of human experience could be added, those that exceed our bare animality and inhabit our consciousness, and even, to a remarkable degree, order it, if even and especially by the haunting allure of their intentional excess over it: freedom, goodness, beauty, desire, sensory experience, the flesh, our temporality, moral decision, and so on—every aspect or dimension of ourselves in fact when not examined through the optic of an a priori reduction to objective categories. What is there that really matters for our humanity that does not stand emphatically in excess of our capacity to understand, to receive and digest, to assimilate and exhaust it? Our humanity is manifest to us as exceeding the world of "about"—and that, precisely, because of our existential redundance within the phenomenological world of meaning: the legitimacy (in a final sense) of all meaning must be grounded through an unconditioned source of meaning, a source that is meaning itself. Meaning must, in other words, be infinite to matter at all. And although, furthermore, we are one among the many beings in the world, we are also the beings to whom the world as a whole is given as world, to be contemplated in its totality. This "constitution" is, unless I am mistaken, another word for consciousness, which is always in act, for being awoken to the whole out of an animality that still slumbers, and awoken equally, then, to oneself as its *Spieler*, its active meaning-engaged correlate.[4] God exceeds the world, and we do too, though we only exceed it as a member within it: our excess then at best faintly gestures toward God's own absolute excess over the world, which itself is not alien to the world but paradoxically its most fundamental reality. If man "constitutes" the world phenomenologically, then God does so ontologically. The world is, in this analogical sense, the content of the divine mind projected as a gifted qualification of its self-experience (being as such, infinite being) that is not itself (finite, contingent being).

The concept of God that arises when we ask what it means to speak of God is not alone in its paradoxical qualities, though it is certainly singular and unique. Bultmann's question makes manifest, I should say, the concomitant mystery of our humanity, which is essentially tied to it. And it is by means of our human paradoxicality already in the world that we can pass to contemplating God. And yet, these experiences "in the world," the negative excess by which they exceed every calculation or final quantification, in short, their mystery, is that by which the world is given to us, and, reciprocally, the world is the condition by which they are given to us, and by which through them, we are given to ourselves as worldly beings, as beings in the world. This marks God's basic difference from these other countless experiences of our human excess, of the ever-greater character of our humanity. If taken up collectively and infinitely intensified in their meaning the meaningful realities of human life are most fully or properly understood. This shows that God, as the plenitude of meaning, is already implicitly the means through which we experience the world in its meaningfulness, though we can only reach this awareness through reflection on our worldly experience, the myriad ways in which its meaningfulness elicits a desire within us that exceeds every desirable thing. These mysteries of the human world are not related to the mystery of God as parts are to a whole, although, already, the whole, the world, is totally different, qualitatively different than the sum of its parts that it contains. This whole only defines the world as the fundamental condition for our experience as worldly beings, which we are. But God is more than the totality of the world. God gives the totality of the world to itself, which is, as creation, contextualized by God's freedom. In this freedom it is revealed as radically contingent, as that which has absolutely no claim on its own existence. God is therefore only found in our concrete situation, *there* where our total existence is called into question and put at stake. *There* God is encountered and known precisely as the One who exceeds this existence, and gives it to be, who is, simply, the master and lord of it. To find oneself aware of the Absolute Mystery, even to confess belief in it, is to recognize oneself as wholly ordered by it. And if this Mystery were to be recognized, through the experience of the mystery of one's freedom to forge one's own creases in the world, as the granter of this freedom, then an awareness of the sacred character of life and of self-responsibility begin to dawn. The totality of the world in its bare thereness, its non-necessity and without why-ness (since it is given to itself out of the utterly sovereign freedom of God), raises in its radical immediacy God's mystery as the secret (so to speak, I have no other word) of its own mystery. This rather ordinary and common religious sensibility elevates and intensifies the groundlessness of the world *in proportion to* one's sense of God's transcendent immediacy as the hidden fullness of all things that establishes them in their contingent integrity. When we come to recognize that we cannot, in the conditions natively given to us, speak truthfully about our situation, but need God to do the speaking about it, which we cannot effect, *there* the truth of ourselves emerges. The truth of God, God's unutterability, is the site where our truth, as a human and worldly truth uttered not by ourselves but by God, begins to emerge.

The upshot of this situation is that all speech *about* God, and theology itself, therefore, at least theology with the ambitions to be scientific, Bultmann is not shy about asserting, is *inherently sinful*. Bultmann's development of Luther's stinging critique of scholastic theology as *scientia* is certainly radical and annoying to professional and academic theologians, but we still must accept the truth of it: human speech as the instrument and means of rationality, as a conceptual instrument, seeks to generalize and to separate in order to elucidate the intelligibility of that which it seeks to understand, and when it models itself after modes of thought defined and developed within the horizon of the world (which is of course necessary for thinking within the world and therefore any *human* thinking), however remarkably truthful these modes are in their articulation of the basic distinctions that the world itself gives, and despite whatever massive qualifications our modeling might ascribe to itself in order to mitigate this worldliness, it is simply not enough, never enough, to overcome this situation, for this situation, our historicity or finitude, understood in the present sense as our *merely* worldly character (as opposed to a *fully* worldly character, which does not have to be merely worldly), cannot be overcome by us.[5] And the terrible truth is again thrown in our faces: we are powerless to speak about God in himself (for we can only speak about God by speaking about what God is not, viz., ourselves and the world). We are at best partially powerless (and what good is that?) to speak about *ourselves* and our native, all-determining context, *the world*, two mysteries that require contrast with God to be understood as they are, in their irreducible openness to God. But it is this contrast or difference that we cannot grasp: everything is apophatic, because God, the key to everything, is unknowable.

This presence, better, presence-as-absence, even better, presence-as-presence-as-absence, of the Unknowable God raises the question: How much does acknowledging this situation do for us toward making our speech appropriate for God? How much does the recognition and even explorations of the depths of our finitude do for theology, for our speech *about* God? We must first admit that this strategic reconciliation with our finitude (a hallmark of Continental thought since Kant, for example), which by definition can never be completed or exhausted (since it is "absolute"), certainly does something for us; it raises our thinking, at least negatively, to God. How? It arrives at a sort of intellectual satisfaction with its essential emptiness in relation to the Question, the mystery of the invisible Donating Source beyond the world's order of intelligibility, and it even opens toward an almost pagan serenity regarding the natural sacrality of our own worldliness, a satisfaction with that which is native to us as beings in the world for whom the world in its finite-infinite wholeness is given as our own.

This recognition and the certain piety inherent to our finite thinking regarding the God who is fundamentally absent from the world, who is present as the Absent One, and even our concomitant at-home-ness in ourselves and the world that results from the inexhaustibility of our finitude, I am tempted to call, following St. Paul, the piety of the "Unknown God" (see Acts 17). "Athenians," said the Apostle in his discourse on the Areopagus, "I see how extremely religious you are in every way!" (v. 22) This observation of the Athenian religiosity is a conclusion directly tied to Paul's discovery in the city of an altar dedicated Ἀγνώστῳ θεῷ—"to the Unknown God," the God worshiped in ignorance, without knowledge (v. 23). This God, the Unknown God, *the* God, ὁ Θεός, indeed, but worshiped as unknown (as one god among others, or as the God, unknowable, beyond all others?), is reached, according to the classical philosophies, by way of negating every inner-worldly distinction, undoing every predication as fundamentally failing to be predicated of the one who exceeds the world, by making a method out of our essential ignorance. This way, which we could call the *way of abstraction*, proceeds by means of surpassing every distinction by which our worldly intelligence moves until it reaches the silent ecstasy of noetic union beyond every determination. It is therefore a way of abstraction in two complementary senses: (1) dialectically expanding our intellect into the empty void of being as such and preparing for the ecstatic leap into its nameless source; (2) and therefore abstracting us from out of our worldly conditions, if only proleptically, by separating out the intellect from its limiting and darkening conditions of the body, which becomes, suddenly, what it has always been, its material prison-house. Take the following passage from Book VII of Proclus' *Commentary on the Parmenides* of Plato as an example of this classical method:

> This whole dialectical method [of reason], which works by negations, conducts us to what lies before the threshold of the One, removing from all inferior things and by this removal dissolving the impediments to the contemplation of the One, if it is possible to speak of such a thing. But after going through all the negations, one ought to set aside this dialectical method also. . . . Here all dialectical activity ought to be eliminated. These dialectical operations are the preparation for the strain towards the One, but are not themselves the strain. Or rather, not only must it be eliminated, but the strain as well. Finally, when it has completed its course, the soul may rightly abide with the One. Having become single and alone with itself, it will choose only the simply One. . . . Parmenides . . . passes from the nature of Being to the inexpressible itself; for by means of negation he too removes all the negations. It is with silence, then, that he brings to completion the study of the One.[6]

This way of abstraction or negation proceeds from the recognition of the failure of reason to comprehend the One, the source or origin in which all things exist, what we (and they) rightly call God. We could even agree, as many Church Fathers did, that this tradition rightly grasps the existential or religious character of reason even when understood as created in the sense given by revelation. The biblical critique of idolatry finds a parallel tradition in the Hellenistic world in the rational critique of the myths that culminates in the philosophical monotheism of the Platonists in particular.

With that said I can throw a divine wrench into the system and introduce dogma to reason.

What specifically happens when reason is given by revelation new and insurpassable content, which it could never reach in its passage into the silence of the One? What happens to this existential situation charted or plumbed by philosophy when, to center on the most important and challenging example, God is revealed as and *thought* as Triune, when God is revealed, through words and deeds ascribed to ὁ Θεός within the theatre of the world, as Father, Son and Spirit, three persons irreducibly distinct and at the same time singularly one in the divine nature? To say "God is X," to define the divine essence, to make qualifications upon it that positively assert in an unsurpassable and permanent way that "God is therefore not Y and Z," seems certainly to fall under the chopping block of this "natural" and simultaneously intellectual *and* religious piety the merits of which I have attempted to recognize starting from Bultmann's remarks. Here, under the harsh light of revelation, we have to intensify Bultmann's question: What does it mean to speak about God, not in general, but as revealed in history, as the God of Christian worship, the Holy Trinity?

We would have to say, in the first place, that the Trinity, as a "dogma," can be conceived as itself *a negative theology stated positively*. Surely the history of the early Christian doctrine, the so-called Christological and Trinitarian controversies, would lend itself to this negative or apophatic conception: we are neither saying, says Gregory of Nyssa at the beginning of his letter to Ablabius that "'there are three Gods,' which is unlawful" nor are we "denying the Godhead of the Son and Holy Spirit, which is impious and absurd."[7] What does it mean to confess: "We believe in one God, the Father Almighty, Creator of heaven and earth ... and in Jesus Christ his only Son our Lord ... and in the Holy Spirit, the Lord, the giver of life?" It is to repeat and affirm, to *confess*, the words and deeds of God as God's own words and deeds; it is *not* to declare concepts that define the nature of God whose *infinity* exceeds altogether the worldly distinctions by which we think and speak. But, even more, to confess the Trinitarian shape of God's words and deeds is to declare that God's infinity therefore exceeds and overcomes those contrasts and distinctions intrinsic to the world's order of intelligibility which proscribe God in a silence determined by them. The dogma of the Trinity could be seen, in this light, as a rule for theological thinking that clarifies the boundaries within which thought can properly move under the horizon of faith lived out in the world; it could be seen, that is, in a regulative manner, as an antinomy: a conceptual condensation of religious affirmations required by faith to be affirmed together *as one*. The articles of faith, as Thomas Aquinas proposes (to privilege an example), are the unique principles that undergird *sacra doctrina*, inasmuch as they translate into worldly categories the knowledge of God enjoyed by God and the blessed dead, the *beati*.[8]

On this view, the very antinomical structure of the authoritative summaries of Christian belief and practice, the holding together of two apparently contradictory affirmations as together assertive of a truth that exceeds each one standing alone, the structure of a dogma like the Trinity, is a manifestation of the excess of rationality that cannot be grasped in the worldly modalities of reason that are ours: we say the Father is God, the Son is God, and the Holy Spirit is

God; we also say that there is only one God; the distinction classically made to elucidate this aporia is that between person and essence: there are three persons equally participating fully in the one divine nature. But these categories are derived from our experience in the world: the way human persons, for example, participate in the one human nature, Peter, James, and John, is only an aid to our reflection in understanding our own concepts of person and nature; our inner-worldly categories do not furnish us with the truth of God's divinity at all. "Following the suggestions of Scripture," says Gregory in the same letter, "[we] have learned that that nature is unnameable and unspeakable and we say that every term either invented by human custom, or handed down to us by the Scriptures is indeed *explanatory of our conceptions of the divine nature, but does not include the signification of that nature itself.*"[9] Faith gives perpetual unrest to our reason, and in this unrest, in the perpetual failure of reason to reach the truth through itself in its attempt to stretch into the divine reality, such dogmas show the cracks in our worldly rationality: they become fissures through which we rationally encounter the divine intelligibility that exceeds us and our world and which is given us to stutter at the level of concepts in our dogmatic formulae, but also to *experience* in worship. Our images, symbols and concepts, even those divinely revealed are, for Gregory, self-referring—it is their very failure to signify the divine, the human failure that they themselves uniquely expose—that composes much of their religious truthfulness. Our dogmas and the words of Scripture before them, *fail* in a unique and irreplaceable manner. And it is important that they do fail, for (to refer to a well-known formula) "if you have comprehended it, it is not God."

Here, through the intensifications of the existential situation of human speech brought about by the articles of faith, we begin to see that the way of abstraction toward the Unknown God is offset by another way, the way that I am calling, following the early name for the creedal definitions (τὰ σύμβολα), fragments that imply a whole, *the way of the symbol*. This path is different because the silence before the "unlimited and incomprehensible"[10] divinity is a silence that does not contradict that speech, theological speech, that itself gives the divine silence. Let us call this silence, to parallel the Dionysian symbol of dissembling semblance, of "dazzling darkness," a "speaking silence." In God's words to us about himself, which are fully human words, but not merely (there is no other way), divine speech made through human speech, God discloses the nature of God's true difference from the world, a difference not at odds with worldly manners of being, but transcending them so entirely that God (the "Almighty" remember?) can take them up in order to utter himself truthfully, and in a way that reveals God's unutterability in and through our speech. This *coincidentia oppositorum*, this union of contraries, the eclipse of the difference between speech and silence, discloses the divine order of truth, not in itself, but in its distinction from the world. On this path for reason, the path of revelation, the very path laid out, we believe, by God in the itinerary of the flesh of Jesus of Nazareth (an itinerary that remains proximately and in principle complete, but only definitely and absolutely complete at his final descent that glorifies the world), we are still speaking *about* God, and hence we are performing a fundamental error, and are implicated in an inescapable failure, but the error is transformed and the failure becomes, through the transformation it effects on the forms of our thought, the visibilization of the invisible God (I am thinking in particular of Augustine's use of Aristotle's ten categories in Bks. V-VII of *De Trinitate*), and in a way that is certainly distinct from though perhaps even complementary to the way of abstraction, since the latter already affirms the fundamental ineffability of the God of silence who exceeds every qualification derived from the world. In fact, this new way sets within its own horizon, the absolute horizon of God's speech, the way of abstraction and discloses itself as the latter's *most* appropriate context: God eclipses the world *and* confirms the integrity of the world *through* revelation, showing there is no "competition" between God and the world, and that therefore the "impossibility" of divine speech in the world according to the world's own conditions, is itself only a condition for revelation to show itself as divine, as not *merely* worldly, if also, in being revelation to us, *fully* worldly.

This collaboration between the two ways is programmatically stated in the prologue of the Fourth Gospel: "No one has ever seen God; the only begotten God, the one who is in the bosom of the Father, has made him known" (1:18). The way of abstraction, in other words, becomes the forecourt or entryway into the second way: the world, the world that "did not know him" (v. 10) becomes silent, or is disclosed in its powerless silence, before the God who speaks, before the Λόγος τοῦ Θεοῦ; the Unknown God is "made known" to us in the flesh-tabernacle of Jesus (v. 14). In this singular path, God is acknowledged as irremediably more than what the way of abstraction can give us, the UNKNOWN GOD, which is a nameless principle, brewing with potency and utterly opaque, a mute silence and terrible darkness, locked up by its transcendence, incapable of eclipsing the world's conditions that render it mute. In the body of Jesus, God is disclosed as not even limited by the silence of our worldly being in relation to God's own absolute alterity, not even by the difference of our world from God. Rather, says Gregory again, "the divine nature is unlimited and incomprehensible . . . in all respects infinite, and that which is absolutely infinite is not limited in one respect while it is left unlimited in another, but infinity is free from limitation altogether."[11] In excess of the first way we have here the God who speaks, who eclipses the horizon of the world in such a manner as to be totally free in relation to it, to be able to enter into this horizon and to speak and act according to its distinctions as the one who fundamentally exceeds them, demonstrating that excess by means of his capacity to assume that which he is not as that which he is, just as, at the beginning, he made that which was not into something that is. And such is what Christians mean, at least partially, when they confess the Triune God.

We should remind ourselves here that our theory—the theological explication of concepts—is *rooted* in θεωρία—the contemplation of God's words and deeds—words and deeds that transcend the rationally possible and by that transcendence expand and intensify reason itself.[12] The mystery of the Incarnation, for example, regulated for our thinking by its own historically forged dogmatic antinomy, is taken up by the Pseudo-Dionysius at the point of explicating the transformation of the elements in the Eucharistic celebration in *The Ecclesiastical Hierarchies*: "For," he says in reference to the bread and cup, "because of his goodness and love for humanity the simple hidden oneness of Jesus, the most divine Word, has taken the route of incarnation for us and, without undergoing any change, has become a reality that is composite and visible."[13] Clearly, it is a paradox that in the incarnation, the divine Word, the unfathomable uncreated intelligence itself, by which he brought forth the order of separation and union through which all things subsist, "without undergoing any change, becomes . . . composite and visible." These liturgical symbols themselves, uncovered, elevated, broken, distributed, paradoxically unveiling the mystery through their sacred veiling of it, become the sacramental means by which we give, as he says "full attention to [Christ's] divine life in the flesh." This unhesitating mashing together of the irreconcilable, referencing items in the order of the world as privileged bearers and communicators of the ineffable—in short, the "symbol" in Dionysian parlance—discloses in the manner appropriate to our human condition, the impossible mystery of God's words and deeds. Trained in this liturgical order, our speech follows the liturgico-mythic horizon of encounter with the God, emerges from it (through θεωρία), refers to it (as theory), and returns to it (as θεωρία again falls back into the greater "silence" of liturgical action brimming with meaning in symbol as with God in matter): in excess of our rational reflection is the living order of the celebrated Christian mysteries.

Along with the Pseudo-Dionysius, we must see that the Christian mysteries elucidated conceptually in our dogmas are not *merely* logical puzzles that give us (negatively) the God beyond being; they are themselves "theandric" revelations, given by a personal initiative of that God who reveals who God is *to us*, and hence in the terms most appropriate to our experience as beings in the world.[14] We cannot speak *about* God—except in the terms that God gives us, and even these, although normative and unsurpassable, are merely "symbols" distilled through the Spirit-guided process of dialectical reflection on that which is revealed in Scripture and experienced in the liturgical encounter of "thanksgiving," εὐχαριστία, to the Father of Jesus Christ who has adopted us into that familial order at the originating font of all things through the Spirit. It is therefore this concrete context of worship from, in, through and to the Trinity that the dogma of the Trinity, through the utilization of familial symbols, explicates or frames or refers. In other words, the strange theological "concept" of the Trinity is shorthand for our "contemplation" of God *in* the act of worship, the *thanksgiving* that defines the Christian faith, which it in no way replaces, but can recall, explicate and even manifest. It is in this faith as practice that we find ourselves and our world, better, that we actively interpret ourselves and our world, even better, we find ourselves and our world being actively interpreted as inscribed in the sacred history given by the apostolic and prophetic witnesses of Scripture.[15] Christian θεωρία is not normatively the silence of noetic union (understood as abstraction from the particular), but a concrete practice, an embodied discipline, an orientation of the mind to God through sacred actions performed in the body, wherein we share, beyond knowledge, in the union of God and man in Jesus.[16] These are actions that, under unique conditions brought about in a ritual ordering of the worldly domain, partake of the historical actions performed in Jesus' body, in its past earthly inherence and presently, again we believe, in its new, inarticulable heavenly inherence that is, in him, joined to earth.

For *our* present worldly inherence, this sacramental dwelling at the overlapping transition between the present world and the world to come manifests symbolic "redistributions of the field of experience" (Lacoste), according to the logic of eschatology, that reorder our worldly, ontic order and anticipate, prepare for and effect—if only in a hidden manner accessible to the wakeful patience of faith—that which they signify.

Let me explain this with some concluding remarks about the conception of the liturgical that I see as the background of theology, making our speaking about God more than it is or can possibly be on its own, worldly terms.

Bultmann, recall, gave some worldly examples that help us elucidate the mystery of God and the impossibility of speech "about" God. He observed there that love, for example, is conceptually impossible to elucidate. We cannot speak meaningfully about love from a standpoint external to love itself. As we have seen, "one cannot," he said, "speak about love at all unless the speaking about is itself an act of love." Do we have here, according to the peculiar logic of this terse statement, the recognition that our speaking "about" can become more than *merely* speaking about even though remaining *fully* so? When we recognize that God is "known through being loved," are our concepts liberated through our love of God to become all the more rigorously conceptual and disciplined while ceaselessly pointing beyond themselves to the contemplative labor of attending to God, a contemplation that is itself an opening of one's rational eye (so to speak) within the liturgico-mythic horizon of encounter with divine things? They must.

So, we must affirm, after Bultmann, that speech *about* God, concepts or theory, is therefore impotent apart from speech to God, the λογικὴ λατρεία emerging from contemplation, itself predicated on God's prior speech to us, *given* in the liturgico-mythic horizon, since faith conceives itself as a gift or nothing at all. Prayer, or prayerfulness, the attitude of attention to divine things, is therefore, according to these considerations, the right context for Christian theology. This conclusion almost passes for a commonplace. Theology, even at its most conceptually rigorous, must begin and end and be interpenetrated with adoration, address *to* God rooted in the primordial divine address to us, and only then as speech *about* God, which always sees itself as an explication of the act of thanksgiving. The God who loves—loving us most supremely in the human words and deeds of Jesus of Nazareth, and in him revealing himself as love—is *known through being loved*. Correct thought about God is dead apart from liberating submission to God, adoration, which is a *response* to God who has spoken. I have proposed that the silence of the "way of the symbol" is the silence pervading words joined to sacred actions, the sacramental silence of the flesh. In this way is the concept of the Trinity—a concept there among other concepts in the world, uttered by human lips, a *flatus vocis* with nothing in the world to correspond to it, worthy in that sense, it would certainly seem to the apparently rational observer, to be reviled, pushed away as inevitably idolatrous, as human speech *about* God—in this way, along this way of transfiguring flesh, is it more than a concept, a *word* that discloses the unutterable mystery of the life of God and the destiny to which he brings the world.

Liturgical experience, normative for Christian theology, and its original milieu, the wellspring of its life *and* the site of its perpetual deconstruction, exposes at once the inadequacy *and* the strange permanence of our concepts. The liturgical, in other words, divulges an irreducibly double-character that points to their sign-like quality, the way in which they presence God to us. The Eucharistic "symbols" make present, or rather make us, through our world, present to the God who exceeds the world. They make the world transparent to God. The "symbol gives rise to thought" to be sure, and it is within contemplation of the symbols of

Christian experience in the liturgical-Scriptural matrix that theology as a rigorous exercise is undertaken. But at the same time, we must add a twin aphorism to the one borrowed from Ricoeur and say that "the symbol presences the unthinkable," in a way, says the Areopagite, "that cannot be enclosed in words or grasped by any mind, not even," he adds, "by the leaders among the front rank of angels."[17]

The distance between these two dimensions of ordinary, worldly realities filled with extraordinary meaning through human and divine, through *theandric* action, is charted by the logic of Christian eschatology. Theology must attend to its work with the recognition of its eschatological situation, acknowledging that we think, to cite Bonhoeffer's formula revived by Lacoste, "in the next to last,"—"in the world but not of it"—wherein theology is called to recognize that the world's conditions, though tragically absolute in a finitude irreconcilable with itself, are yet only provisional and have been eclipsed and even marginalized proleptically by God. Theological thinking is called then to think from within the world that which the world cannot contain, which has been disclosed and continues to be disclosed *through* privileged items in the world in excess of our conceptual order as its ground. We *think* this way by contemplatively "bracketing" the world's conditions, undertaken by symbolically "redistributing" the field of experience to *signify* more than what the world can give, which is only ever more world. This redistribution occurs through sign (invocation) and action, ritual movement that causes the material symbol (water, wine, bread, fire, oil) to carry eschatological, that is, definitive significance, the significance of the kingdom in the midst of the cosmic order. The dipping of the Easter candle, lit from new fire, three times into the church's baptismal font during the Easter vigil, symbolizes the descent of Christ into our world, ruled by death. The waters are the waters of judgment, of death *and* life. Christ makes death life-giving. It is the new life through death that the newly baptized enter in that same vigil. As a natural symbol, water can signify destruction (the storm, the tsunami, the flood) and, equally, life (the pool, the well, the teeming sea). Mythically, it is equally the primeval waters of chaos and the waters of the river of life that spring from the earth to make life possible. The water is itself one. Like all truly great symbols, in it, opposites coincide and are pre-contained in an inscrutable higher unity accessible only by way of the opposition of its manifestation. The sacramental signification of water builds on this double identification and does not reject it. It transforms it, redistributes it, providing the indication, the hint of the wider and deeper setting in which it will ultimately find its home. The water-symbol, like fire, ultimately symbolizes the divine reality, which is both infinite fullness and absolute potential one, and in it are integrated the antinomous concepts of death and life: to be in God's presence is to die for God is the source of life. To understand this paradoxical statement (in a way "beyond understanding") is to comprehend the sacramental "mystery;" it is to have a religious pulse. The identification of death and life in God is the sacred meaning of water. The divine presence is born by water in the sacramental-eschatological eclipse of the water-symbol. Humans "pass through" that presence in the sacramental share of baptism and in this way they become partakers, then, in its reality.

Our thinking may be made "liturgical" in the expanded sense.[18] It is an embodied practice of "dwelling" in the world considered as "the next to last," as *in eclipse* by the God who is coming. This thinking, in taking up its task, recognizes that only God can close the eschatological distance between, on the one hand, concepts, which take up, from out of the narrative milieu, the tools of elucidating the world's intelligibility (Aristotle, Husserl, or whoever) and apply them to God (always recognizing the impropriety of such a necessity, the work of negative theology), and, on the other hand, contemplation, which attempts to *see* in the liturgico-mythic horizon of the world the God who exceeds the world, recognizing in this impossibility and paradox the disclosure of the world's own destiny. The eschatological resolution of concepts and contemplation that our dogmas at least imply—by what they signify through their antinomical structure unified in the symbol—leaves open the question of the nature of this resolution, the closure of the gap between Christ's "already" and our "not-yet," which is not ours to give but God's alone. The symbol is ever provisional, for it gives the self-excess of God through the material.[19] We can speculate about it, by thinking from what our dogmas—like the ascension of Christ, the resurrection of the dead, in particular here—give us to think while acknowledging of course that they presence the unthinkable: what they give is beyond our conceiving and we must show through reason that this makes sense. In what the tradition calls the beatific vision, if I can allude at once to St. Augustine and St. John of the Cross (to famous passages from *City of God* and *The Living Flame of Love*), the vision of the world and the vision of God become one in the eschaton; while the world clouds over our vision of God in the present state, where God is accessed only by passing through the world, in the future state, we will be definitively turned "right side in" (since we are in the present disorder turned "inside out"), as it were, and the world will be seen, known, enjoyed *through* God—and therefore most *fully*. To use the classical description, in the present order our materially immersed minds move from visible effects to invisible causes: we see the world order and discern through its patterns an ultimate source. In the kingdom the soul's vision of beatitude is immediate, its bodily life in the resurrection is coincident with this vision, when that beatitude is made to redound as an echo of God's own essential self-eclipse. This reordering between world and kingdom occurs through the embodied disciplining of our desire, which I call liturgical and which can anticipate, and thereby proleptically participate in, our eschatological metamorphosis. In the eschatological *visio Dei* that is our human end, which is, biblically speaking, merely the accomplishment of the beginning, the *coincidentia oppositorum* of the fundamental, guiding images of our thinking, say the "darkness" of Gregory or the "light" of Augustine (to generalize about the two main reference points indicated earlier), will be shown to be two perspectives that signify more appropriately the divine plenitude together than when opposed inasmuch as they express a saturation of meaning to which the *concepts of transcendence* can only be *means of approach*. When we hold them together, therefore, when we plunge the universal into the particular, holding it there in our thinking in the present, we anticipate more adequately the eschatological truth. Something similar is said, classically, about the "coincidence" of body and soul in eternal life: experienced in opposition in the present, our confession of the "resurrection of the dead" demands of thought that we conceive these two dimensions of our one humanity in a new unity that we can contemplatively intuit only at the edges of our worldly thinking. This thesis of more or less Dionysian inspiration also points, I think, to the essential theological labor of anticipation of the eschatological coincidence of our concepts and contemplation where the Triune God will be, of course, seen and known. "For now, we see in a mirror dimly, but then face to face. Now I know in part; then I shall understand fully, even as I have been fully understood."[20] But then, again, such visionary knowledge is only the condition for something ὑπερεκπερισσοῦ ὃν αἰτούμεθα ἃ νοοῦμεν, "superabundantly beyond the things that we ask for and think."[21]

In this quasi-*conclusio* (vv. 20–21) standing at the end of the closing prayer of the first half of the Letter to the Ephesians (chs. 1–3), we can see clearly how the hyperbole of praise—as pertains to God—is in no way overstatement, nor can it be. God is, as I have argued essentially, superlative; being divine means being in an "ever-more" and boundless fashion.

> Now to him who by the power at work within us is able to accomplish superabundantly beyond the things that we ask for and think, to him be glory in the Church and in Christ Jesus unto all the generations of the age of the ages. Amen.[22]

To the measureless power introduced by the historical events pertaining to Christian witness (δυνάμενο ὑπὲρ πάντα ποιῆσαι) in the first phrase of the *conclusio*, there corresponds the glorification of God (αὐτῇ ἡ δόξα) "in the Church and in Christ Jesus" εἰς πάσας τὰς γενεὰς τοῦ αἰῶνος τῶν αἰώνων, "unto all the generations of the age of the ages," at the end the prayer (as also at the limitless end of time). The accomplishment of the eschatological αἰών is the consummation of all ages, of everything that was and will be, and therefore the fulfillment of the divine οἰκονομία τοῦ μυστηρίου (3:2), the administrative order by which he carried out his ultimate purpose, the hidden plan of the ages (κατὰ πρόθεσιν τῶν αἰώνων) finally made known now (ἵνα γνωρισθῇ νῦν; vv. 10-11), that is, in the final chapter (as it were) of the present age. Divine power is "made known," then, in the revelation, the ἀποκάλυψις of Christ, the disclosure of the μυστήριον (3:3), which brings about the completion of the divine purpose integral to the created order itself, disclosing its ultimate meaning, which is, strictly speaking, "superabundantly above" the intellectual striving of man, both epistemic (interrogative inquest, "what we ask for") and noetic (visionary seeing the truth as such, "or think"). This superabundant beyondness is accomplished, precisely, by being kenotically far below the intellectual terminus that requires, in the creaturely movement from below, passage away from the particular, and therefore away from love.[23] It includes, rather, the glorification of the world through the Church (through Christ), the complete reconciliation of universal and particular through the total immersion of divinity into the world. *That* is the accomplishment of God's purpose, hidden in him from the beginning, through his elevated special consort, his elected partner, humanity, to the bewildering stupefaction of the spiritual powers that be, the ἀρχαῖς καὶ ταῖς ἐξουσίαις ἐν τοῖς ἐπουρανίοις, the rulers and authorities in the celestial domains (v. 10).

Of course, upon consideration, one may decide it to be impossible to submit their "modern" horizon of possibilities, determined, as any epochal horizon is, by the subtle interweavings of expectation, desire, and experience, as by, here, consumerism, liberalism, and materialism, to the Pauline μῦθος that, I think, I have more or less faithfully adumbrated in this closing remark to another stage in my argument. But its total replacement by another, more abstracted and rationalized μῦθος of post-cosmic-soul-release-to-visionary-seeing-of-un iversal-truth-as-end, as if this μῦθος is a more sophisticated interpretation of the ordinary Christian confession made by the unthinking rabble of that lesser and exoteric caste: *that* Averroism is something else entirely (though its account can, and must be incorporated, as a transitional stage, into the primitive and perennial Christian frame outlined here, as I have already suggested). Let that one troubled, and perhaps, if possible, offended by the Pauline σκάνδαλον, not think, though, that the replacement is in accord with either the Apostle's own or that of classical Christian creedal confession as it has reached us today centuries further εἰς τὸν ἐνεστῶτα πονηρὸν αἰῶνα.

4

Anthropomorphism and Some Aspects of Modern Thought

If you can conceive it, it is not God.

—Anselm

For human thought about God, it would seem, anthropomorphism is inevitable. My argument thus far, if judged moderately successful, has established this claim. It has also provided an initial statement about the way of conceiving the (eschatological) validity of such an inevitability. And it has, finally, made some first points of description about the character of this "way of conceiving." I have yet to do justice to the comprehensive scope of the issue of anthropomorphic inevitability. There remains, it seems, half a book left to be written. Even "classical theists," for example (whose central concern is the avoidance of gross misrepresentation of God by reducing him to the scope of our human imagination), in pursuit of a purified intellectual conception of God, consider that God has a "mind" and "will." The idea of God has to conceive of God as "more than an idea." It is a fundamental tenet of Christianity, sine qua non, that God not only is living but also lives as "three persons." And if by "hypostases" we mean, minimally, "concrete instantiations of the divine being," these are still to be addressed in terms familiar to the most ordinary human, worldly experience as "Father," "Son," and "Spirit." By recognizing that we do not know exactly what we mean when we use the concept of person to signify a basic characteristic of divine reality, we have to confess that God is more, not less, "personal" than human persons. God is the superabundant archetype of personality. Christians even pray to Jesus of Nazareth, a *fully* human person—but not *merely* human—worshiping him as "fully God." Somehow, a single ὑπόστασις can be both divine and human at once. Take as a radical case the famous modern devotion in Catholicism, the "Sacred Heart" of Jesus, which worships Jesus' human organ, the physical heart, and through its highly symbolic, sacramental significance as the core of his human affection that is one with his infinite divine love finds at the center of his humanity the heart of his divinity and there the most intimate passage directly into participation in the depths of the Triune life of God.[1] Of all classical religions, it is tempting to suggest that Christianity makes a case for being the most crudely anthropomorphic. *On its own terms*, and, perhaps, also, in generically human terms, this is a judgment in its favor. And there is little doubt that Christianity's profound humanity has been a—if not the—central reason for its remarkable historical vibrancy beyond any civilizational scale. Its conception of the divinity arises directly out of the historical accounts of the Creator's interactions in a history, mediated through the memory of a community concretized in Holy Scripture, a story culminating in God's total identification with a discrete particular, bounded by time, space, matter, by culture, language, biology, the historical person, Jesus of Nazareth. God is the replete and limitless unity of the universal and particular, of whole and fragment, of nature and person, of one and many, of identity and difference, with no intrinsic necessity but love compelling him either to create or, having once created, to redeem, to glorify the creature. And yet both creation, in its "sophianic" mystery, and redemption (through the divine Wisdom's incarnate, personal identification with Jesus of Nazareth), which alone discloses the full secret of the world's "sophianicity," its divine and sacramental potential, the capacity of the material cosmos to bear the divine fullness, awoken in humanity, are bound, irreparably, to God's desire to make the world replete with himself by partnership with his creature. The latter, that is, redemption, is, properly understood, only the completion of the former, the act of creation. Redemption *is* the beginning, just as, in the sacramental ritual of thanksgiving, the transformation of the elements into the living presence of Jesus Christ, in realizing, proleptically (if only, then, still under the forms of temporal historicity), the world's divinization, is itself only the dressing of the table for the banquet's repast. Theology must not only be done with the sacred page as its "soul" but also, as Bulgakov said, from the bottom of the Eucharistic chalice.[2] If revelation is primary, controlling our comprehension of God (in the service to such comprehension the traditions of human wisdom are employed), we must confess that it is actually *more divine* to transgress the absolute alterity of divinity, abstractly conceived, than to remain imprisoned within it. The transgression of "divinity" by the divinity becomes the deepest expression of divinity. Theologically, then, I should say that the negative castigation of such anthropomorphism is finally felled by its own critique, since it, in the end, is based on an all the more egregious conception of the divine as ἄνθρωπος writ large, since it creates *humanly conceived* boundaries that the divine cannot cross and . . . remain divine.³

This latter perspective would be, from the vantage of revelation, too *anthropocentric*. For is it not, in actuality, the reverse that is truly the case? Humans are theomorphic says the originating word of all Christian anthropology. They are made in the "image and likeness" of the one who created them. God is, therefore, personal in a way that humans only dimly reflect. The same goes for his mind and will. Our human minds and wills are only images of his Mind and Will. God, in himself, is the ever-greater transcendent archetype of anything that human being is. Such a justification of Christian anthropomorphism, which is not without substantial force, only makes my initial observation, of the necessity of anthropomorphism, redound all the more loudly. That is, the theological justification that I have by now, I hope, established only highlights the philosophical (i.e., perennially human) problem in its great insolubility and thus brings it into greater clarity as a problem.

The viewpoint I hope to counter—if only I could destroy it completely—is certainly a presumptive force among the intellectually inclined remaining, often problematically (on their own terms), among the Christian community. Though they are more like the fish who, on mouthing the wriggling worm, is so engrossed in its endeavor to swallow it that it has yet to feel the hook through its lip already pulling toward the muddy bank. This *point of view* has become, as is inevitable, I think, at the far end of the second Christian millennium, integrated far into the ordinary piety of the unlearned many. The religious comfort of knowing Jesus Christ for mortals striving on this earth has become, indeed, hardly distinguishable from the love of comfort and security, the fullness of stomach and affect that we animals labor to sustain most of the time. And it simply transplants from this life to the next one the sense of wholeness, of security, of well-being, so often refused to so many mortals so much of the time (and all mortals some of the time) and generalizes it to a maximal vagueness. It considers God (as an abstraction of nebulous beneficence) the necessary instrument of its accomplishment: "just hold your nose and go to Mass." Nietzsche considered it hollow. It justifies that struggle to find meaningful our fight to survive by asserting, much if not most evidence to the contrary, that the reason for the universe's existence (and, granted, our odd place within it) is somehow mystifyingly benevolent, even personally engaged with us all, impotent but caring, *especially* for the ones who suffer so mercilessly at the hands of those who do little more than use them as stairs to climb to the top of this world-gutter for a momentary glimpse of the sunlight—and are even ready to forgive these for being in the way, if they can only but come to see the egregious error of their burdensome existence. You could be forgiven, in light of this late-stage religious decadence, for wondering if this "projection of value" into the shocking "absolutism of reality" is actually all that religion, any religion, ever was. Well, whatever religion is, the religion that claims to offer man the fullness of being, a total surpassing of his finite mortality by, precisely, filling it from within with divinity like a ceaselessly flowing and ever-increasing fountain, this religion will, of course, speak fully and completely to man's biological survival as much as to his higher search for truth and goodness in their absolute, unqualified forms, for all of this is what man *is*. If the *Lebensverachtung* of Western civilization diagnosed by Nietzsche is patently real, if meaning is finally sacrificed to comfort and security, then it is such as a post-Christian phenomenon, indebted, to be sure (and however paradoxically) to an eviscerated ascetic strain of "hatred of the body," wherein the Christian μῦθος of resurrection, strained through the bourgeois elitism of the resentful πνευματικοί as belief in the next world of spirit (requiring) hatred of this world of body, has rung hollow, becoming no longer believable. In response, the civilization has simply filled the cavity pre-formed by the hatred of the body and its world with the stultifying materiality of the hatred of life.[4] You could also be forgiven for thinking that such filling is the essence of modern liberalism, a debased and secularized end-form of Christianity. The myriad-formed Christianity presently struggling for survival within Western civilization, if not yet finally identified with this "hatred of life," certainly labors against it like a cat beneath a wet blanket.

As I write this, I must confess, that I struggle not to see the claim I have undertaken to elaborate as hardly requiring the painstaking argumentation with which I have labored to serve it. The apocalyptic distinction of Second Temple Judaism between the *ha-olam hazeh* and the *olam haba*, the present age and the age to come, which has so fundamentally informed the logic of the New Testament; the fundamental Christological dogmas (the Incarnation, the Resurrection); the sacramental action of the Church's ritual in which parts of the created order, strained through human cultivation, reach their eschatological *telos* (through human collaboration with God) to become, themselves, in their very materiality, media of divinity; the teachings of Christ—especially obvious is the prayer he taught his disciples and that Christians of all time have prayed daily, in which the *descent* of the Father's βασιλεία to earth is the all-defining end sought; the definitive apocalyptic portrait with which the Scriptures conclude, in which the goal is a renewed, glorified creation wherein the New Jerusalem *descends* from heaven as a Bride for unifying consummation (and whatever then is to come after) with the God who has himself taken up residence at the heart of a renewed world finally and fully made his Temple—all of this is patent, the daily bread of the most basic Christian sensibility. But perhaps it is the utter apparentness of the vision in the sources that has made it so easily disfigured. Traditions develop in surprising ways, and they do so by changing focus through the many historical crucibles of controversy and challenge, which invariably push formerly emphasized dimensions to the ambiguous backdrop through the foregrounding of aspects once considered marginal or supplementary. Christianity is no exception. That said, traditions also develop by backtracking, by reform, by recovery of the origin's wellspring, by refocusing on the forgotten or obfuscated essential.

Classically, the basic intellectual problem motivating Western thought was specifically with the anthropomorphisms of the sacred myths: the gods of Homer were simply ungodlike in their all-too-human actions and preoccupations. Philosophy's great raison d'être was, it could be said, first religious and theological.

Modern Western philosophy styles itself as a continuation of the ancient Greek freedom to contemplate the cosmos and thereby to discern its most fundamental principles by which one can best order one's life. Although, for the Greeks, contemplation was most philosophical particularly at its apex, when contemplating the divinity, and in the most divine manner, namely, with reason—that is, the most divine part of humanity—free from base constraints that a (moderate) degree of wealth may provide. We can see that, paradoxically, revelation reveals something to philosophy here, something that philosophy must take into account for its own sake: only revelation can disclose the *anthropocentric* anthropomorphism of philosophy, in its ancient or modern guise. This anthropomorphism of the anthropocentric character of philosophy is located precisely in its concern to evade its own anthropomorphic character. That is to say, as we have seen, the concepts which philosophy purifies and by which it ascends to a more rational picture of the divine, are themselves, fundamentally, as anthropomorphic as the basest images by which humans have ever conceived the divine. Our concepts arise—whether by abstraction, for the realist, or by categorization of particulars, for the nominalist—from out of the body's phenomenal experience, to which human beings, and their minds, are irreparably tied. Kant's intuition was right in a fundamental respect: our greatest concepts are as tied to our embodied human experience (albeit as its transcendental conditions) as are our crudest images. Gregory of Nyssa taught that our intellectual conceptions, the names we give to God (infinite, eternal, one, causal power, etc.) are derived, by negation, from the sensible objects of knowledge. We must equally leave these behind to enter the divine darkness, and, when we do, we must return to images (of, for example, Abraham's sojourn or Moses' ascent of the mountain) to signify anything at all. In this he agrees with the Pseudo-Dionysius the Areopagite, who, as a result—again I cast a desirous eye further down the path ahead—elevates anthropomorphic images beyond abstract concepts, first, because the latter are more deceptive in that they conceal their anthropic limiting conditions, but second, more profoundly, because God himself prioritizes them in the Incarnation, in Scripture and in their liturgical extension in time and space through the sacraments.[5] The Areopagite, in other words, saw as a radical solution that which Kant (whom I will shortly consider more fully) conceived to be a fundamental objection. The basic difference between the two styles of thought, acknowledging the anachronism, is simple but definitive: one begins with revelation, finding reason's very rationality emerge from the fundamental commitments of faith, whereas the other preconceives the scope of reason and disallows revelation from challenging it. We have already seen the contemporary science of phenomenology begin to perform its criticism of the Kantian procedure, an aspect of phenomenology to which I, for one, see as a recovery of something that had been lost.

For the former perspective, the "transcendental" account of our knowledge of God, for which the conditions and limits of human reason and experience are established critically, that is, before experience, is mistaken to the degree that they contradict what is given in live human experience. Hence we have what may be called "transcendental idolatry," to quote Jean-Luc Marion again, and according to which "God is submitted to the conditions of the possibility of experience, such as they define, a priori, the finite human mind."[6] These general conditions of human experience are universalized without exception. They make man, finally, the measure of all things, ἄνθρωπος μέτρον πάντων. The post-Christian abyss, in which Nietzsche's *Lebensverachtung* flowers, as of this writing, so ineluctably into Heidegger's *Gestell*, finally perfects Protagoras' epistemological subjectivism all the way, as Foucault had said, to the eclipse of the human subject itself.[7] They are even applied to divine revelation, which forms the basis of a conception of religion within the critical limits of mere reason. Kant finds himself, therefore, in the position of philosophy abstracted from revelation, with what we could call an "anthropocentrism-in-itself." He claims to know *in itself*, without contrast to anything other than its own self-alterity within the transcendental regime, its own inviolable aspiration for the unconditioned that it itself is in its own incomprehensibility—the limits and conditions, which define human finitude. Kant presents us with an anthropocentric instance of a radical, hidden anthropomorphism precisely in its attempt to be reconciled with human anthropomorphism as absolute, which he reduces to an anthropocentrism(-in-itself). Kant's anthropocentrism-in-itself requires God, in order to appear, to appear under the general conditions of human, sub-cosmic reason that are staked out before God appears, so that God can come to reason. In this scenario,

God cannot appear in himself but nevertheless must and can be presupposed as an idea governing right living. God can only be a concept that guides practical reason. Yet if we begin with revelation as opposed to an a priori account of human reason-in-itself, we find that revelation may reveal to human reason its conditions and limits for the first time. Revelation (ἀποκάλυψις, *revelatio*), paradoxically, reveals philosophy (i.e., a perennialism of the questions that become unavoidable when the definitive meaning of our humanity comes into question) to itself as its most radical concept. Christianity, as philosophy, thinks from within a σοφία ἄνωθεν κατερχομένη, a "wisdom descending from above."[8]

In the *Prologue to Any Future Metaphysic*, Kant, of course, notes that any *theism*, that is, the proposal of a *personal* God, will always suffer from the inevitability of anthropomorphism. On the one hand, theism is required for the justification of moral responsibility. Moral responsibility requires belief in an ultimate arbiter of justice, a God who is just. On the other hand, the specific morality of intelligence requires recognition of its own fundamental limitations, the essential human conditions of the body's specific human attunement to the world. Theism is strictly impossible because in eclipse of these conditions. Kant resolves this dilemma by making a distinction between "dogmatic anthropomorphism," on the one hand, which, he says, facilely claims to make affirmative statements about God in himself, and "symbolic anthropomorphism," on the other hand, which reaches beyond, or rather, behind, dogmatic anthropomorphism by reconciling it to the given principles of the possibility of experience. How is this reconciliation accomplished? According to Kant, symbolic anthropomorphism is concerned, not with the thing itself, namely, God, but only with *language*. In other words, because human intelligence, insofar as it is dealing with beings that transcend its framing conditions, like God, for example, or the self, or the world in its origins, deals only with the appearances, and thereby can *only* think of God as a being in this world (since thought, in its positive content, is tied to and limited by the sensory dimension of embodied experience). The concepts that we use are, in a word, indeterminate, for all we are doing, when we think of God, is thinking of a phenomenon that belongs to the sensible world, which is *not* God. To take the divine grandeur, for example, we take our intramundane concept of greatness, either of value or measure, and expand it as vastly as our imagination can extend it. But since God is outside and beyond the horizon of the world, our thought does not terminate on God, in himself. It is, in the end, *only* a concept, and we have no way of knowing if it truly signifies God as God truly is at all. We have then, with Kant, a rather thorough expression of the medieval nominalist and pseudo-apophatic impulse, which protects divine transcendence by delimiting humanity's epistemic capacity. Kant's phrase, I think, was *das Wissen aufheben um zum Glauben Platz zu bekommen*, "to deny knowledge in order to make room for faith."[9] By Kant's day in Europe, for complex but intelligible political and cultural reasons—reasons already starkly anticipated in William of Ockham's political and economic controversy with the Avignon papacy that inspired his later political writings—the "protection" of divine transcendence was another word for protecting human liberty from external constraint, especially by the heteronomous assertions of overreaching hierarchical authority.[10]

For Kant, there is, properly speaking, no concept of the supreme being, but only an element of the world that we exalt to its place. Kant, in a now familiar revolutionary move, limits the scope of reason's reach to the "relation that the world may have to a being whose concept itself lies outside all cognition that we can attain within the world." And so we have to think, he affirms, "according to analogy."[11] Kant's notion of analogy is, of course, not what he takes the classical one to be and is in fact built in direct contrast to it: his notion, he says, "surely does not signify, as the word is usually taken, an imperfect similarity between two things, but rather a perfect similarity between two relations in wholly dissimilar things."[12] The way Kant phrases this readily suggests his rejection of the "analogy of proportion," or the (Neoplatonic) analogy of causal likeness (affirmed in Thomas Aquinas' mature thought), and an affirmation of the "analogy of proportionality," or analogy of indirect proportion, readily preferred in the Aquinian's early writings, according to which there is an analogous relation between God and his actions or attributes and, for example, between a good man and his actions. Kant's analogy, of course, only relates to practical reason, whereas Thomas' is speculative and therefore concerns real knowledge of the divine being. For Kant, analogy validates the idea of God for practical reason; it gives no real knowledge of God. He thinks, perhaps like the early Thomas, that a doubly mediated conception of analogy, the proportion of proportion, would be more apt for articulating the relation *inter finitum et infinitum*, in which, directly speaking, *non est proportio*, "there is no proportion." For Kant, one cannot cognize God, but only think about the idea in a meaningful way, a way that essentially orders our actions. Human liberty is protected: it is man, as finite and correlated to the world through the limits of his experience, that thinks God as creator, as judge, as lawgiver, and regulates his own actions by virtue of his own generated idea. Thomas' youthful use of the analogy of proportionality (in his *Commentary on the Sentences* and in *De Veritate*) is a degree removed from an apparently direct analogy between man and God, but nevertheless gives true knowledge of God as he is in himself, however limited. The mature Thomas (in *Summa Contra Gentiles* and in the *Summa Theologiae*)—after reading, apparently, both pagan Greek

Neoplatonism and Greek Fathers in newly available Latin translations—will come to see the analogy of attribution (simple proportion) as the best expression of the relation of God and creature, reading it as an expression of the Neoplatonic conception of the cause, in which an analogical chain of likeness persists within the difference, even especially absolute difference beyond proportion, since the cause "precontains" the effect in a "more perfect" way and the higher the cause, the greater extends and more direct its (as it were) intrinsic contact with realities down the causal chain. The highest cause precedes the immediate causes by virtue of an excessive immediacy at every level. Thomas' final preference for the analogy of proportion evidences his conclusion that Neoplatonic causation is the best possible philosophical resource (available to him) to express the revealed notion of *creatio*. This explains his intermittent use of the concept of *emanatio* in this context as well as his consistent use of the concept of *participatio* in these works. Perhaps like the anthropomorphic exacerbation of the concept, veiled if improperly grounded in imagination, the analogical doubling of the proportionality of proportionality, though it would seem to intensify the analog difference and thereby be more appropriate to divine signification, in reality (perhaps, indeed, like the meaningful saturation of symbols with more adequate signification) the direct proportion is paradoxically more radically analogical, the proportion bearing an "ever-greater" disproportion within every acknowledged proportion, a proportion that itself expresses, then, the eclipse of the contrast between disproportion and proportion altogether in a hyper-immediacy that overcomes the duality of creator and creature, and even overcomes mere identity between them toward—as I have tried to express in earlier stages—something eschatological, something apocalyptic, something ever-greater. To take, frankly, the scholastic axiomatic (*gratia perficit naturam*) seriously as a valid expression of the patristic "supernatural paradox" of created nature as finding its completion in its origin, beyond itself in God, as a created god—and this patristic articulation as a valid interpretation of the biblical revelation, the descent of God into flesh for the liberation of all flesh and matter and space and time by an elevating overcoming of the distantiation from God caused by human sin, which is nothing but the elected pursuit of human nature's fullness by freedom from God (human-divinity, if you like) as opposed to freedom through God (divine-humanity)—is to understand the scholastic axiomatic, the concept of the cause and its concomitant concept of analogy properly.

I confess that to return to Kant after cracking again this window, is, to say the least, rather disappointing in its anthropological stuffiness. Yet Kant's importance is found in his failure. And, like all great philosophers, perhaps, he is in no way unique in this regard. For Kant, a theistic notion of God, with its personal attributes, as opposed to a deist, wholly abstract one, which is a god with no living connection whatsoever with the world, is necessary in the sense that morality requires freedom, and freedom comes from our consciousness of the moral law, and this awareness is only properly derived from the context of interpersonal relation: we must first "respect" a lawgiver in order to respect the moral law as absolute. This necessity justifies our speaking of God in personal terms, and, at the same time, we are free from the faulty transfer of predicates from the sensible world onto the being wholly distinct from it. The idea of an ultimate legislator of morality, an idea which justifies human action, is what Kant will call in the Third Critique a *symbol*.

Kant should certainly be seen as the one who introduces the problematic of the *symbol* into modern thought. For him the symbol is the sensible presentation of an idea that cannot be represented directly, that is, by concepts. Symbols are the *product* of the imagination, and derive from its power to perform (something like) what the Scholastics called the *conversio ad phantasmata*, to retie the intelligibility of concepts to the sensible domain. The structure of the symbol bears an *analogy* with the formal structure of what it seeks to represent: so the despotic state, in which a single man kills any resistance to his rule, is analogous to a grindstone where the wheels obey the single turning of a crank. The role of the symbol is to give us a comparative image in order that the weakness of our understanding, tied to the sensible world, will gain an inkling of the conceptual truth. So he says in §38 of *Anthropology from a Pragmatic Point of View* (publ. 1798): "Symbols are only means of understanding, in an indirect way, by means of the play of an *analogy* with certain sensible intuitions to which a concept is able to be applied in order to confer on this concept a signification by the presentation of an object."[13] For Kant, symbols are a primitive stage of reason, which, when an adequate concept arises, can be set aside. When it becomes a matter of talking about God, Kant sees the peculiar necessity of "symbolic anthropomorphism," if only for the reason that an *adequate concept of God* is impossible. It is perhaps worthy to note that still in Kant there remains an election of the concept and its regime of knowledge over the symbol and its regime, as far as what qualifies as real or at least adequate knowledge. The symbol is a necessary stand-in from the practical domain that does not count as knowledge properly speaking.

Let me note a criticism. *Primary remark*: Kant's critique of reason, it should be said, did not go far enough, since it simply reasserted the *modern* priority of conceptual knowledge over the figurative, even though his recognition of the ubiquity of anthropomorphism should have led him toward the radical questioning of such a metaphysical assumption. As a constructive response, two historical observations would have to be elaborated. I will only state them: (1) this specifically modern form of the priority of concept over figure emerges in the late medieval turn to the concept as foundation of knowledge, where, as Francisco Suárez put it, fundamentally transforming Aristotle, the "better known" (which are no longer the beings of sensory experience but the content of one's mind, its concepts) can ground the knowledge of the "lesser known" (no longer the ἀρχαὶ καὶ αἴτιαι, transcendent "principles and causes" that explain, but objective realities outside the subject). The transcendentalism of Kant is only the completion of this Suarezian transformation of the epistemic principle.[14] (2) The priority of the concept, its autonomy and self-sufficiency, is made possible, most importantly, by the erasure of the priority of eschatology for philosophical reason, a possibility that emerged only with the separation of the theological domain (the realm of God and supernatural revelation) and the philosophical domain (the realm of human reason) in the late middle ages at the foundation of modernity—and, furthermore, grounding the epistemic conditions of theology (as Suàrez will fully secure) in philosophy, or metaphysic's account of *scientia*. Philosophy, as autonomous discipline, is founded on the rejection of the centrality of an *eschatological* disclosure of truth from above for reason itself, a disclosure that frames the historicity or worldhood of human rationality but also eclipses it.

Second remark: Kant's critique of reason from the vantage of the limits of the epistemic and conceptual regime stands within the moment of philosophical reflection we can call negative philosophy, a necessary moment when the received data is purified and elevated by the dialectical work of reason in its quest for reality. This corresponds to the Greek origins of philosophical reflection when λόγος emerges from μῦθος, that is, when our received traditions are critiqued for the sake of the higher truth that they contain. It is not a final stage. Or, if it becomes one, the subjective transcendentalism that founds it manifests itself as a materialist objectivism, wherein the real is and can only be the measurable and utilizable, which finally resolves into the surpassing of humanity by the very power of technology it created but emerges near-apocalyptically as independent from its producer.

It is only with Nietzsche, I think, that the Kantian revolution is radicalized to the point that we can call into question, or rather, properly relativize the epistemic-conceptual assumption of modernity. Nietzsche's advance on Kant is found in his affirmation of metaphor as a constitutively anthropomorphic process at our cognitive base, but his limits are found in identifying "truth" with the assertion of the will in the war of all against all when it finds that common definitions serve his own existence, and therefore, with a non-metaphorical conception of the truth, truth that, like Kant, is wholly determined by the metaphysics of the concept.

Truth, Nietzsche will claim, is an invention born out of the animal impulse to self-preservation, which finds its perfection in humanity, when the necessity for social existence presents itself: truth is an arbitrary generalization that organizes experience in a way that serves the individual by serving the herd.[15] Truth becomes necessary because we have to organize the world in order to survive, which we do through language. Our linguistic organizations that are given common assent by a group are for us *the truth*. Truths are only useful tools, instances of technology that establish and extend our control over existence. To presume their reality outside ourselves is to produce the illusion that we have access to anything more than our very- own finitude, to anything at all beyond the scope of our mortality.

Nietzsche's metaphysical modernity, I would call it, is found in his assumption of Kant's controlling distinction between the noumenal and phenomenal realms, the world beyond and within experience, which he assumes, like Kant, to be absolute and inviolable. It is from this vantage, in light of the transcendental account of knowledge, that he criticizes the traditional conception of truth— *adaequatio intellectus et rei*, "correspondence between mind and thing."

For Nietzsche, it is clear that words belong to the subjective dimension of the self, while things (in themselves) belong to the world outside of the ego, and are inaccessible to it. Words and thought are representations or repetitions of nerve stimuli of the senses when they encounter the unknowable realities of the world. Words therefore express the relation of realities to human beings at a more abstract level, giving them to us as discrete, manipulable things, better capable of being negotiated, *utilized*. Every word is therefore a metaphor for Nietzsche, the *transposition* of nerve stimuli into language. This process actually occurs through multiple levels, each of which is an act of transposition that is metaphorical on its own terms: first, the stimuli is transposed into a concrete image, which is, second, then imitated in a sound. Metaphors are words created by the human subject and used to navigate and control the world of experience that assails him through the senses. Words become concepts when specific things, which are wholly incommensurate, are grouped together in general categories, which is always done by discarding individual differences in order to affirm what appear to be—or rather, are useful to be considered—essential similarities. Not only does every word have metaphorical origins, but every word and concept is made by reference to human experience. Words only tell us about ourselves, about what we are—survivors seeking a better grip in our environment. They give us nothing else. Here we arrive at Nietzsche's famous anthropomorphic definition of truth: "A movable army of metaphors, metonymies and anthropomorphisms: fundamentally a sum of human relations which have been poetically and rhetorically intensified, transferred, and embellished, and which, after long use, seem to a nation to be fixed, canonical and binding. Truths" he continues, "are illusions which we have forgotten are such, metaphors that have become worn out and drained of sensuous force."[16] The anthropomorphism of all truth discloses the fact that every truth is not a truth outside of the human horizon. Speaking of concepts in particular, such as the definition of mammal applied to a camel, he calls them "thoroughly anthropomorphic truths" [*durch und durch anthropomorphisch*] which

> contain nothing "true in itself" or really and universally true apart from man. At bottom, what the investigator of such truths is seeking is only the metamorphosis of the world into man. He seeks to comprehend the world as something analogous to man, and at best he achieves in his struggling the feeling of assimilation. In a similar way to the astrologers who considered the stars to be in man's service and connected with his happiness and sorrow, such an investigator considers the entire universe in connection with man: the entire universe as the infinitely fractured echo of one original sound—man; the entire universe as the infinitely multiplied copy of one original image—man . . . he forgets that the original perceptual metaphors are such and mistakes them for the things themselves [*die Dinge selbst*].[17]

Nietzsche discovers the metaphorical sea upon which rationality floats. He accepts the existence of the technological monsters that swim in its depths. For him, metaphor is more than non-essential as if it were a non-literal mode of signification (defined over against the literal, which determines the true), whose relation to truth (in the classical sense) is simply ornamentation to that which literal descriptions and statements achieve at the proper level. At the same time, however, he accepts the classical valuation scheme: he evaluates this discovery of the necessary anthropomorphic shape to human speech and thought in an absolutely negative sense. For him, the fact that truth is only a mobile army of metaphors means that truth is the product of human making, truth is the product of the technology of language's mental grip on the world, in short, the will's assertion and control over reality. To be a lover of the truth, then, a true philosopher, means to accept this fact, to embrace it and to live it out.

One can usefully evaluate Nietzsche's criticism in light of Kant's distinction between dogmatic and symbolic anthropomorphism: he continues Kant's metaphysical assertion that the necessity of anthropomorphism requires self-consciously symbolic signification, for which the images and concepts of reason (only purified images) are understood as wholly extrinsic to the realities that they signify. A fundamental fact of human experience is this: everything manifest in human experience can be set in mutually illuminating juxtaposition with everything else. The necessary anthropomorphism in our understanding the world is tied to and reciprocal with a necessary mondo-morphism in our understanding of ourselves. To say that a very smart person is "sharp" is first to know and experience sharp things, like a knife. You may set that thing in comparison to your friend's intellect, which is like the knife since it cuts through problems, dissects difficulties easily, and so forth. In the same way, our new understanding of your friend's intellect informs the way we understand sharp things in the world. We look at the knife in human terms in order to understand ourselves in terms of it. If realities are not unchanging substances, defined by literal definitions, with attributes attached to them, then the event of linguistic transposition defines reality itself. It certainly comes before and makes possible the later conceptual approach to things, when we take a contemplative stance and ask what they are in themselves. It is of the anthropomorphic essence of language to perform the illuminative work of transpositional comparison, and it is the mechanism of the progress of the discoveries of reason. The process has always been intrinsic to the tradition's understanding of knowledge, whether dialectical or abstractive. As in vision, discernment of truth emerges through contrastive comparison. I always know what something is by direct contrast with what it is not—even if implicit, even if this is forgotten or obscured by virtue of my grasp. The lesser known always comes to be known by way of the better known, by way of this illuminative juxtaposition, that is, by metaphoricity. The better known, however, is not our concepts, but rather the primary rational process that occurs in the juxtaposition through which appears, like fruit on a stem, a like-unlikeness, as it emerges from the concrete images of sensible experience. Rarefied through a process of expanding application, this affirmation-negation, *sic et non* becomes the concept.

According to Bergson, the history of philosophy will disclose to any interpreter two basic manners of knowing. The first is analysis, knowing things externally, at successive moments. The second is intuition, knowing things from within. The latter I referenced earlier and it is now time to collect on that down payment. Bergson calls it metaphysics, considering it "absolute knowledge," for it makes contact with, uncovers (in a kind of Heraclitean way) the prior unity of mind, in its affective depths, with the living flow of reality.[18] Analysis, he says, "as the ancient philosophers taught" is rooted in intuition—so much so that there is fundamentally one way of knowing, and all the various sciences are first rooted in metaphysics (75). Dialectical reasoning, analysis, not only leads to knowledge as seeing but presupposes it. Bergson's absolute is, of course, not the timeless, frozen reality that illuminates abstract ideas. This is only a representation of absolute reality in concepts. Metaphysics is rather the seizure, by an effort of the mind, of the reality of a thing, which is, for Bergson, in a flux of movement itself. Metaphysics, in the first place, is the experience of oneself in the flux of one's enduring temporal subjectivity, the feeling of life. According to Bergson, analytic knowing uses symbols, or concepts, abstract, general and simple ideas; the inner life of subjectivity, "the original feeling I have of the flow of my own conscious life" (15), the object of metaphysics, cannot be grasped by concepts, and it cannot be represented even by images, although the latter, for Bergson, have an essential advantage over the concept, in that, he says, "they keeps us in the concrete" (16) dimension of lived experience. They hold us there where the event of reality happens. If, for Bergson, the intuition is immediate, without any mediation, the image is the first level of distance from the reality, which somehow maintains the thing's concrete dimension of duration. The concept, last of all, simply substitutes itself for the reality, retaining within only that part of the object that it shares with other objects, making it members of a class, categorizable, that is, by the concept itself.

Concepts fool us into thinking that what we have with them, by virtue of their essential act of "substitution," is the "intellectual equivalent" of the thing itself. But the substitution itself already shows that we have with them mistaken, as it were, the shadow for the prey.[19] In this way, he says, concepts present to us "the shadow alone" of the thing, providing an "artificial reconstruction" of the object, which is symbolized only impersonally and generally. Even the property or aspect that the concept elects to draw from the object observed (say, Garfield), grouping it together in a general class of things ("cat") deforms that very property in direct proportion to the distance it erects to put that property in place: housecats and lions are both cats, is (or was) the Tasmanian tiger a cat or dog? The problem is that in the thing itself, the properties are one with it, and the various properties coincide with each other. The best concepts do, even if we multiply them in order to present together various aspects of an object, is only, as Bergson puts it, to "inscribe round it so many circles, each much too large and none of them fitting it exactly" (19).

Whatever we think of Bergson's metaphysics, of the possibility of intuition of reality, apart from concepts and even images, we can at least take on board his critique of concepts and his subtle prioritization of images in terms of their proximity to and communication of reality beyond the sensible. Images for him "suggest" reality "indirectly" (22) and when we multiply images, diversifying them by borrowing from different orders, putting them into conversation by reference to the reality, they can lead us little by little to the "precise point where there is a certain intuition to be seized" (16). Sounding, to my ear, very much like the Pseudo-Dionysius, Bergson notes, further, that

> by choosing images as dissimilar as possible, we shall prevent any one of them from usurping the place of the intuition it is intended to call up, since it would then be driven away at once by its rivals. By providing that, in spite of their differences of aspect, they all require from the mind the same kind of attention, and in some sort the same degree of tension, we shall gradually accustom consciousness to a particular and clearly defined disposition—that precisely which it must adopt in order to appear to itself as it really is, without any veil. (16–7)

Beyond the concept, and its distortion of reality by its replacement with a lifeless dead letter, images achieve a proximity to the reality, and it seems, experience within themselves a certain intuition of the reality they are meant to represent. Better put, images participate in the intuition itself, in which they are immersed. One communicates with the reality itself by the images and through them, and only very vaguely by concepts, if indeed, as Bergson indicates, our concepts are the progeny of our images in the first place.

Metaphysics, therefore, in the Bergsonian sense, is achieved in actuality by a reversal of the conceptual way of thinking, that is the passage from concepts to things, a passage that is realized by taking an arsenal of ready-made concepts and mixing them into a formula that becomes the equivalent to the reality. Bergson notes the essential pragmatism of this normal activity of the intellect. The movement toward knowledge begins and is motivated by a specific interest applied to reality. We approach an object of inquiry seeking the appropriate action or attitude it suggests to us and thereby try to fit a concept onto it. "To try and fit a concept on an object is simply to ask what we can do with the object, and what it can do for us. To label an object with a certain concept is to mark in precise terms the kind of action or attitude the object should suggest to us. All knowledge, properly so called, is then oriented in a certain direction, or taken from a certain point of view" (41). We first see reality through the order of contrasts, the foregrounding and backgrounding that emerge out of the *salience* the world has for us. We approach the world for a reason, with intention, and the world is manifest around that reason. Concepts, as Nietzsche said, are the induration, the reification-product of such successful salience orientation. For Bergson, concepts are the highest form of the exigencies of normal human experience in its navigation of the world: we make the reality of experience manageable and useful to us precisely by the process of *reification*, reducing it to something that we can control, by approaching it with specific interests and utilizing it toward those ends. Thinking, normally, the "ordinary function of ready-made concepts" consists in the "practical knowledge of reality" asking about something "in order that we may know what to do with it" and entails, merely, the "enumeration of the principal possible attitudes of the thing toward us, as well as our best possible attitude towards it" (54). Concepts, he continues, are "practical questions" (66) to which reality must answer in a certain way. To utilize realities, we reduced them to objects; it is even more useful to us, completely useful, as Heidegger will finally say, if the reification process becomes complete, and we can come to equate the reality itself with that which we grasp of it. This is why, for Bergson, "our mind has an irresistible tendency to consider the idea the clearest which is most useful to it" (53). The representative and substitutionary work of the concept, by which it freezes reality, says Bergson, corresponds "to the most inveterate habits of our thought" (52). In these habits, he continues "we place ourselves as a rule in immobility, in which we find a point of support for practical purposes." Here we construct an imitation, a *representation* of reality, which is more *useful* than any intuition or image, for, to be sure, it "catches in a net something of the reality that passes" through it (66), which are normally its features salient to our end in mind.

For Bergson, reality is the farthest removed from our conceptual abstractions, which only correspond to a certain face of it, which the concept, by its very nature, freezes and pulls out into itself. Instead, reality is life itself, intuited by feeling, which plunges us, enstatically, into it; at absolute infinity, life is Life, God itself, which we can reach by finding the living duration of our life in the absolute concentration of life that is eternity; at the opposite end, the intuition is that of materiality, the pure simple homogeneity of quantity, or the pure dispersion of duration. At any rate, for this (as it were) inverted and enstatic Neoplatonism, we start in the middle, through the intuition of our own life in its concrete, enduring flux (see 62–4). We experience intensities of life at certain moments, for example, in joyful moments, orgasms, or mystical experience. These affective experiences are the place, historically, where one recognizes the touch of the divine, the inexhaustible and unapproachable source and origin of life—this is why the sexual act is sacred, for example, in many of human civilization's religious traditions: here one comes into contact with life, which is, in itself and as such, divine, and therefore our experience of it is holy, equally dangerous and vitalizing, equally destructive and life-giving. Within each of us, and within all life is a spark of the burning bush. And this is why, reciprocally, sexual union has been a key image in mystical and apocalyptic theology. The image of the sexual act, as the culmination of an elaborate social ritual that consumes much time, energy, and resources for its participants, comes closest in all of our experience to the reality of the "consummation" of the ages at the end of time, closest to an encounter of love with the Living God.

Remark. Bergson's critique of Kant is predicated on his rejection of Kant's identification of metaphysics with conceptual determinations; our critique of Bergson would be found in first tying intuition to images, and then second, concepts to image-intuitions. Intuition is achieved through and in images, and not without them; concepts arise from our sensible experience of the world and the fundamental images that it gives to us. Bergson criticizes Kant's metaphysical assertion that all knowledge, properly so called, must be according to the level of concepts and relative to the human understanding, a "single and closed system of relations imprisoning the whole of reality in a network prepared in advance" (83). We can criticize Bergson for a concept, "intuition," the content of which can only be described by images, and for his assertion of plastic and living concepts that exceed the critique of concepts by virtue of their disinterested character, what he calls "fluid concepts, capable of following reality in all its sinuosities and of adopting the very movement of the inward life of things" (69), which arise out of the reversal of the habitual orientation of thought, by moving, now from thing to concept and thereby eschewing any utility for the concept vis-à-vis the reality. What are these at best but images and, indeed, symbols? At worst, such fluid concepts are still substituting representations for the thing itself falling under the same critique that Bergson wages against Kant. If Bergson critiques Kant for "pouring all possible experience into pre-existing moulds" (85), then we would have to ask how far Bergson removed himself from these essential metaphysical presuppositions of Kant's, according to which the image, after all, is subservient to the concept, however renovated. On the other hand, Bergson seems to equate truth with feeling, with intellectually *touching* the real, and banishing the theoretical to the domain outside of the paradise of naked, ever-magical intuition. The maintenance of the irreducible tension here between new, plastic concepts and the naked intuition itself is not enough. The fundamental tension is something, besides, *that already abides within the image itself*, in a more concentrated way. Bergson himself attests to this when he turns first to images to express his thought and to describe metaphysical "intuition."

We should recall Whitehead's observation that scientific reason is as symbolic as religious or poetic reason, the difference being only the fundamental determination made for reason by the *use* to which the symbols are put: science is the use of symbols to know reality for specific material ends; poetry is the use of symbols for the sake of the humanization of the basic and lasting dimensions of experience in the world.[20] If the scientific and technological application of symbols comes to define what we consider true in the world, then we are allowing ourselves a very narrow slice of reality. Poetic symbols have a more universal scope than science, for they give expression to fundamental human experience by entering into a reciprocal relation with the world: they offer the world human meaning and offer humans meaning in the world. To take a simple example from the hearth, my wife remarked once remarked about our infant son, with whom she spent a lot of time through the night: "when he fades to sleep his face is the moon; when he wakes up, peacefully, and looks at me, his eyes are stars, and his smile, lighting up his entire face, it is the sun." The poetic symbol, in a broader way than the narrow ends of scientific application, anthropomorphizes the world, making it a human dwelling, a cosmos, and makes, thereby, the human a microcosmos, which, through symbols, "contains" the world within the human sphere. Humans exceed the horizon of the world through the symbolic function that "redistributes the field of experience," charging it with human significance. In religion, symbols are *used* in order to enter into relation with the common, transcendent Source of our life that binds us with the world. The use of symbols in this way is called "ritual." Ritual is the symbolic action par excellence. Through human action the material world of common experience becomes open to the divine in a special if also normative manner. Ritual is thereby the spontaneous reception and passage of the living Presence lying at the root of the world and which nevertheless wholly surpasses it. It is in and through the action of man himself that the world becomes receptive of the divine. In the religious "use" of symbols, which has the broadest scope and is therefore the least utilitarian of all symbolic modes (unless, that is, it devolves into magic, but that brings religious "use" in close proximity to science), we see in the most complete way that the human being is itself the symbol par excellence. The human as symbol, we could even suggest, defines him as the image of God: he is the presence of God in the world, the passage by which the world enters into its defining relation with God. And here may be, not incidentally, the grain of truth in Hegel's phenomenology of Spirit: the human being is the symbolic application "used" by the divine spirit, *pneuma* to enter into reciprocal and "gnostic" (little g, i.e., in the original and catholic account of the term, "coactive knowing") relation with the world. Humanity itself is therefore the instrument of divine symbolic and creative thinking, the linking of matter and ideal, and the means of the expression of the divine reign in the world, the means by which the God of heaven becomes the God of earth, the way his reign becomes manifest "on earth as it is in heaven." The symbol itself anticipates the end of all things, when what it signifies—its own repletion—is enacted. Its priority in knowledge points to the apocalyptic emergence of the *eschaton*: *Gloria enim Dei vivens homo*, "the glory of God is a living man:" *vita autem hominis visio Dei*, "and the life of man consists in the vision of God.²¹ By "vision of God," of course, the ancients probably first meant the accomplishment of the visionary experiences of the prophets. To "see" or "behold" God meant to be present at the final vindication of his ways, to see the accomplishment of his purpose, the δικαιοσύνη τοῦ θεοῦ, "justification/righteousness of God," which is, at the same time, the accomplishment of his final justice (δικαιοσύνη) through judgment (δίκη).²² A Church Father, like Irenaeus, works from out of the extended sense of this meaning, since blessing means to be or to remain in God's presence (when he comes to bring, in a final way, his presence to bear, eschatologically, on the world) and curse means to be removed from this "parousiac" presence.²³ For them, vision of God means the accomplished, ultimate state of total cosmic union with God, with humanity at the center of a new, glorious administration of the creation, or, in other words, a "new heavens and new earth."²⁴ It is finally worth observing that γνῶσις means, in this Pauline context, knowledge that is both personal and receptive, the γνῶσις τῆς ἀγάπης, both participatory and creative, the love that God possesses to bring into being a world, a people, order out of χάος, the love that God possesses that forgives, that restores, and that draws his interlocutor into a collaborative partnership. This is a γνῶσις in which humanity is intended to participate, and in which it participates when humanity performs the good, "fulfills the *nomos/torah/*instructive wisdom" by ἀγαπῶν τὸν πλησίον, "loving the neighbor."²⁵ Ὁ θεὸς ἀγάπη ἐστίν, "God is love."²⁶ "The one that does not love (μὴ ἀγαπῶν), does not know (οὐκ ἔγνω) God." After belief in the God of love, in a post-Christian context, there is a vacuum of divinity created that fragments the now individualized psyche located outside of a community that celebrates that love as the most real, joining that one into a unity grounded in recall of an origin and the pressing expectation of the αἰών when charity will rule all. This vision, however imperfectly, and not, of course, without draughts of the tragic, large and bitter, once unified a civilization to a significant degree.

Before, each was an object of divine love, elevated in their singularity. Now the elevation of singularity remains but without the condition divine ἀγάπη. That Christendom's metaphysical subtext remains as the submerged substructure to Western civilization, both in its understanding of human persons, though their original vocational dignity to "co-rule" with God has become self-consciously self-assertive in a command of the world as resource for individually competing ends (as I will later discuss), and in its understanding of the world, though the creation, once a field of sophianic plenitude laden with possibilities for flourishing needing only activation by human creativity working under the divine instruction, has become a field of raw potential for rapacious exploitation. And God is reduced, finally, to the merely benevolent and hidden, quasi-personal force ensuring that, despite personal frustrations of expectation, the universe is working to fulfill every individual's every dream (or at least my own). There is much cultural, material, and psychological suffering in a post-Christian milieu, despite the wealth, liberty, and health that it has most certainly afforded many.

In his lectures *On the Essence of the Truth* (1931/2), a commentary on Plato's allegory of the cave, Heidegger responds to the objection that his thought, which ties the meaning of Being in general with the particular being, human being in particular, is an "anthropomorphization" (*Vermenschlichung*) of the nature of truth. For Heidegger, this criticism emerges out of an unreflective conception of truth itself (that it is not necessarily something human) and of human being as well (that the truth of what is human is laid out in advance). He says, "Do we know then that without further ado what man is, so that one is in a position to decide that truth cannot be something human?"[27] In his lecture course commentary on Schelling's *On the Essence of Human Freedom* (1809),[28] as also in his essay "On the Essence of Truth" (not to be confused with the lecture course on Plato), Heidegger follows Schelling's view that freedom is not in the first place an attribute of humanity, but rather that humanity is an attribute of freedom, as it were: we are "appropriated" by historical existence in its unfolding, for it unfolds *through* human freedom, which is understood, not as autonomy, or the ability to manipulate, but as a contemplative stance toward reality, an orientation that allows reality to articulate itself through us.[29] Though hard to comprehend from a modern voluntarist post-Cartesian and post-Lockean standpoint, we are essential components, in our freedom, of the reality of Being. What humanity "is" for Heidegger is only understood in recognizing that human being is what it is through being *more* than just human. In this context, we will see with how little variation he repeats his response to the objection of his anthropomorphization of the truth laid down a few years earlier in the lectures on Plato: "Behind this accusation stands the conviction, which is not further discussed, that everyone knows in general what man is."[30] For Heidegger, adapting Schelling, the nature of particular realities ("beings") is unfolded through the very act of human being's bringing these realities into the phenomenal light of awareness, an act through which he comes to comprehend himself as the one through whom beings' become themselves, and thereby through whom Being, reality in itself, comes to light, that is, *is* itself, in this coming to light. The truth of Being itself in the event of its un-concealing (ἀ-λήθεια) occurs through the human freedom to let things be themselves (what he calls, appropriating Eckhart, *Gelassenheit*). And yet human freedom to "let be" is essentially a kind of appropriation *to* Being's "sway" (as he expresses it in *Mindfulness*, 1938/9), a placing oneself, as observer and participant, in Being's purely finite and temporal flow, as witness to and an articulation of it. As he will say again and again in that text, divinities and mortals encounter one another in the "strife" of two basic modes of experience of the human context, world and earth, in the site of human "in betweenness" that "crosses"—that is, passes through and crosses out, annuls—metaphysics, the self-destructive mastery of humanity over all things through the reduction of everything to the same value determined by usefulness, replacing it with the experience of the unreserved giftedness of existence, "serenity," and a religious expectation for a new kind of divine appearing, "the last god." Humanity's proper place, despite the aberrations of Western civilization, is the sacred, the mortal *mysterium* of water, fire, flesh, light, air, darkness, shadow, birth and death, sky and star, tree, animal, dirt, of an earth that is either womb or tomb, or both, the place of the emergence and passing away of being.

Forgive the pun, but it is in *Mindfulness* that we may gain some clarity. Heidegger is not merely responding to the critique of his own thinking as "anthropomorphic," but himself criticizes the anthropomorphic character of Western thought. "Anthropomorphism," defines Heidegger, "is an explicit or implicit, acknowledged or unknowingly adopted conviction that 'beings in the whole' are what they are and how they are by virtue of, and in accordance with, the representation that, among other processes of life, proceeds in man, the animal endowed with reason."[31] This being or that being, this mathematical formula or that soiled napkin, this idea of God and that god presencing in the temple—the essence or nature of this or that being and its manner of being—whatever being there is and the totality of beings as such, are "in accord" or agreement with the "representation" of the particular being, the human being, by virtue of its uniqueness as animal "endowed with reason," with the capacity to measure and control what is in its conceptualizing representation. The standard or measure, so to speak, of the meaningfulness of beings to the human is the human measure itself, namely, human reason. Furthermore, this reason is one among other "processes of life"—a dimension, in the last analysis, of human animality, though precisely that dimension that makes the human distinct from the "other" animals. The upshot of this "belief," argues Heidegger, is that "everything represented, stated and inquired is indeed merely 'human,'[32] indeed, merely animal but distinctly human, which is, simply, a unique division of animal being." But, Heidegger contests, this conception of humanity as the animal that knows through representation rests on a certain understanding. One cannot have an understanding of the "rational animal" except as the animal that represents to itself the contents of its world in the internal sphere of consciousness. Anthropomorphism proposes itself *in this way* as "immediately intelligible." Its self-evidentiality is even more, "strengthened and sustained by the opinion that what man is in his ownmost can by no means become the object of a question."[33] What we have here on Heidegger's account of the peculiar anthropomorphism of Western thought is a kind of first principle: an apophatically assured basic intelligibility regarding human rationality that defines human being and all that it represents to itself but which cannot be properly examined. Yet it is this that determines the totality of all possible and actual "representable" beings. Representation is tied to reason (indeed, the fullness of its content) as the human standard of beings. What is known is not the beings "in themselves" but only their phenomenal appearing in the form of representation. And yet reason says this representation is all these being are, the anthropomorphic form is their truth. Representation itself (as the nature, so to speak, of rationality) is the principle of, and the key to, the humanity of man and therefore to "beings in the whole."

Anthropomorphism, then, is the power of representation to give the truth of beings to themselves. What is is what it is by virtue of the capacity the rational animal has to give beings to itself as objects, manipulable for its use. The "subterfuge" of this anthropomorphism is its apparent "unassailability": it is obvious (no?) that, to quote the medieval adage, "what is received is received according to the mode of the receiver." Humans receive human-sized and human digestible chunks of reality into themselves. This properly human proportion is rational representation, a repetitive mirroring in the human mind of the intelligibility inherent in things out in the world. The problem, for Heidegger, is that this "Vermenschung," literally, "hominization" of beings that defines the anthropomorphic form of Western thought pseudo-apophatically hides its transcendental conditioning. It rests on, as a more primordial condition, the

"Vermenschung" of being itself (and makes human being into the particular type of *bios* that bears "logos"—humans are the product of this *Vermenschung* as well. Classically speaking, this *logos* is divinity. Humanity is the form of animal life, below the moon and in the sphere, therefore, of mortality, that partakes of what is highest and best in the world, the divine kind of nature, through participation in *logos*, the intelligence of things, active and ordering, gathering and holding in place for a time. The *Vermenschung* of beings and of being involves a *Vergötterung*, "divinization," of humanity. And yet, it is this identification of human essence (as *animal rationale*) with divinity (as *logos*) behind the anthropomorphism of Western thought that sustains the *Entgötterung*, "de-divinizing" or absence of the gods from the modern world, ruled by technology, the essence of which, in *Mindfulness*, is articulated by the term *anthropomorphism*. Humanity reveals to itself a ("hominized") world to which it then offers itself as lord and master. *Logos* has become *ratio*, calculative reasoning. But, as much ironic as it is truly apocalyptic, this self-empowering determination of the world as usable material for human projects only destroys humanity and its world through the all-encompassing power of such "technicity": the last stage or condition of human "knowing-awareness" that "secures" anthropomorphism, Heidegger concludes tersely, is "the final harnessing of man into the unleashed machination of beings."[34]

Western anthropological anthropomorphism does not inquire into the truth of being, but remains on the plane of beings, veiled, alienated (as it were) from its own human "allotment" to Being, and its "place" (as it were) as receiver of beings in their truth in the clearing where Being gives it to beings, and gives it a world. It presupposes a metaphysical assumption that veils the questioning and its properly receptive attitude that together can escape from the nihilistic upshot of the reduction of Being to beings and beings to representation, the "contrivance of the rational animal," with its divine power to determine what is in its truth. Being, here, is nothing but the capacity of beings to be represented, "representedness," where representation becomes the real, where the artificial displaces the natural, where, now, virtual reality blends with the "human" sphere, performing, through participation, a capitulation of human desire to transcend nature through mastery. Mindfulness, *Besinnung*, in response offers a practice akin to the later fully conceptualized "thinking": a being mindful of the *Ereignis*, "en-ownment" of man to Dasein, which means recognizing the always present and primordial "owning-over" by Being that gives humanity to itself and to beings, a "being-owned-over-to," an experience of finitude that liberates a "letting be" of things in their sacred presencing that is experienced as an "in-between." Mindfulness gives rise to an escape from the destructive reign of anthropomorphism-technology and its unrelenting erasure of human freedom.

I can only ask your indulgence for the rough (but serene) poetic Heideggerian riffing of the previous paragraph, but there really is no replacement for it. And this is an illustration of the point. Reality itself possesses a certain *metaphoricity*, a certain lavish opulence, a wild generosity in the giving forth of things to the human awareness, and brought to light through speech, that always discloses something of itself, something salient to human intention, and yet recedes in an excess of reserve with equal force, in proportions to the limitations inherent in the scope of utility structuring the approach. Training in mindfulness can dilate this receptivity all the way to a poetic correspondence, a kind of dance of gift and return, call and response that itself begins to lift the veil and to slide awareness back onto the sacred quality of things. Metaphoricity, then, is more than a mere description of Heidegger's mindfulness of the enownment of Being. Representation, the equation of truth with the conformity of the mental concept to the thing in question, denies this metaphoricity (when it does not recognize its ground in it, and conceives itself as basic), and replaces it with a corresponding fit between thing in the world and idea in the mind. Truth, for Heidegger, is an event, where the clearing of being happens that is the sphere of human awareness, where human being becomes human, becomes self-conscious as a being in the world. The clearing happens where beings come forth as they are in their self-appearing. Human awareness, or Dasein, is allotted the truth of being by being itself. Being (as finite, as groundless inexhaustibility with nothing behind it, as "grounding ground" without remainder) is the condition for the arising of human awareness as "being there." Human being is receptive to beings' appearing in and through themselves into the clearing of human awareness by his being given to be as the being for whom beings appear. He is receptive, but his receptivity is conditioned first not by him, but as a condition for his human kind of being. Being is the presencing power that gives beings to themselves; human Dasein shares in this presencing as awareness, in other words, in the human way, in the way that has world, and has a clearing that "poetically" lets things be.

Understanding the risk of anachronism, I use an expression of Ricoeur but shall interpret it as a precise exemplification of Heidegger's insight. Ricoeur wants metaphor to be involved in our "appropriation of our effort to exist and desire to be." Present in reflection is a pre-theoretical hermeneutical moment before cognitive comprehension.[35] The figurative (metaphorical or symbolic) is an event of re-appropriation, disclosing more deeply the "bond" my human being shares with the being of being. We may sift through this event "dialectically" and through this we discover the gains in understanding pre-contained in the figurative as its possibilities. Metaphor, the "transposition" (ἐπιφορά) of a set of meaning-associations in one context to another, establishing a linkage between the known and lesser-known resulting in the expansion of meaning that preserves the discontinuity and unknowability that pertains to the sphere of transference while also illuminating it, is a repetition in the sphere of language of our (already linguistic) existential gripping onto the world, our human making the world meaningful—not through an extrinsic pasting onto the alien world of sensible experience a hominizing meaning, a turning nature into liveable human culture, but rather by deepening lived experience of human language-formed community that blends a vertical dimension of (for lack of better word) hierophaneous appearing and horizontal passage of history through the inbreaking of the "destiny" of being, a future from which new or renewed meaningfulness in the present comes (even in the form of absence). Reality, metaphorical reality, is the appropriation of us, human being, by our being given to ourselves and (same thing) to our world of meaning—not by ourselves—but by being, which is, for Heidegger—reminiscent, in fact, of Plotinus—a non-intentional source about which one can only speak intentionally, teleologically, for the reason that (unlike Plotinus, perhaps) our being in our place is intelligible and can give us a meaningful place, but is not our construction except through our poetic receptivity, our response to the "call" of being that gives rise to the appearing of the truth. The call of being is *our* being. We are not masters, nor lords, but "shepherds" of the historical unfolding, "allotted" our place, stewards. It is worth noting, finally, that, for Heidegger, it is a human—a finite, mortal—meaningfulness that is perceived all the more deeply, that is, humanly, when we keep the place of finitude without remainder that is ours free from any predicated final identity behind it (such as God). This does not, as a thesis, determine the metaphoricity as such. For the infinitely redundant finitude, a complete reconciliation with mortality eliciting *Gelassenheit*, "serenity," does not exhaust the order of human possibility. Man can choose, apparently, to be serene or anxious. He can also be, as Lacoste said, joyful, "overdetermining," by the "symbolic subversion" of eschatological expectation, the essential topology of humanity, existing instead "before the Absolute," dwelling at the proto-eschatological margins of earth or world, two variations of the human τόπος equally experienced, in a symbolic, protological way, as "jointly given" with God (as opposed to excluding him in an a priori manner), and thereby eclipsed in their claim to priority for humanity. *Thinking within the world of its eschatological eclipse, thinking theologically, requires thinking in the bond of symbols.*[36]

With Heidegger's critique of anthropomorphism, we find ourselves, then, in the midst of a "re-appropriated" account of the anthropomorphic character of the human horizon, of the world, which I have wanted to call a metaphoricity that *at once* gives meaning through human participation and preserves the apophatic alterity of what is given in its presencing, making the unfolding historical experience, thereby, truly human. The key, I think, is found at the bookends of Aristotle's definition of metaphor: "Metaphor consists . . . on the grounds of analogy."[37] Metaphor expands meaning, and therefore understanding, through the recognition of analogicity, the elicitation of a likeness between two otherwise unlike things, involving a seeing of one thing in light of another. Pseudo-Dionysius, as we will see, will use the term ἀναλογία as a synonym of σύμβολον.[38]

Remark. Paradoxically, the anthropocentrism of modern anthropomorphism since Kant can only be overcome if the regime of the concept is deconstructed and the priority of the metaphorical is rediscovered, a priority that acknowledges even the metaphoricity of reality itself, that truth *is* likeness (as God is self-redundant excess even beyond non-duality), that truth is *more like* images, symbols, metaphors, narratives, than it is like a concept, which, again, is only a metaphor at a critical remove from concrete experience. It is therefore truer to say that your lover's face is the moon, her eyes are stars, and so forth, than to say that she has straight teeth, or fleshy, pink lips. It is truer to say that light is "wave" or "wave particle duality" than to say that it is electromagnetic radiation visible to the eye with a frequency between 380 and 740 nanometers. The latter definition by concepts is supremely useful for applications of appropriative control but remains wholly external to the phenomenon. The former enters the phenomenon, by way of asserting, or rather, accepting, its anthropomorphic character and, at the same time, our optomorphic character. The phenomenon of light tells us about ourselves, and the phenomenon of ourselves tells us about light; it only requires the metaphorical juxtaposition of the two phenomena in order for their reciprocal properties to emerge, properties which emerge *only* via the specific juxtaposition put in play. The juxtaposition of ourselves to light reveals the anthropomorphic corollaries within light and the optomorphic corollaries within us. The juxtaposition shines the particular shape of man onto the phenomenon of light and determines what it will show of itself, just as the answers the nature gives to science are determined by the kinds of questions we ask of it, and before that the "style" of attention we give to it. In every juxtaposition, even when we ourselves are not an explicit part of the metaphorical pair, we are implied, since it is by our speech that we perform the metaphorical illumination of the world of things. Experience as a whole is human, yet it is not anthropocentric, that is, not delimited to the limits and conditions of human knowing set out in advance, to the degree that we, even in our freedom, are simply the site where language and reality pass over into one another. We exist, that is, we have our particular being, in and through the passing of being into language and vice versa. The act of transference that determines metaphor is an ontological reality and in the first place the site of our being. Things persist in and things become in the metaphoricity of language, which in the first place defines us. We come to be *in* this passage, and *as* the passage where things come to be.

What does it mean to say reality IS metaphorical? We must be careful not to understand this according to the metaphysical presupposition that being and the concept are correlate. Instead, to say that reality IS metaphorical must be understood on metaphorical terms (and we must be careful, against the normal habituation of our thought, to understand metaphor according to the order of the priority of concept, for which metaphor is an extravagant ornamentation upon reality which is penetrated by concepts). Perhaps the real is meaning that things symbolize. To use an image from religion: to say that Jesus is Lord, seated at the right hand of the Father in heaven, can be understood literally. Here God has an anthropomorphic form, and heaven has literally what we understand when we understand thrones, and all other exotic accoutrements. This image can also be purified: God does not literally have hands, and he is not literally reigning in heaven on a throne shaped like a chariot set upon a sea of glass and surrounded by thunder and lightnings, dwelling in impenetrable cloud and darkness, and so on. All this signifies the divine majesty and authority and power in terms drawn from our experience of nature, that we earth dwellers can understand. But if we are simply to reduce the image to the concepts that I just mentioned, such as "God has all authority, and Jesus, as the King of Israel shares in that authority as the Father's human regent even now" or that God is all powerful and Jesus is the manifestation and even mediation of that power, and so forth, then we lose what is essential in the image by way of boiling it down to some purely conceptual base. This second moment is of course critically important to avoid what our ancestors called idolatry that almost nobody today would be guilty of (at least in my experience, but I hear stories . . .).

At any rate, the critique of our conceptions of God is necessary to ascend to a greater understanding. And such has been, for the Christian imperial and post-imperial orthodox traditions east and west, the value of an intrinsic and spontaneous consonance between the Jewish conviction of uncompromising transcendence and fidelity to it unto death, on one hand, and the "interiorizing" spirituality of Greek metaphysics, on the other. Yet, we must avoid the greater and more pernicious idolatry implied, if we are not careful, in the critique itself.

Here we are tempted to equate or identify our conception with the reality itself. Here we say or at least imply that what I understand of God's power is what God's power is; or that the resurrected Jesus' authority becomes determined by my conception of it (or more generally: God's power to reveal himself becomes determined by our preconceptions of its scope). Here things like the resurrection of the dead, the ascension into heaven and Christ's eventual return to consummate the ages and to usher in the New Heavens and New Earth where God's original intention for the creation, that it be his temple and that human beings incarnate his presence and life and justice in the world, and so forth—all these things become only variations of the abstract idea which becomes determinative of the reality. So a third moment is required, where the realities themselves can hold first place in terms of the signification of the truth, and the idolatry of conceptual determination is called into question. This means (and we would do well to make this a principle of theology) that God is given the last word and that the last word can actually be spoken by God. Christians believe that the last word *is* Christ, the living human being, that the resurrected Jesus of Nazareth is God's full truth, his ultimate statement about himself and about ourselves and about all reality. Generally speaking, this means that the original images of revelation are more truthfully replete than the conceptual abstractions, but they are more truthful not in a crude literal way, but still truthful in a way that requires their crudeness to be given its full scope. And this is the difficult part. The most we can say is that reality itself is closer to the images and symbols of the poets than the concepts of the philosophers, and that the concepts of the philosophers are closer to the truth when they are used to bring about our fidelity to the truth, which the images and symbols give us, *to account*. Yet after the critique, and through it, the recognition that the images and symbols are *truer* than concepts must emerge, and this emergence is actually only possible by way of the critique applied by philosophical conceptuality in the first place. So how is the image of Jesus enthroned at the right hand of the Father *truer* than the abstract conception of his authority and power over history? We can only say here that the image participates in the reality (in a more immediate and living way than the conceptual reduction), anticipating it in intramundane terms, giving it the flesh that it requires to be true for history, for human beings in their fully embodied state and for the cosmos in its destiny as "support" of the descended divine plenitude. The image most indirectly evokes the most metaphorical of all, the divine presence. And this makes it a symbol.

History, embodiment, cosmos are three ends for revelation, ends not destroyed or abandoned, but transfigured. And this flesh is part of the reality that cannot be superseded. If ultimate reality is alive, if the truth of things is grounded in this Life, finding their origin and end in it, precisely in the way that the resurrection of Christ points, then the living reality of the flesh in our experience gives us more reality than the dissection of reality into the frozen or suspended state by concepts. This appears to me to be a wholly consistent theological a priori. Even more so, the resurrection of the flesh for Christianity, already achieved in Jesus of Nazareth, who becomes in that event and nowhere else, the paradigm for all reality, means that the flesh is worthy of the truth of things, more worthy than the attempt to de-flesh the truth by conceptual abstraction—a kind of intellectual Docetism, an idolatry of the angelic.

Something analogous to what I suggest for religion ought to be possible in relation to other domains of knowledge. We at least must say that if we leave ourselves determined by the second moment of critique (for which concepts equate with the real or determine what is possible of the real for us, as in Kant), then we are in danger of not allowing the real to surpass our preconceptions of its limits by virtue of our anthropocentric requirements that the phenomena must comply to. We would not allow experience the possibility of being impossible; we would never allow what happens to transform us by virtue of the absolutization of ourselves in our (Kantian) transformation of reality into "human" experience. One would have to wonder whether this is human at all. Approaching any and every domain of human inquiry in light of the metaphoricity of reality in this way of course ought even to mean that we should be open to the possibility that they have a final compatibility even with theology, though this is only fully possible in the eschatological future, though it can be anticipated in smaller or greater ways in the present, the achievements of which even ought to be ever revisable (in order to avoid the higher idolatry to which we are prone), and this requires and is even only possible, paradoxically, when the scope of inquiry be given its own relative autonomy and self-sufficiency to explore its own domain to which it is appropriately attuned. Here (for example) the horizon of faith is a goad and aid to scientific and intellectual freedom, for it calls every domain of inquiry to continue forward and never rest in what it has achieved of the truth, precisely by providing the paradigm case, in its very unsurpassable radicality, for the possible: revelation's stretching out of rationality and our conception of what is possible for experience is, one would be compelled to say, though this would have to be demonstrated, precisely what makes room for science. Revelation questions and dilates experience to give room to reason. It also affords a de-Copernican return to a Neoplatonic hierarchical conception of reality that places humanity's material cosmos on the outer rim of the hierarchically real, which recovers a sacral sensibility of the symbolic and συμπαθής character of the material order with the spiritual, and permits, then, the radicality of the

Incarnation and the eschatological venture to be made properly manifest. This we will shortly discover in the next chapter.

The necessity of anthropomorphism is a problem only if we consider the order of the concept to be determinative or even primary in knowledge. If the concept is primary in knowledge, if it defines the nature of what is knowable or not, if the concept, with its ideal of *clarity* and *distinctness*, and its procedure of *abstraction* and critical *distance* from its object, is the paradigm of *knowing*, and hence the object is the paradigm of *knowledge* (according to which the *grasp* of the concept *corresponds* exhaustively with the reality that it grasps (at the level of the absolute, whether that is God or man), hence reducing the reality or thing in itself to that which is grasped of it),[39] then anthropomorphism is indeed the fundamental and unsurpassable problem for thought, definitively delimiting the scope of human reason, making the speculative penetration of reality—what Kant called "metaphysics"—impossible. If, however, the figurative dimension of language is more appropriate to the divine transcendence (and even, perhaps, the nature of all things in general), then anthropomorphism actually fits best with the nature of reality—in other words, our necessary anthropomorphisms are the very substance of metaphysical knowledge that the concept can only ever explicate. In this case anthropomorphism is not something to be overcome, as if knowledge requires the shedding of our humanity and the achievement of a sort of state of divinization above the materiality and instability of the world. *This* was the Greek philosophical ideal, rather barbarous, before the original enlightenment that penetrated the classical world through the Jews and then the Christians, transforming its categories from within by the sacred teaching of creation-incarnation-re-creation. Rather, if by way of the critique of our concepts, we turn in the first place to the figurative dimension of language and accord it intellectual and philosophical primacy, as art, literature, religion, *and today, even science*, require of us more and more strongly, then the necessary anthropomorphism tells us something about ourselves.[40] First, indeed, it provides the critical lesson: it tells us that we are merely human, that we are finite, limited, that our reason is tied to the density and dumb impenetrability of our flesh, and of the relentless change of historical existence to which our language and especially its fundamental metaphors, figures and images are tied. Second, the necessity of the anthropomorphic form of our thought also tells us something, perhaps, about the nature of reality itself. For if the figurative dimension plunges its roots more deeply into the dark mystery of reality, and if the concept, with its abstract generalizations, achieves its distance by means of pulling these roots out of their soil in a mechanical and de-temporalized manner, then the *living* and *personal* aspects of reality, essential to it (as revelation expresses and religion experiences), are bracketed out or covered over by the very structure of conceptual objectivity. This means that, as Nietzsche, Husserl and Heidegger have equally indicated, the concept is created by means of an original veiling of its own metaphorical or figurative roots, its necessary material character or the fact that its origins lie in embodied human experience. Likewise, with the priority of the concept (both radically critiqued by Kant and yet remaining, for him, in its place of priority), the *qualitative* dimension is excised from reality and made merely a subjective aspect of experience (as in Galileo, for whom only measurable quantity is real).[41] Here anthropomorphism would be less a fundamental problem for thought than thinking determined by the priority of the concept, requiring a critique of reason and demanding the "end of [bad] metaphysics" as only a more sophisticated mythologization of experience than myth, since the embrace of the priority of the figurative dimension of language and reality and, further, the anthropomorphic form of reality, is straightforward about its own limits, conditions and origins. We have already seen how even the transcendental approach of Kant is an extension of such "metaphysics," veiling, at a second remove, its own all the more "anthropomorphic" substitution of formal abstractions for the images of the poets and of Scripture. Instead, if the figurative dimension of language is closer in proximity to the truth of reality, then our anthropomorphisms, when acknowledged as signifying the condition of our finitude, but also its essential bond with meaning, are invited, through placing them within the wider eschatological conditions that reveals the "principle of the uniqueness of things" (Yannaras), to become for us a sign of the divine truth that can never come to an end, a sign of the insolubility and inexhaustibility of reality that perpetually motivates philosophy, and with which the dense intelligibility of the figurative dimension of language fits, even participates—I almost said "corresponds," but that is only a term for the extrinsicism of conceptual knowledge.[42]

Recall, for a moment, that the Pseudo-Dionysius understood theology to have cataphatic, or naive moment, where the symbols, metaphors, images, and even concepts and names of God are given, and an apophatic, or critical moment, where these significations are negated. God is a rock, Scriptures says, or love, or, our theologians and philosophers say, more abstractly, "infinite goodness," or Being itself, sheer "to be," or even "that than which nothing greater can be conceived." At the second moment, we say that God is *not* a rock, for he is immaterial, but here we affirm that the rock's rockiness somehow signifies God's fidelity, constancy, permanence, and so forth; likewise, God is love, indeed, but whatever we know of love, God is infinitely more; he is the archetype of love in which all created love only dimly participates. Hence, our original affirmation is negated: it is more true to say what God is not—he is NOT what we conceive as love—than what he is. But even so, our negations are made out of a sense, a conviction, even a certainty, of a greater affirmation that cannot be articulated. We must negate even our greatest concepts inasmuch as they are, for us, only aspects of our world magnified to greatest conceiving, and then some (to paraphrase Anselm). God is "ever greater" than any of our concepts. How then are any of them "true"? Traditionally, they are true inasmuch as (1) they know their limits and (2) are justified by God's authority. It is perhaps not too misleading to say that the former is emphasized by modern thinking (only ever greater emphasized to this day) and the latter, by premodern thought. It is perhaps truer, however, to say that premodern thought, acutely so in Christianity especially through the Middle Ages, was characterized by a self-conscious attempt to balance the two principles. In this case, we would only be more barbaric today than in ages past. At any rate, the Pseudo-Dionysius sought to capture this dynamic of divine excess in relation to our images and concepts by affirming a third degree of knowledge, which he articulated by appending a prefix hyper-(super- in English; Uber- or Ur- in German) to the original affirmations themselves: God is "super-goodness," etc. If considered the end of our signifying capacity, the negation of our positive affirmations of God would simply deconstruct everything: we would be necessary agnostics. Ending here, however, would only put limits on the divine power to reveal itself, even to finite, fleshly beings like ourselves, poor in intelligence, marginal (naturally speaking) in the vast and imponderable hierarchy of reality. This, according to the Pseudo-Dionysius, is only a particularly terrible form of idolatry, almost on par with the other pernicious idolatry that afflicts our humanity: namely, that our abstract concepts correspond in themselves to the divine reality, or even do so any better, in the end, than the images, symbols, and narratives of Scripture, which purport to make the divine tangible, in a participatory way beyond knowing and therefore anticipative of the eschatological, in the liturgy. Hence, the hyper-prefix reflects a third order of knowing God beyond the critique of mere negation, back to the simplicity of the affirmations with which one begins, but more deeply illumined, at least as deeply as human marginal intelligence allows, which is not exactly nothing. This, third order, as we observed earlier, was already implicit within the negative critique of the original affirmation. Hence, one returns to the originally given concrete data with the critical knowledge gained, but surpasses even these negations themselves *through* the crude images whose density harbors a unique intelligibility that the rarefied concepts, expanded to infinity and become only ever weaker and vaguer, can neither grasp nor hold within themselves. For the Pseudo-Areopagite, this perspective, which fundamentally surpasses his pagan interlocutors (themselves tied to the priority of the abstract rational dimension over the concrete), is precisely what sets Christianity apart from them, for such a third way is both necessitated and justified by the Christian revelation in which God takes on flesh in Jesus of Nazareth, and by the Scriptures themselves, which obviously prioritize the figurative, the narrative, the symbolic dimension over the conceptual—a perpetual scandal to the intellectual elite of late antiquity. The point is that this perspective perpetually dismantles the human attempt to constrain the divine by human categories, *especially* the intellectual temptation to circumscribe and indeed replace the living God with formal determinations, as much for our most exalted concepts as our most humble, or seemingly humble, *self*-limitations (which are too often actually delimitations sketched out in advance and applied to God). BUT: it is God who reveals *himself*, not we who reveal God.

The general schematization of religious knowledge I comment on here, which Aquinas called the threefold way (*triplex via*), is of course well known. A tempting thought experiment would suggest that its form may be applied (1) as a general hermeneutic of the history of philosophy and also, as I noted previously, (2) as the general structure of human knowing. The latter is obvious and strictly necessary if the concept of God is what it purports to be, paradigmatic, normative, and controlling for thought in general. I will close this stage of my argument with a few elucidatory remarks.

(1) The general approach to philosophical self-understanding, our philosophy of philosophy, or meta-philosophy, is typically related to the Greek self-conception (at least in Aristotle) and then the Enlightenment conscription of this narrative, through its proposal of itself as a fundamental repetition of it, a renewal of the original Greek impulse toward knowledge. *Logos vom Mythos*. On this view, philosophy arrived when λόγος, awoken in human reason, extracted itself from the explanations of reality established by the sacred myths from time immemorial and sought to consider reality *in itself*, and on its own terms, *free* to plumb the depths of hidden potential of intelligence that the narrative milieu only presupposed but was incapable of explaining. Indeed, it is true that the early Christian intellectuals understood themselves to be bearers of the true Enlightenment in this respect, the "true philosophy," the means by which human beings are fundamentally delivered from the darkness of mythic consciousness and the cacophony of accounts of the divine by the countless "schools" of philosophy. By contrast with their pagan critics, these thinkers equated the love of wisdom with the love of God in the flesh and understood Christianity as the path toward the fulfillment of human life in the truth, a wisdom that is only

granted "from above." True philosophy, the essential human wisdom, and the way of life that incarnates such wisdom, then, was made possible by the gift of revelation. It should not be overlooked that Christianity also articulated itself as a continuation and radicalization of the philosophical impulse at work in the late Hellenistic world, which already in its greatest precursors (Plato, Aristotle) tended toward monotheism and was (arguably) an essential reason for the wide allure held by Judaism and then Christianity in the classical milieu. Yet Christianity understood itself to surpass paganism and complete its impulse by means of revelation, the words and deeds of God that are also the words and deeds of humanity. Hence the *Logos vom Mythos* model is, as a description of Christianity, too simplistic.

An index of what I want to say here is seen in the way the Christians treated their sacred texts, by contrast, again, to the late pagan philosophers. For the Christians, mere *allegorēsis*, that is, the *philosophical* critique of the mythic stories, finding the exalted truths of philosophy as an esoterica behind the letter of the text, was *only half-way* toward the divine *res*, the realities of faith. The Pseudo-Dionysius is, again, a paradigm articulation of the patristic Christian view. For him, as I have suggested, there is more, beyond the critique of images and symbols of the poets and the exaltation of abstract conceptual determinations of the divinity; indeed, the fundamental thing is to penetrate into the heart of the reality, by returning to the simplest, crudest images and symbols themselves, which God has sanctified and, in disclosing himself through them, has revealed their capacity to bear forth the divine truth, precisely by transforming, as has been said before, myth into history, and hence showing the foolishness of humanity, in its quest for wisdom, in the revelation of the divine wisdom in the cross (1 Corinthians 1–3). It is the authority of revelation itself which allows this penetration: ultimate reality is personal, conscious, free, engaged with the world. Hence, the concreteness and dense intelligibility of the material world of ordinary human experience in its embodied condition, and its linguistic adaptations of poetry, symbol, narrative, parable, and metaphor are more appropriate to ultimate reality than rarefied generalities. If the critique of μῦθος by λόγος is a second and necessary step for reason, corresponding to the Pseudo-Dionysius' apophatic negation of the simple affirmations, then also, a third step is needed: the return to "μῦθος," by a higher λόγος, a critique of λόγος by way of hyper-affirmation, beginning with the λόγος of revelation itself as the definitive word (λόγος) about reason (λόγος). If we were to apply this simple scheme to the history of Western thought, then we would have to suggest that the first phase, that of affirmation, is tied to the biblical revelation itself, and was closed with the apostolic age. The second phase, begun with the transformation of the Hellenistic milieu by the Fathers of the Church, was extended and deepened by the medieval period, reaching its articulation in the principle, I suggest, of analogy, and *is only radicalized in modern philosophy*, with its emphasis on critical reason, into the present. We are, then, intellectually speaking, not simply medieval, but patristic. Western human reason, even in its hyper-critical form, its focus on the critique of reason and human finitude, reached its radical form in Kant's transcendental account. The argument can be made that postmodern thought is itself still transcendental, and therefore dominated by the second moment of Dionysian schema, the critique of reason. Even with Derrida, we intellectually inhabit the early Church.

(2) Classically speaking, divine revelation, at least according to the Christian conception, is God's free self-disclosure in Jesus of Nazareth, made in a definitive, unsurpassable and true manner. However great the difference between Creator and creature, somehow God reveals *who he is in himself* in Jesus. This revelation, of course, is not in the first place "data," but it does have definitive intelligible content. We can also say, and we must say, that God's revelation in Christ, if it is fully true, is not complete. In other words, God gives all of himself in Jesus, holding nothing back, but all that he gives in Jesus is not fully manifest. As Rémi Brague said, following some indications in John of the Cross (to whom the idea is owed), there is a distinction, then, between givenness and manifestation in revelation.[43] There is nothing more that God can or will say that he does not say in Jesus Christ—this is precisely the scandal, and if I can say so, of the "essence" of Christianity. Even so, this Word, the Word of God, God's total word about himself and his last word about everything, like an echo in reverse, growing, magnifying, expanding from the point of its historical utterance, is not, in history, fully understood, not only because of human limitations but also because God is infinite in himself. The Pauline concept of κένωσις names this distinction between givenness and manifestation in revelation. The "self-emptying" of Christ ἐν μορφῇ θεοῦ, "in the form of God," by the cross and death reveals God's glory in the world, which appears as a contradiction.[44] And yet this self-giving, this self-diminution is true of what God is. Divine revelation in history is therefore, perhaps, like that old video of the Tacoma Narrows Bridge Collapse of 1940: the wind created vibrations that compounded and multiplied exponentially through the bridge-system like waves in a bathtub. The force of the wind—rather mild in the bridge's case—caused the bridge to vibrate; the bridge's vibrations would travel through the structure, and return, accepting new energy provided by the wind, in a rhythm that inserted energy into the waves of the vibrations running back and forth through the bridge, and which negated

the bridge-system's ability to absorb the vibrations and led to exponential growth of energy until the structure was stressed to breaking point through the compounding rhythm of swaying and buckling.[45] It is hard to say where we are, in the reverberations of history, in terms of the total sequence: Perhaps we are still among the earliest vibrations, which in their crests and troughs, and the crashing of their encounters, only begin to register the amplitude of the first increases of compounding oscillation. Perhaps, in the present state of the world, we are inscribed within a trough of only the earliest of reality's oscillations. Viewed from within the system, and without knowledge of the whole sequence, the low bound of the wave, at the point of its moment of return, gives the illusion of stasis. There is really no way to tell but from the end, when the whole sequence is finished, by bringing the system to breaking point. All this is to say that our knowledge is radically limited in itself; though at the same this radical limitation of our knowledge, due to our historicity, the radical finitude of our faculties, including the immersion of our reason in the material limitations of our flesh, *does not necessarily entail a critique of the claims of faith.*

Traditionally, human reason is divided into two divisions, dialectical reason, which works according to the logic of the order of concepts, and a greater reason, often called intuition, which is a mysterious mode of participation by which the mind is pulled out of its intrinsic limitations and penetrates reality. The first order is conceptual, that is, it abstracts from the rushing temporality of experience some stable points from a particular perspective guided by specific ends; it is derived from the human need to order the complex data of experience in useful ways. It is, in this sense, practical reason. It makes reality stable enough to be grasped, which it grasps by *substituting* ideas for the reality, which are nothing but practical questions posed to reality. This level of reason, at root, is fundamentally symbolic, as we have seen. The second order is conceived as an event that occurs *through* the basic process of dialectical reason that the embodied mind ceaselessly uses to navigate experience. It is commonly understood as an "immediate" intellectual *perception*, beyond language, of realities or reality itself, even divine reality itself. Intuition is an event beyond language, but it nevertheless must be translated into the lower order of representation in order to be understood and communicated. In this higher order of reason, intelligible intuition is typically articulated using the language of the material senses and its images as, paradoxically, the most appropriate to describe it. The tradition of the "spiritual senses" in Christian mystical writings is a case in point. Here God is less "known" than perceived—and the traditional hierarchy of the senses, from touch to sight is reversed; one enters the "dark cloud of unknowing" in order to smell, taste, and touch the divine reality in a way beyond normal rationality. According to this tradition—eminently represented in the writings of even Thomas Aquinas and John of the Cross—it is love, and its peculiar rationality, that leads one beyond the noetic limitations of finitude into the nuptial embrace with God, while mundane rationality is left behind as a leaping off point. This division that I am describing here is central even to Kant's philosophy, with its fundamental partition between understanding (*Verstand*), which unifies the fragments of experience into a unified world, and reason (*Vernunft*), which, completely abstracted from the world of experience, restlessly and irreparably seeks the unconditioned principles of existence.

It should be clear to us now that the *Logos vom Mythos* schema is not, if I may be permitted a colloquialism, total trash. It is a specifically "natural" way to conceive reason, abstracted from the input of revelation, according to which λόγος, when liberated from the hegemony of μῦθος, is set free to contemplate the real in itself. Reason is truly a capacity of ours, then, for the real itself, which is accomplished in the specific mode of distantiation from the sensory realm, but which, importantly, only possesses a derived status, a distantiation achieved through the transcendence of concepts, if such a transcendence is realized by way of a purification of the data of experience into general ideas that possess a unity that determines the particulars they categorize as an expression of the pragmatic and technological character of conceptualization. When the negating power of concepts acquires an absolute status it is equated with the things for which concepts substitute themselves. Even with intuition, or knowing-as-seeing, one does not come to realize the essential practicality of reason, nor the dignity of the material domain. Instead, at least on the traditional view, intuition is a passage through the conceptual dialectic which, for all its transcendence, is itself tied to the material domain of sensible manifestation. Kant described the limitations and conditions of this domain, that of radical human finitude, in a radical way. Already for Plato, too, the body englobed the soul in history as myth enframed theoretical intelligence. The former, in both cases, became the site for the proto-eschatological passage of the appearing of the highest things, for example, in Beauty or in Justice (in politics), where the Good's excess over being in formal (the invisible ἰδέα) or informed (ὁ φαινόμενος κόσμος) modes, is supremely manifest.[46]

In Kant, this dualism at the heart of human reason is assuaged, at least relatively, by the introduction of the notion of the symbol in the Third Critique. At the end of his critical project, it is the beautiful itself that becomes a "symbol of morality," manifesting to the whole person that which reason cannot reach in its quest to grasp the unconditioned (a failed quest which nevertheless provides the important basis for moral action, for the humanity of the human). As a sensible manifestation, or incarnation of the moral law, the beautiful reconciles the theoretical dimension, concerned with navigating the world of experience, and the practical dimension and its concern with ultimate reality, precisely by implicitly subverting the order of sensory and intellectual domains, or at least bringing them together into one, embodied perception of the noumenal truth (under the conditions, of course, of worldly finitude) that elicits "metaphysical" desire and transforms and motivates action.

One should argue that this quasi-rapprochement between the elements of his most pernicious dualism at least implies and probably (as in Plato) requires an *eschatology*. Kant's description of the sensory encounter with material data as "intuition" already points in the direction that we are looking. And here we can return to the thinkers just mentioned earlier, Aquinas and John of the Cross. For them, the division between intellect and charity—charity, which is *eminently* practical, since it is a manifestation of desire—is neither absolute nor permanent. Instead, the return to images and the senses in the intuitional embrace of God achieved by mystical knowing—proposed as the ideal and hence paradigmatic conception of humanity—itself implies (in the weakest possible sense) philosophically what faith proposes dogmatically: the resurrection of the body and life without end in a new heavens and new earth, and so on. In the state of eternal life, beatitude, the body and soul of human beings are no longer in competition with one another: the body is no longer a necessary veiling detour for the mind as it seeks to know intelligible realities. Instead, the body and mind are united in the "vision of God,"—God's "vision," as when a rector "casts a vision" for the organization under his or her care, which includes "epistemic" elements, of course—which is one with the "vision" of all things, the γνῶσις τῆς ἀγάπης that is fully reconciled with embodied human experience that has been, according to the μῦθος, awarded, in Christ, the vice-regency of sharing in this "vision." Revelation, with its prioritization of the sensory realm, of its images, metaphors, symbols, and narratives, forms a fundamental anticipation of this future reality, which, as Scripture indicates, is best signified only by way of the wild intensification of symbols and images (as in the Apocalypse of St John). The central point is *that intuition is refigured by revelation as incarnate thought*. With revelation we are no longer finally concerned with an intuition of intelligible realities made by climbing through dialectical reason and the ever-greater purification of concepts and at the farthest remove from our materiality, but rather that as a preparation for a concrete event of the flesh. This "third way" of the coincidence of thought and flesh is made possible by the presence of a Third (like the Good "beyond being"), a presence which composes the active content of revelation, insofar as revelation is not the communication of propositional knowledge (at least in the first place) but is rather the event of divine action inclusive of the personal communication of God in himself to the creature, and precisely in the context of the creature's own normative conditions (historicity, finitude, etc.). To this "Third," the material and intelligible realms are equally distant and equally proximate: God, as absolutely transcendent, is so totally other that he is also totally immanent; his immanence and transcendence are not in competition, defined, then, over against one another. His radical immanence, even absolute proximity to every created thing—expressed in Augustine's famous dictum that God is more intimate to me than I am to myself—is an *expression* or manifestation of his very divinity, his total or absolute uniqueness and transcendence. As I will attempt now to show, this conception of divine transcendence is the theological justification for the Pseudo-Dionysius' practical and eschatological prioritization of the sensible sphere and its images over the conceptual, and it is what sets his hierarchical conception of the Neoplatonic system apart from his pagan interlocutors. For him, the divine reality is *equally superabundantly present* to every level of the hierarchy and is emphatically *not* an ever-distant reality mediated according to successive gradations of being all the way to matter. And this is, precisely, what the spiritual exercise is meant to awaken within the student of his writings. In other words, his radical hierarchization (he coined the term "hierarchy") of reality according to multiplied angelic triads recapitulated in humanity through the Church and in the material cosmos (and expressing the diffusive excessiveness of reality), contains a radical democratization at the same time. To be sure, the *paradoxical presence* of the Third to the material and intelligible realms is a mode of presence that is distinct to both according to their own material and intelligible integrities, respectively. This, of course, requires elaboration.

The first thing to suggest is that which unites them: this presence, across both domains, is one of a presence in mystery in which the transcendence of God is protected while at the same time truly revealed. God is present in absence or present as the Transcendent One, as the one who transcends his presence. In other words, he is present as ontologically holy. With Christ, we are dealing with the Living God. And here arrives the essential point: the presence of the Third is an eschatological presence. And it is an eschatological presence because it is original. It is a presence, the transcendence of which makes a promise, the content of which is that the presence not fully understood can be more fully understood, can only ever be more fully understood without end, since, on the one hand, God infinitely transcends his presence, and he infinitely transcends his own self. On the other hand, this God is the self-revealing God, who reveals himself as this self-transcendent One.[47] It is this "eschatologicity" of the Third that is determinative of the whole thing. Most fundamentally, this means that the eschatological structure of revelation will provide the determinative conditions and limits for the knowledge of God, within which even the a priori conditions of finitude (historicity, temporality, materiality, etc.) will find themselves articulated anew as means of the deepest comprehension of God.

In this way, revelation, if it is to be taken seriously—and we are free to do so, according to the particular intellectual impulse that comes from faith—proposes itself as a paradigm of meaning and intelligibility for human experience in general. If revelation reveals humanity to itself precisely by revealing God to it, then one aspect of this revelation is that humanity is no less a mystery than God, though precisely as a mystery (like the cosmos) that is tied to the mystery of God. The mystery of human existence is that experience itself—with revelation as the *paradigm* case, understood as that which happens that proposes itself as a sort of absolute for the nature of experience in general and which therefore determines our understanding of human experience itself—reveals that the conditions of human finitude are not enough to prohibit experience from manifesting a given impossibility. If, in other words, there are experiences that contradict the essential conditions of human finitude, conditions that finitude itself must, no doubt, impose, then these experiences, these *impossibilities*, and the sort of knowledge that arises from them, which we can call *paradoxical*, proposes itself as the truth of human being, the truth of an unfathomable mystery.[48]

Third

5. Symbolical Apophatics (Pseudo-Dionysius the Areopagite)
6. Anthropomorphism and Realism

5

Symbolical Apophatics (Pseudo-Dionysius the Areopagite)

Join me in observing how appropriately the symbols convey the sacred.[1]
We contemplate the divine mysteries solely by way of the perceptible symbols attached to them.[2]

The reader will agree that it is high time, in this argument, to turn our direct attention to the Pseudo-Areopagite. We have found ourselves appealing to him consistently in the previous pages. By turning to him directly, our immersion into the apophatics of the sensible begins to fly, a little like a rollercoaster that, after slowly climbing to the crest of its first major hill, drops near-recklessly toward the first curve.

Ἰησοῦς, ὁ θεαρχικώτατος νοῦς καὶ ὑπερούσιος, ἡ πάσης ἱεραρχίας.[3] Luibheid and Rorem translate this sentence with the lapidary, "Jesus, the source and the perfection of every hierarchy."[4] The unsurpassable paradox of the Dionysian corpus without which it cannot be understood is contained in this sentence. Their translation is remarkable enough: the incarnate God, the man Jesus (and not, simply, the disincarnate Son), *is* the "source" and "perfection" of every hierarchy, whether angelic or human, cosmic (whether it includes, implicitly, in this Platonic sensibility, the repetition of political hierarchy is worth pondering) or ecclesiastical, intellective or material, creational or soteriological. There is no hierarchy—and there are many, but also they are all one, in him—of which he, that man that is God, is not the principle origin and perfecting completion. The words translated as "source" are θεαρχικώτατος νοῦς. The word "perfection" is ὑπερούσιος. Literally, the words involve a veritable Neoplatonic train wreck of superlative and hyperbolic expression. *Thea-archē-tatos* are the parts of the first term, "divine"—"rule/authority/principle/beginning/origin"—with a superlative suffix meaning of the highest degree. *Hyper-ousios* is equally as interesting. It is redolent of the Platonic ἐπέκεινα τῆς οὐσίας, "beyond being" of the *Republic*, indicating an absolute transcendence that originates, orders and sustains the whole—as origin, as end and as excessive presence intrinsic to each thing and level. It also means to indicate the prepossession of every perfection scattered throughout the hierarchical whole in itself, in an utter, infinite unity without any extrinsic limitation. Lapidarily, yes, this could be translated as "perfection." With these terms, the Pseudo-Dionysius is balancing, like much apostolic literature (albeit here with an emphatic Neoplatonic triad-ontological ring), the unity of beginning (as creative principle), middle (as incarnate savior), and end (as recreative principle) in the one Jesus, the human identity of the hypostasized creative intelligence of God, the "origin and beginning" of all things, as Λόγος or Word, on the one hand, and the end of all things in the new beginning, the "firstborn" or "only begotten son," on the other.[5] To call Jesus the "source and perfection," or, more adequately, "the thearchic all-ruling and absolute essence (or being) beyond essence (or being) intellect" above and within, the beginning and goal and total repletion of every hierarchy, is to make a claim about the role this divine man has in holding all things together, creation in its very intelligible structure *and* creation as the seed through which, by his power, germinates and sprouts into the world to come. It is to conceive of the world, of man, and of God from an understanding profoundly transformed by the confession of—and "theurgic" or liturgical participation in—the incarnation and its outworking telos. It is to conceive of intellect, of thearchy, of being in a radically distinctive way.[6]

One thing we must not do is reduce the novelty, the "renewing newness" of the Pseudo-Areopagite's Christian thinking to the horizon of possibilities intrinsic to his Neoplatonic sources. To lean over the rim of the well laughing at that doofus Thales is to ignore the intensity of his gaze streaming beyond you to the stars.

The Pseudo-Areopagite proceeds to explicate this new vantage by a contrast. For him, there exist two fundamental modes of approaching God by the created mind: symbolical and conceptual. *Symbol*: A symbol is the language of the flesh; a "sign of recognition" (Plato, *Symposium*) that makes present what it signifies by performing a "redistribution of the field of experience" (Lacoste). In the sacred domain of Pseudo-Dionysius, that is, all things reduced to their fullness in relation to the Creator, a symbol is an earthly thing whose likeness is *transposed* to heavenly realities by virtue of the incarnate descent of heavenly reality. The first principle of sacred symbolics is the Incarnation, which announces and enacts, as principle (ἀρχή), the end to which revelation is ordered and to which all things tend and therefore determines *all* theological knowledge. A symbol, establishing the knot or bond of higher and lower, is therefore an *unfinished transposition* of heavenly reality in earthly forms, eschatological in orientation and divine in origin. *Concept*: A concept is an idea that can be applied to an entire set of particular objects; it signifies a class of objects according to common features (and is therefore "abstract") and determines inclusion into a class (and is therefore "general"). The concept is fundamentally angelic and the symbol, anthropic. Programmatically stated by the Pseudo-Dionysius: "The heavenly beings, because of their intelligence, have their own permitted conceptions (ἔννοιαι) of God. For us, on the other hand, it is by way of the perceptible images that we are uplifted as far as we can be to the contemplation of what is divine."[7]

The mystery of *anthropos* is that he can endeavor to utilize both modes of approach, σύμβολον or ἔννοια, though the former is the anthropic ideal given his natural embodied condition and it serves as a category term for human cognition that embraces ἔννοια, concept. On the other hand, ἔννοια, cognitive perception, a more direct visionary knowledge, serves as a category term for the angelic, since the angel knows without the mediation of the body, although at every level of spiritual hierarchy, there is spiritual or immaterial mediation for angelic noetic acts. These are, therefore, *relatively* more immediate or mediate given their place in the scale of worlds. Thus, the conceptual mode of approach, for man, is wholly conditioned by the symbolical: for him, concepts (as in Gregory of Nyssa) are formed through carnal experience and therefore the figurative dimension precedes and determines the abstraction of concepts. Angelic intelligence knows God through "permitted conceptions" proper to its immaterial nature and unique to it. Both modes of approach, however, are decidedly apophatic, though in different registers. The apophasis of the symbol is found through immersion in the material domain and its aesthetic principle is the *aesthēsis* of the senses themselves; whereas conceptual apophasis is found in transcending *distance* from the material. The latter's principle is abstraction; the former's principle is the intelligible *density* of the material. If, as is our principle, Christian eschatology (as a realization of the beginning) is the starting point and condition for theology, then a symbolic (in the realist sense) unity of heaven and earth, of the intelligible and material domains, is the ideal state of knowledge, for the material adds to the merely intelligible a particular *density* that intelligible abstraction needs in order to overcome its ever-greater *distance* from the divine *res* that the process of conceptual abstraction brings about. The coincidence of these two separate domains is (as proposed by St. Augustine) one with the vision of God.

Given that the angelic economy of the old creation has been replaced by (or, for Pseudo-Dionysius, grounded in) an anthropic one of the new creation, the native human modality of the symbol has succeeded the angelic conceptual mode at the apex of creaturely knowledge of God. The vision of God, as the ancients attest, is fundamentally a mystery of the resurrected body.[8] For these reasons, which are really but a *précis* of the previous stages of my argument, I suggest, the symbol ought to be privileged over the concept, and beyond these reasons because God speaks first the language of myth and figure. And God's speech is inexhaustible. On the philosophical plane, the inexhaustible *intelligibility* of the symbol is the condition of the concept, being both its foundation *and* ever-receding horizon. The concept only goes as far as the Greek λόγος in its critique of mythic consciousness, which I consider, following the lead of Daniel Cohen's study, *Formes théologiques et symbolisme sacré* (2010), to be equivalent to the negative speculative moment in Pseudo-Dionysius the Areopagite's conception of apophatic theology, which, by contrast to Proclus' relation to the mythical literature of Greece defined by allegorization, prioritizes the symbolic dimension of the Christian sacred texts as a result of his uniquely Christian conviction regarding divine revelation (wholly *embodied* in Jesus, ὁ θεαρχικώτατος νοῦς καὶ ὑπερούσιος, ἡ πάσης ἱεραρχίας, and thereby accomplishing a full, a pleromatic fullness, as it were, of All-Unity, which, although replete already in God, is in Jesus accomplished for the creation). An elaboration of this claim, which on the reading I render here is of the essence of the Dionysian corpus, leads to a general theory of sacred symbolism according to which the symbolic dimension is the privileged mode for the expression of the divine mysteries, with greater power to immerse the human mind into the "non-discursive" domain of divine mystery well beyond the point where the regime of the concept and discursive reason is rendered mute.[9] This stands in contrast, again, to Proclus' allegorical manner of approach, according to which the symbolic figure of myth is only a preliminary projection of human intelligence requiring purification by speculative dialectic in order to terminate in σιγή, the hymn of silence, an end of elevation through the *henads*, which used them, by theurgy, in the form of the descended gods of myth, to ascend to an equality of place, which is "participation in the unparticipatable" (the transcendental "many" of the One), for a *henad* is the latter's participatable mode, the highest possible acquisition of the unity (by the not-One) that is the privilege of the One alone. (I am ever-impressed at how profound a reading of Plato this late Neoplatonism is.) In Proclus, the mythological form is a garb for the philosophical ἀναγωγή; for the Pseudo-Dionysius, the intellectual acrobatics of Neoplatonism is utilized in service to the revealed given, incomprehensible action of God in the flesh (and in the liturgy).[10] The "henological" or unificatory knowledge "beyond vision," where discursive activity is stilled and intellection is silenced, reaches its apogee in participatory immersion in the revealed symbol that first evoked the process of anagogical ascent. Both discursive conceptuality and intuitive perception are not absent but rather caught up into a "knowledge beyond knowledge" participant in the superessential principle that is both thought beyond thought and vision beyond vision. The Pseudo-Dionysius seeks to maintain, in foregrounded clarity, the simple content of Christian faith. As he states programmatically early in *The Divine Names*, "The most self-evident idea in sacred theology," namely, "the incarnation of Jesus for our sakes" is wholly beyond all creaturely understanding, even that of the first angels, and yet is, simply, the sea of presence in which the Christian liturgically swims and the content of his "secret" intellectual tradition.[11]

Let me add to Cohen's remarkable study of the Areopagite a corollary orienting guide, Dragos A. Giulea's essay on Gregory Nazianzen, where the relative prioritization of the symbolical dimension that gives access to the key difference between Denys and Proclus paradoxically becomes a distinction given normative clarity for the interpretation of Patristic thought itself.[12] According to this study, which also includes a brief genealogy of speculative apophasis from Philo to Nazianzen, the biblical tradition, *in continuity with its Ancient Near Eastern atmosphere*, conceived of approach to God in terms symbolic apophaticism, according to the order of the forbidden divine glory, whereas the Fathers of the Church, again, *in continuity with their own Hellenistic atmosphere*, translated this apophaticism into their own contemporary philosophical language of the incomprehensibility of the divine essence. This latter apophaticism, with which we are all most familiar, turns on the conceptual negation of concepts. Both apophatic languages attempt to express the *inaccessibility* of the divine, basic to any religious sensibility, not merely because of our distance from God, but rather, in the first place, because, as has been my claim from the start, such inaccessibility, an inaccessibility that transcends the binary that gives meaning to the term and yet establishes it, expresses itself through it, etc., is intrinsic to the divine nature itself. The "hermeneutical context," Giulea notes, for the transition from the symbolic apophaticism of interdiction to the conceptual apophaticism of negation, turns on Patristic exegesis of the biblical theophanies of the divine *kabod*, which explicitly equated it with the divine essence by way of a negative conceptuality common to the Neoplatonic philosophical parlance of its day. Giulea demonstrates this through exegesis of Nazianzen's second theological oration (28.3), which repeats in a Neoplatonic key the common theological trope of Jewish-Christian *merkabah* mysticism in which the visionary enters the cloud of divine glory and sees God in a paradoxical manner by which God is still concealed in mystery. Gregory, says Giulea "instills the Greek philosophical idea of divine incomprehensibility with the mystical and visionary context of theophany." The upshot for Giulea is that there exist "two different languages" for the signification of divine transcendence, both of which are present in early Christianity. These "represent two semiotic forms of apophaticism, one expressed through the *mysterium tremendum* inspiring symbols and images of fire, dazzling glory and enigmatic heavenly creatures, guardians of the enthroned *kabod*, the other through negative philosophical terminologies."[13] At the heart of Patristic orthodoxy, these two parallel streams become deeply intertwined. The Fathers *transposed* the former, semitic style of apophaticism of sacred inaccessibility into their own Hellenistic mode of noetic incomprehensibility which they took, as anyone would do with such spectacles strapped to his or her head, to be its functional equivalent, thereby indelibly transforming Greek/Latin thought and culture from within, a revolution within which we live and move and think still today. However, one should less argue that this transformation, however fundamental, defines Christianity as such than that these two apophatic sensibilities themselves are present in Christianity in various actual and possible modes of relation. Not only does the symbolic mode itself become dominant at various times in various movements and even in particular thinkers (Nazianzen's poetry itself is a perfect example), but arguably the entire Syriac tradition of Christianity itself preserves overtly the priority of the symbolic-semitic form, even while subtly absorbing (as does Scripture itself) at least some Greek conceptual elements (look no further than the, to us, exquisitely exotic hymns of St. Ephrem the Syrian). Further, the Greek language itself becomes a carrier of the semitic-symbolic apophaticism as the Jewish and Christian apocalypses demonstrate. Finally, as I have already suggested, Pseudo-Dionysius the Areopagite's own "system" turns on the assertion of the priority of the symbolical at the centre of Christianity's own transfiguration of Hellenism, which I would suggest both the Greek and Latin traditions themselves ought to take as normative. "For Dionysius," it has been said, "there can be no divorce between theological and philosophical approaches to the knowledge of God, for the substrate of philosophical reflection is God's revelation of himself in Scripture."[14]

The philosophers of the classical age, as I have said, are commonly and rightly understood in relation to their criticisms of the mythic anthropomorphisms: their central concern, more often than not, was with proper speech about the divinity. The philosophy of ancient Greece, if we can say so, is born from a fundamental theological concern. It is this theological concern which was self-consciously considered to be the height of the philosophical impulse and, at the same time, its origin. Hence the very word "theology" is first found in the Greek tongue as the apogee of the philosophical quest for divinity: θεολογία—the divine speech—is an ecstatic hymn to the divinity, the *telos* of the philosophical ascent, and the realization of the philosophical task. In other words, and in Neoplatonism at least, the dialectical work of reason in its ascent to the One by abstraction from the corporeal is consummated in praise of the Incomprehensible. Proclus, to return yet again to the Pseudo-Dionysius' great source, standing at the very end of late Antiquity, considers philosophy as "prayer" understood as the "one theological hymn to the One through the negations [of all else.]"[15] Philosophy, for the ancients, was about knowing God, though in a paradoxical manner, befitting the divine. Theology takes philosophy beyond itself into its own completion, beyond knowing, as a sort of ἀποθέωσις of the human into the divine. Theology, therefore, is potentially realized once the philosophical purification of concepts is achieved, that is, once reason has emancipated itself from the illusory enchantments of mythic consciousness and has entered into the openness of θεωρία, that free contemplation of the *is* of what is in its primal bursting forth. Yet this contemplation in freedom, this φιλοσοφία, is not realized, already for the Greeks, in the freedom of contemplation itself. Even in Aristotle the summit of contemplation is what he calls in the *Metaphysics* σοφία or θεολογία the contemplation of the highest being as the key to the thought of being in itself, of pure thought thinking itself. Expressing a common but undervalued trope of classical philosophy, the philosopher is elevated to the status once held by the gods of the myths in his imitation of the divine in its pure, "useless" freedom of thought, which is sheer enjoyment for its own sake. Even so, Aristotle's divinity (anthropomorphic in its own way, a projection of the philosophical ideal) is hardly the God of ancient Israel, the God of Jesus Christ. The Scriptures of Israel and Christianity are united in their persistence—even on the far end of the philosophical purifications undertaken in the Septuagint—in privileging anthropomorphic descriptions of God. For the Greek critics of early Christianity this fact is an affront to reason; for the Christians themselves, it is itself a critique directed *at* reason, though ultimately the means toward reason's own expansion. Even (as just mentioned) the well-documented purifications of the anthropomorphisms of the Hebrew Bible by the Septuagint were hardly enough to shield the Fathers of the Church from the biting stings of pagan philosophical critique. Much of Patristic writing is taken up in response to brilliant philosophical criticisms of the Christian faith made by pagan philosophers: think only of Origen's *Against Celsus* whose philosophical evaluation of Christianity tested to the limit Origen's vast intellectual resources, or of Augustine's sustained engagement with Porphyry in *City of God*, and, even intrinsic to the battleground for the Christian confession, Gregory of Nyssa's critique of Eunomian rational, *philosophical* orthodoxy with the orthodoxy of the Triune God, whose divinity is best approached by way of a paradoxical concept, the "Infinite" (which includes the sub-categories of "Unbegottenness and "Begottenness"), instead of the concept, which at least had recommending it an apparently much fuller precedent in the biblical material, of "Unbegottenness" (understood as exhaustive of the category of Uncreated divinity) These criticisms of Christianity had one thing in common: they wanted to put the content of Christian faith and the Christian Scriptures on the side of mythic consciousness, set over against the freedom of philosophical enlightenment.

Of course, this situation at the heart of the debate between the pagans and Christians of late antiquity bears strong analogy with today's situation in which classical Christian faith has ceased to be intellectually compelling to the civilization at large to which it has given birth. The typical answer of theologians and philosophers, those within and outside of the Christian faith, is to allegorize the tradition's confession. This is precisely the track that the late antique pagan philosophers attempted vis-à-vis their own traditional myths, once they ceased to be compelling, and precisely what the Fathers refused to do, it seems to me. Instead they submitted reason to the realism of the Christian confession, trusting with all their weight in its own intrinsic rationality as the salvation of reason.

For the great pagan minds of late antiquity as for the post-Christian minds of today, Christianity, with its God who seemed to bear all-too-human characteristics, its dying and rising Saviour, its obscure and seemingly base rituals, and so forth, is too anthropomorphic for cultured wisdom; its claim to catholicity, that is, to embody the universal truth of humanity, is *philosophically* repugnant. As Porphyry put it in his *Against the Christians*, how can the obscure stories about a rabbi from a marginal region of the Empire be the truth that unites all humanity to God? How can insignificant events of a localized historical time and place be the truth for all time and all people, and therefore the philosophical truth par excellence? The necessity of such a truth for philosophy *and* the possibility of its existence was a conviction shared by the Christians and their pagan interlocutors alike: their debate, in the end, was about what was possible, or not, for God, or in other words, their a priori conception of the divinity, a conception ultimately determined either as a pure idea extracted from reality, which reaches its pinnacle in the negative theologies of the late Platonists of Hellenism (achieving its greatest intensity in the radical negations of Damascius, who asserts an unknowable non-principle, the "Ineffable," above the All-One[16]), or as living personality in critical excess of *every* attempt to reduce it to the concept (and the negations of the concept), as in the Biblical faith. The enlightened picture of God of pagan late antiquity is marked, of course, by an absolute transcendence, which can only communicate itself by means of intermediaries in a hierarchical system, yet the Christian God is understood in fundamentally personal terms, for whom transcendence is not an impediment to his appearance in history. Rather the latter is itself an expression of an all the more radical transcendence. The conception of free creation, it is worth recalling, proposes a vision of divine transcendence that differs considerably from the Neoplatonic One who necessarily engenders the world.[17]

Νοῦς, as I said at the beginning, is, for the Pseudo-Dionysius, an expression, a name, for the divine thearchy. It is a symbol, inasmuch as a symbol is an essence, οὐσία that participates in the energies, ἐνέργεια of an ontologically higher reality. The relation between the two is called cause, αἰτία: the symbol names the relationship of effect or manifestation to its ἀρχή, its source. νοῦς is one among several privileged Neoplatonic names appropriated by the Pseudo-Dionysius, including ζωή, life, and οὐσία, essence, or rather, being. Such divine names are ἐνέργεια, activity, emerging from the unfathomable godhead *insofar as* they have been revealed, that is incarnate in human speech (intellect) and action (life) and experience (being) that draws from the world the impression of its source. I know what life is by picking up a snail or watching a fish in a pond; I know what being is by kicking a rock or crushing a fallen leaf in my hand; and I know what intellect is by having a conversation, considering a concept or by praying. The more metaphysically crude our significations—the more incarnate, I should say—the more power they have to serve as anchors for our intellectual ascent to God. While Iamblichus promoted asserting blasphemous tokens or cacophonic strings of babbling in unknown tongues in the practice of calling down the gods to inhabit and animate their statues based on this principle, the Pseudo-Dionysius, by contrast, conceived of the symbols of the revealed given as harboring in themselves the self-excessive presence beyond absence of God—on the model of the Incarnation, participating, indeed, in its "theandric energies." There is a sense, of course, wherein the cataphatic expressions are less apt, contain less truth than the apophatic negations. But this is only to say that one cannot take them merely as given, but rather as invitations to scale the hierarchy, ἀναγωγή aided by the dialectically purified concepts by which one measures (so to speak) the unmeasurable distance between the symbolic disclosure and the infinite God. And yet, he notes again and again, the crass materiality of the cataphatic expressions possess an advantage over the purified negations: they are less likely to be taken for the thing they signify than are the concepts themselves, which are generated out of discursive activity provoked by the mind's desire to comprehend the given symbols. Symbols reach beyond the conceptual-discursive plane, then, both in the direction of the imagination and in the direction of intellective intuition. It is only through the duality, indeed, opposition of direction that the mind can overcome its worldly conditions, structured by these very oppositions, and exceed them, in the direction of the ineffable, which is seen, tasted, touched, contemplated in the "ineffable union" of God and man in Jesus.

The Pseudo-Dionysius, of course, considered "symbolic theology" as the middle term in a triad (a programmatic triad meant to reflect—as all things invariably do, at every level, including that of speech—the triadic character of the Divine Thearchy. The first was cataphatic, the second, symbolic, and the third, mystical.[18] If *The Divine Names* explicates the cataphatic understanding (ἐπιστήμη is the Pseudo-Areopagite's word) of God as Cause, or emanative source of all that is. The symbolic theology (he mentions a non-extant title by this name) is represented in the corpus by both hierarchical treatises, which are as one unfolding text, and in one of his letters, conceiving God as end that elicits our ascent into the images, the intelligible they marvelously contain, and into the hyper-intelligible God that they express.[19] The mystical ἐπιστήμη is undertaken by the brief, *The Mystical Theology*, which ends with a total eclipse of all thought beyond distinction and requires the mind to recognize this eclipse as absolute, no longer negating the world of experience but identical with it. The human mind as the site of the convergence of God and all things in the theurgical recognition (σύμβολον) of Jesus as the all in all of God. The central and mediational role of symbolical theology in the ἐπιστήμη corresponds to the central role of the Son in the Divine Triad and humanity in the cosmos.[20] Just as the participated (μετέχτος) shares in both the unparticipated (ἀμετέχτος), being the way of participation in the unparticipatable by the participating (μέτεχον), so the Son, in the incarnation, forges that path of unification (ἕνωσις) for us, who become, in him, the principle of the unification (through liturgical practice) of all creation in God.

The style of thought of the Fathers of Church could arguably be best described as the penetration and transformation of Hellenism, its culture and philosophy, by the new categories of revelation.[21] This in no way exhausts their fundamental and unsurpassable contribution to the Christian thing. Yet the Fathers must at least be seen to be advancing and bringing to completion the task of the people of God already well underway since the earliest encounters with Hellenism, as witnessed by the Septuagint, its Wisdom literature, and even by the apocalyptic texts of Second Temple Judaism and of Jewish Christianity: the cultural and theoretical conquest of the Greco-Roman world by the culture and θεωρία of faith. I suggest that liberating "conquest" here, rather than "integration" or "synthesis" is a better explanation of the Gospel's relation to Hellenistic culture, since this exemplifies Christianity's own continuity with the prophetic and wisdom traditions of Israel, whose very concern was with the *universal* implications of Israel's *local* faith, or, to put it in other terms, the profound tension between her monotheism, on the one hand, and her sense of election, on the other, God as Lord of the covenant and God as Creator of the world. Israel's covenant Lord is the Lord of all the earth, but how is this so? Christianity, developing out of the apocalyptic traditions of Israel, considers itself as the definitive resolution of this problem. The path of the resolution of this tension is incarnate in the life of the Church and is the way that the kingdom of God advances through the ages, bringing into its fold the riches scattered abroad by the Creator Λόγος and hidden until the appointed time of their harvest.

In light of this fundamental tension between the Gospel's particularism and universalism, in a similar way to Scripture, Patristic theology must be seen *in its original setting and cultural context*, that is, late antiquity, for its very *universality* to be properly seen and understood, appropriated and imitated. The Fathers of the Church demonstrate how Christianity out-philosophizes the philosophers, as it were, in their quest for an appropriate conception of the divine, how Christian speculative apophaticism is a greater and more fitting thought of the divine than that of their pagan counterparts; how Christianity, based on the revelation of God in Christ, gives greater and farther purification of concepts, takes reason farther into God, and penetrates the meaning of human existence in a greater way than the mode of contemplation based on the allegorization of the myths of Greece and on the free contemplation of the cosmos in its "natural" revelation of the attributes of the divinity. The theology of the Patristic Age, in other words, brings to completion the conceptual ἀπόφασις of the Greek tradition, demonstrating how it finds its roots within and bears its greatest fruit from the soil of the Christian Scriptures and in the context of the sacred mysteries of the Church. Yet this *conceptual* apophaticism does not exhaust the contribution of the Fathers. There is also a concomitant apophaticism in a different mode. Based on symbols, it is that type of apophaticism that follows and develops the *biblical* apophaticism of the Ancient Near East, the apophaticism of immersion in the rituals and practices of the liturgy, of sound and smell and wood and paint, of repeated words and stylized action. It is the apophaticism of sacrifice, of narrative, of metaphor, myth and images, of poetic ecstasy, of worship and hymn, of silence and vision: the apophasis of symbolical apocalyptic. This concomitant apophaticism in the Fathers is *not* reduced to the speculative allegorization of their content, as seen in exemplary fashion in, for example, Philo of Alexandria's philosophical exegesis of Israel's faith. Though sometimes this process—let us call it *negative philosophy*, given its essential continuity with the negative impulse of Greek philosophy—is undertaken powerfully, it is never brought to completion, nor can it be. One would have to argue that the conceptual modes of apophaticism, clearly dominant in the Patristic tradition, rest on and return to the *original naïveté* of the Apostles, and to the ever-renewed naïveté of the simple faithful, the little ones, in the concrete faith and practice of the Church, of belief in the resurrection, the Virgin Birth, the angels, the application of water and the fall of the Spirit on the human body, of oil and fire and feeding on the human flesh and blood of God, of the return of the Son of God in judgment, of the awakening of the dead, of the renewal of all things in a world without end. Continuity, in eschatology, must be as radically stressed as the discontinuity, or, frankly, we are doing little intellectual justice to the divine transcendence we claim for God beyond a competitive view of his transcendence and immanence and which locks him away in a distance pre-contained by our concepts as they express our reason's own finite self-sufficiency. And we are certainly not thinking in concert with the tradition. However transfigured the cosmos will be, the faith that believes in the incarnation of God and in the resurrection of the body knows that the central content of the faith, the "New Creation" of the "Kingdom of God," is—here again we find a fundamental affirmation of it—more adequately signified by the density of material images than by our however useful concepts *abstracted from* material experience and expanded to an infinity of emptiness (that signifies a fullness, and thus points, in the *coincidentia oppositorum*, to the hyper-apophasis of All-Unity, the apophatics of the sensible belonging to the eschaton). For Christian faith, speculative apophaticism does not leave behind once and for all the symbolic material in which it is enfleshed, nor is it the essential element, the kernel surrounded by chaff, to which only the philosophical elite can penetrate. Christianity is not an esoteric religion; or rather, the incarnation—and the resurrection of the body only reasserts this with all the more force—demands in Christianity a final coincidence of the exoteric and esoteric moments.[22] In Christianity the most sublime mystical union with God is grounded in the rite of baptism, in the same exoteric ecclesial structures as the most mundane, unreflective faith. And this union, according to the Pseudo-Areopagite, is "completed" in the "most divine eucharist," which hierurgizes (ἱερουργούσης) the gathering of the initiated into the One and granting him as a gift from God its mysterious perfecting capacities, perfecting in fact his communion with God."[23] The rites, in short, effect ontological union, ἕνωσις, through participation in Jesus' incarnate principalization of "every hierarchy," while the cognitive work of purgational interpretation is epistemic preparation for that lynchpin action, and, as such, integrated with it, since divinizing enlightenment remains incomplete as long as the present age persists.[24]

For the biblical and liturgical tradition, the function of sacred symbols is to demarcate the holy, and bear us to it, veiling us as well as elevating us to its presence, making the visionary, who perceives the divine through the symbols, paradoxically, *in his person* the mode of the expression of the divine transcendence through his transfigured existence, manifest in his response to the divine theophany or revelation that unfolds according to the vocation of witness (μαρτύριον), a seer who, in a liturgical context, ascends to the divine presence and returns in order to report what he has seen, which always involves the apocalypse or *veiling disclosure* of a message for the community of faith. The symbol, for this tradition, is the greatest possible mode of approach to the divine transcendence precisely because God is, as I have tried to say, *ontologically holy*—by his very nature, impossible to approach and unable to be seen. This tradition is mediated into the milieu of Hellenism in the form of Jewish and Christian apocalyptic texts, as the Book of Daniel and the Apocalypse of St. John canonically demonstrate, which are themselves concerned specifically with the question of wisdom, a wisdom that is necessary for humanity but impossible to access apart from the opening or ἀποκάλυψις of heaven and its mysterious translation or transposition into the images and symbols that populate apocalyptic writings, the truths of heaven in the mode of earthly signification. This mystery only "the wise," that is believers, by virtue of their *faith* in the God of Israel and intimate knowledge of the symbolic system(s) of Scripture, can access and rightly interpret. Here we see all of the major elements of the Pauline teaching on wisdom, mystery, apocalypse, and gospel (Romans 1:16; 1 Corinthians 1–3; Col. 1:3, Ephesians 1–2, etc.), categories, which he rather substantially shares with the Apocalypse of St. John. This observation suggests that a major impulse at least of the Christianity of the apostolic age lies in fundamental continuity with the tradition of the symbolic apophasis of Second Temple Judaism, as it develops, looking back to the great prophetic traditions (Isaiah, Ezekiel, Daniel, etc), and looking forward, through the great apocalyptic texts emerging from the intensifying crises that marked the people Israel in their travails in the wild battle zone of empires that seemed to define the fertile crescent—and still do, to a considerable extent—of which the encounter with Hellenism is a major moment—to the great, final victory of God in his elevation of Israel, through the Messiah, as shepherd over all the peoples of the earth. In this sense, it would not be wrong to consider Christianity, in the first place, as a Jewish apocalyptic movement that has spread throughout the globe, with the symbolic apophasis inspired by visionary apocalyptic as its major mode of intelligible signification, as Scripture and liturgy attest. I am really only trying, in these pages, to elucidate, then, a fundamental impulse in the Christian tradition.

For negative theology, it is true that we arrive at our greatest concepts through the process of purification or "negation," by which we expose or uncover the radical limits of every affirmation we humans make about God. Negative theology arises, then, from the conviction that the ultimate foundation of reasoning, its first principles, are *beyond the grasp of reason*. "The supreme Cause of every conceptual thing," says the Areopagite at the conclusion of his treatise on *The Mystical Theology*, "is not itself conceptual:" "It cannot be grasped by the understanding . . . it falls neither within the predicate of nonbeing nor of being. . . . There is no speaking of it, nor name nor knowledge of it . . . free of every limitation, beyond every limitation, it is also beyond every denial."[25] For this tradition therefore, in the first place, we know God better by stating what he is not, rather than by stating what he is (if we say "God is love" then we also have to say God is not "love," that is, he is not what *we understand* by the term "love," because he is infinitely beyond *our* concept that is derived from our experience of love: and yet the love of our experience is itself participant in the Love that God is. And we will only eschatologically know, in God's "last word," the meaning of this love through the experience of its place beyond the purgational fire of divine judgment that ushers in the renewal of all things.).

A "passing through" from the material to the spiritual, and therefore the unifying tension between the two is all conceptual reasoning can possibly be for us, embodied intellects that we are.[26] "Hence" affirms the Areopagite, "it is quite impossible that we humans should, in any immaterial way, rise up to imitate and to contemplate the heavenly hierarchies without the aid of those material means capable of guiding us as our nature requires."[27] These "material means" are the embodied images and symbols of Scripture and the liturgy, the "sacred veils" that "upliftingly conceal" the "divine ray of truth" as it "adapts to our [embodied] nature as human beings."[28] In this way, ἀναλογία is a term for this total passage of human reasoning between the material and spiritual domains in the three moments articulated by negative theology, of which the "symbol," as a manifestation of the intellectual through the material, is itself the best name.[29]

For the Pseudo-Dionysius, it is the συμπάθεια of all in creation with all in the One Ineffable Cause, that forms the condition for Christian theurgy. Ascent, for Pseudo-Dionysius (and this certainly seems to distinguish him from the Cappadocians for whom anagogical movement is found in the perception of the intelligible through the sensible theophanies and then entering the divine darkness *through* the intelligible, recognized now as theophanies themselves) is effected through the ritual activities of the interlaced hierarchies, human and angelic. The ecclesiastical hierarchy, mediating the material and intellectual realms, is a copy of the exemplar celestial hierarchy. Yet these are intrinsic to one another, as all worlds, as effects, are hyperessentially intrinsic to God, the Cause, in his supereminent fullness. And this leads us back to the contrast with which I began this chapter. The symbol, σύμβολον, is the natural and unsurpassable mediator of human cognition (ἔννοια) encountered in the living matrix of sacred text, theological representation, and ritual action. Concepts, *ἔννοιαι*, are reflective-interpretive abstractions that extract the meaning and isolate its significance "marvelously contained" in the symbols (as the Godhead in Jesus) in order to serve as intellectual frameworks that aid the created mind (νοῦς) in its attempt to comprehend, to see (*noein*) the incomprehensibility of God's action that is also humanity's (theourgia). These intellectual frameworks, encompassing all cognitive activity of purifying ascent (ἀναγωγή) organize the experience of God. This is not an end in itself. The end is union (ἕνωσις). The kind of union they achieve is anticipatory and preparatory. They "angelize" humans so they may become all the more, beyond that, "divinized" *sacramentally*.[30] Symbols are for joining two orders. Concepts are for grasping, intellectually comprehending for the sake of joining and, same thing, communicating.

The σύμβολον is, of course, a concept in its own right. It is a name and an abstract comprehension at the rational or dianoetic level of the ritually encountered realities. The concepts forged at the level of human cognition are also names. And as such they fall under the wider human category of symbols. Symbol is, in the first place, the ritually encountered reality transposed to the plane of the concept for the sake of comprehension that results in deeper immersion or (same thing) better joining (ἕνωσις), which happens in an unsurpassable and incomprehensible way at the site of the flesh.[31] Joining and unification happens beyond knowledge, beyond intellect, by occurring, marvelously, incomprehensibly below it. It is fully (though not merely) human (and therefore embodied, temporal, spatial—though not merely) and precisely as such, profoundly like angelic cognition (ἔννοια) with its supersensible immediacy of vision because of the Incarnation and the all-hierarchy-defining union of God and flesh. Indeed, Jesus is already the source of the first angelic illumination.[32] From this vantage, angelic cognition (ἔννοια) is, simply, an anticipation of such a marvelous union. Even more, this all-upending unification as principle of all joining, all union, does not destroy but re-establishes the invisible order itself. Just as the Son is, in God, the intelligible principle (λόγος) of divine order (for the Father gives to the Son without reserve), so also, in the creation, the second (humanity) is revealed, in the intention of God to be all-in-all, one reflected in each, to be principle for the first creature (angelic). Just as the Son as Λόγος reveals the Father's *mon-archia* in the Godhead, so does the human's elevation in the Incarnate One's universal reign (βασιλεία) reveals the natural place of mediational angelic hierarchy.[33] The angel, in its transcendent greatness, *serves* humanity, as the Father delights in nothing other than giving all to the Son. Hierarchical mediation is the *most direct* mode of revelation since God's absolute causal *immediacy* is paradoxically expressed by the mediacy itself.

According to the Areopagite, our theological concepts emerge from out of our reflection upon the anthropomorphic images, symbols, metaphors at the center of biblical revelation. *Lex orandi lex credendi*. How we pray, or rather, the work we do as prayer (λειτουργία) determines what we believe and in fact already contains it. The point is that such a "negative theology" perpetually deconstructs the human attempt to constrain the divine by its own categories, the intellectual temptation to circumscribe and indeed replace the living God with formal determinations.

I am aware that the account I have sketched here grates against the common reading of the Dionysian corpus. For that reading, the purpose of the liturgical is (at best, when it is brought into consideration) to set the stage for intellectual ἀναγωγή that abandons the material, the mediational, the middle. This places the Pseudo-Areopagite in a more Porphyrian than Proclean camp. And yet, I have tried to suggest here the fundamental way that his Christian theurgical vision is differentiated too from Proclus as well. Theirs is a difference of eschatology. And the heart of Christian eschatology is the incarnation itself. My argument rests, as all accounts of a complete system of thought invariably do (especially those with an esoteric concern, protecting the teaching from profanation, like the Dionysian corpus, apocalyptical literature and the parables of Christ), on a hermeneutical assumption. It is this assumption that sees, expressis verbis, Jesus as absolute hierarch that I have only but given voice to here. I write as no more than a pseudo-apprentice to an authentic master. My interpretation in the space of this book, surely raises many valid questions and is, perhaps, not without a few mistakes. Yet its validity is found, in the end, in the way it illumines the corpus as a whole. I have said enough, perhaps, to suggest this validity. It is up to the reader to return to the corpus as an apprentice that shares its aim, in order to determine if, in the end, there is something to what I have said.

In theology to be sure (but with radical implications for philosophy), it is necessary that God be given the last word (as much as the first word) and that the last word can actually be spoken by God. Christians, of course, believe that the last word *is* Jesus Christ, the living human being, that the resurrected Jesus of Nazareth is God's fullest truth, the Creator's ultimate statement about himself *and* about ourselves and all reality. Philosophically, this prime data of revelation means that the original images of revelation are truthful in a way that requires their essential crudeness, their *material density* to be given its full scope—even if, and especially because, this truthfulness is only partially disclosed, according to the fundamental structure of eschatology. And this is the difficult part. Repeating our core example: the image of Jesus enthroned "at the right hand of the Father." We may approach it by letter and by spirit, and tradition, if it urges us to pursue the spirit, it also warns us to find it by lavishing in the letter. We may apprentice ourselves to the figure, the mythological frame that holds it and we may distill it, conceptually, to the abstract conception of an "authority and power" over history, Both registers certainly refer to the same reality. The conceptual register does so by explicating the mythological, which remains, as the first appearing of its meaning, implicitly present in it as the source of the concept's own meaning. But it certainly remains that the living reality of the flesh in our experience gives us a taste of the salt on the skin of ultimate reality. And through this new "immediacy" established by the Incarnation, the whole order of hierarchies of power, visible and invisible, is, to speak eschatologically, which is the only language appropriate, finalized at God's right hand, or rather (and this is most important for the Christian vision) *finally coordinated, finally established, finally initiated in that "place."*[34]

The symbolic order may be defined (supplementarily to the way I defined it earlier) as that mode of signifying that allows the alterity of God to be communicated while remaining wholly his.[35] Hans Urs von Balthasar refers in this context to Proclus' notion, found prominently in the Pseudo-Dionysius, of the ἀμεθέκτος μετέχεται, "participation in the unparticipated"—the paradoxical manner after which beings participate in the divinity: that which he gives—existence, life, knowledge—remain at the same time his alone.[36] It is the function of the symbol to perform this action. Let me explicate this by reference, briefly, to Jean-Luc Nancy's conceptions of images and the sacred. According to Nancy, in *Au fond des images* (2003), images are marked first and foremost by their manifestation of a general "unavailability." That is to say, they give that which is unavailable for technological utilization for specific ends.[37] Images, as products of human making, paradoxically constitute, in themselves, the reality of human experience. In this way, images have the power to transform our existence. The mode of manifestation of images stands in contrast to that of mundane reality in its general "availability." Nancy calls this mode of manifestation of images "distinction," for images set themselves apart, are circumscribed in themselves and only cross over this "distinction" precisely by means of, paradoxically, remaining separate and unavailable. The image, therefore, is manifest as radically *discontinuous* with experience, as separate, as other, and gives an opening, a presence in the mode of unavailable absence.

We may extend this general conception of images readily to sacred images. Sacred representations, like icons, make an unavailable, transcendent presence available by virtue of the mediation of sensible reality, which is only present, paradoxically, *through* transcending its presence, and are therefore all the more radically present *by means of* the "distinction" between heaven (and its denizens) and the materiality of the image. It is perhaps illuminating therefore to juxtapose Nancy's philosophical reflections on the sacred and images with Christianity's theology of sacred images developed so richly in the East. The Church's understanding of icons turns on a distinction developed out of reflection on the relation of God to his own revelation in the world in the economy of salvation that culminates in Christ, the essence (οὐσία)/energies (ἐνέργεια) distinction, which emerges, arguably, as a more generalized expression of a prior distinction demanded by theological controversy, that between essence and person (ὑπόστασις). The first distinction expresses God's essential transcendence of his own revelation through his "energies." The latter is a more specific distinction used to articulate the logic of the incarnation as well as the trinitarian constitution of God, but it performs the same task of expressing the paradoxical nature of God's sacral self-presence. In sacred images, the ὑπόστασις, not the essence is "circumscribed" through its incarnation in the sensible wood and paint. God (for example, with the icon of Jesus Christ) is in this way truly present through the sacred image while simultaneously wholly transcending it, just as he is in the living human person, his image par excellence.[38]

In the second volume of his *Theo-Logic*, Balthasar provides the following articulation: "every finite being," he says, "participates in the duality of expression (appearance [*Erscheinung*]) and self-expressing ground. Expression becomes image in the field of sensible reality, where appearance is apprehended imaginally [*bildhaft*] and, through the interiorizing movement of the imagination [*Ein-*

bildung], becomes inward image [*In-bild*]. Image, finally, becomes word in the sphere of the spirit." Our concepts are expressions of the images, apprehended as means toward self-expression, which precede them.[39] As the Areopagite emphasizes, speculative concepts of negative theology run an even greater risk, by virtue of their avowed "spirituality," that is, their *distance* from the material domain, of deceiving the thinker about their proximity to the divine. The great testaments of mystical theology of the Patristic and Medieval periods together demonstrate this by virtue of their return to the most basic images at the zenith of the spiritual ascent: "darkness," "touch," cloud," "embrace," and the most vivid sexual imagery of nuptial mysticism are cases in point. Nicholas of Cusa, in his radical speculative negative theology, for example, in describing the "coincidence of opposites" that I alluded to previously, had no problem using the imagery of a secret garden surrounded by a wall in order to express the event of coincidence itself in the vision of God in order to evoke the reality that is only evocable in excess of conceptuality, where it runs aground. John of the Cross is also an interesting case: trained in Iberian scholasticism, he composed poetry to make an initial and in some way unsurpassable communication of his mystical experiences and primarily as a heuristic for those under his spiritual care, and then provided dense theological-philosophical commentary on the poems, informed, above all by scholastic categories. His commentaries themselves, however, pile images on images in order to explicate the spiritual experience that itself, as in the Fathers, expresses an eschatological-oriented theological horizon within which the experience is given: an experience, again, governed above all by the images of nuptial mysticism provided first by apocalyptic eschatology. If John of the Cross is more aware of the anthropological categories of affect and emotion in the experience of the dark night, he is no less centered on the dense imagery of embrace, touch, and the paradox of "unknowing" in divine darkness than is Gregory of Nyssa or the Pseudo-Areopagite. This return to images at the height of speculative abstraction (which already emphatically occurs in Plotinus)[40] strongly suggests, as I have indicated, that just as speculative ascent by negation of concepts derives from images, it also must return to them in the end. This is because of the absolute excess of God over the names that signify him. The utterly transcendent source, "beyond all intellect and being and knowledge" is reached through an eclipse of the creaturely order that he himself is as he marvelously sustains the latter in it.[41] As the Pseudo-Dionysius puts it: "And so it is that as Cause of all and transcending all, he is rightly nameless and yet has the names of everything that is."[42] The "distance" of speculative abstraction, its sacrifice of proximity for clarity, exhausts the mind and requires that it collapse back into the images and symbols out of which it first emerged. Not that these two apophatic modes are necessarily at odds, precisely as John of the Cross demonstrates. A symbol is an image perceived as bearer of higher reality. The image may be sensory or conceptual. As sensory, the image bears the conceptual, and through it, the transconceptual, the hyperconceptual, which is more immediate to the sensory (given its higher causal status) than the conceptual "explanation" (αἰτία) of the sensory, its intelligible content explained by the presence of the ideal that orders it. *Lord of the Rings*, *The Tempest* and my memory of an encounter at the gas pump brought to speech at dinner are all instances of narrative understanding, with a beginning, middle and end, with characters in a setting overcoming a challenge, obstacles, etc. Their disparate genres (epic fantasy, play, conversation piece) do not necessarily permit us to determine the greater story-value of one over the others. (One could imagine a conversation piece to be of more fundamental value than a work of fiction, say in the testimony of the witness to a miracle, a tragedy, and so on.) But their manners of the presentification of meaning in the narrative mode evidently do. In Neoplatonic language adapted by the Pseudo-Dionysius, a symbol is the activity of an essence. (The essence at one level is, in its independence and freedom to write itself, the activity of a higher essence, its cause.) The essence in going out of itself (as participating), withdraws into itself (as unparticipatable), and this dual movement of emergence and return unveils the arrival of its effect (as participating). The turn of the participating effect to the cause is it sown unification that permits the lower order of its effect to emerge. The symbol has two meanings here. First it is the lower seen *in* the higher. Second it is the *union* of lower and higher, the relation of the two. From the Neoplatonic perspective these two meanings are vantages on the same dynamic. A symbol is therefore the unification of disparates at the horizontal level in light of their origin that explains them, the source that is the reason for them, the giver of their freedom, freedom to write themselves inasmuch as they unify themselves in aspiration for their source. This occurs at the level of individual things and of higher unities like categories or kinds, and beyond these, indivine names, like goodness, being, life, and so on, that are the causes of all unities and all order (as participants in God, beyond being).

An image is perceived as a symbol when the higher is seen in the lower. To progress, one must distinguish the higher from the lower, by perceiving the lower, now, in the higher. One must perceive the independence of the higher, and the dependence of the lower. One must, in short, see the lower in the higher. In the apophatic theology of the Pseudo-Dionysius, this activity works in the following way: I see stringed potato in steaming gravy on my plate. I perceive that it *is good*, to taste and to nourish. It will give me a temporary feeling of satisfaction, of fullness to consume it, to become one with it. As I am chewing, or perhaps afterwards, as I am digesting, assimilating with the potato, I recognize that it *is not*, itself, the goodness, the fullness that it presenced. It is participant in the goodness of culinary art and, more generally, the overall good of food. And the potato, I might notice, is participant in a unique way, even in a substantial way. (It was cooked and served by a marvelous French chef, let us say.) More broadly, the gravied potato participates in the goodness of life. It sustains life and all its activities. It participates in the goodness of being. I had to be to enjoy the potato, and it permits, in its small but not insubstantial way, my persistence in the goodness of being at all. This activity is repeated with the conceptual content. I can ponder fullness, life and being in themselves. What is their meaning, their purpose? What is their source? I can recognize their participation (if they are to be ultimately meaningful) in some higher unity, some plenitude that gives them to be. I can ponder the hyper-fulness of life and being that precontains them in a way beyond the conceptual order that is theirs and the sensory order that is the potato's. I can see them as symbols, participant effects of God's infinite superfulness, as I can see the unity and goodness and fulness of the potato in them. And I can come to recognize the immeasurable fullness of God as the measure by which I must measure the fulness of goodness and being and life themselves and the very potato I may still be savoring on my tongue. I realize that I experience the goodness—no doubt about it!—but I realize that I do not possess the measure to comprehend the meaning of that goodness that I am enjoying. There I see the lower in the higher. Its difference from the higher is no barrier to the super-presence of the higher. In fact, that super-presence is all the difference in itself is. The lower *is* the higher, outside of itself. The higher *is not* the lower, for it remains in itself. We have named the logical antinomy. Both statements must be affirmed. Notice that at each level *the negation does not* destroy *the affirmation but* establishes *it*. I reach the higher by negation but included in the negation is the recognition that the lower is a participant expression of the higher in its nature. It is the higher. The higher is not it. With this double recognition we immerse ourselves in the experience that is both explicable and wholly inexplicable at once.

The Pseudo-Dionysius' is a program of liturgical contemplation, of properly seeing the symbols and participating in them. There's a recapitulatory passage in *The Mystical Theology*, for example, where he will use, like Gregory of Nyssa, the language of Moses' ascent up the mountain into the dark cloud of God's presence, as a roadmap for the liturgical progression to its apex, the eucharistic communion. He will discuss the progress from affirmations to negations to abandonment of negations into an inexplicable experience of unification as knowing beyond knowledge, unknowing, described as seeing darkness beyond the light of being. Unification, knowledge, vision, our highest conceptual achievements are all suddenly understood as, like the sensible symbols they explain, symbols themselves from a lower order that express the higher as its derivative participants. "The holiest and highest things perceived with the eye of the body or the mind are but the rationale," he says, "which presupposes all that lies below the Transcendent One. Through them, however, his unimaginable presence is shown."[43] The contemplator of such things must, apprenticing themselves to Jesus Christ, who unifies the most disparate realities, come to join them with their opposites (being/nothing; knowledge/unknowing, light/darkness) in paradoxical expressions in order to indicate the way that the higher supereminently is what they are in a way that owes them nothing but gives them everything. He must see God in the gifts, and, beyond that, the gifts in God. In this moment, he says, "Moses breaks free of them, away from what sees and is seen, and he plunges into the truly mysterious darkness of unknowing."[44] To say anything more at all, therefore, he must call on images long abandoned (the "breaking free" of a prisoner, the "plunging" into disorienting waters or, the space or darkness of a desperate person). He must, like God, put "robes" on the naked ineffable in order to indicate something about the experience in which the God beyond being is sacramentally encountered in the mediation of the sensible. The Pseudo-Dionysius describes this awakening to what is beyond the antinomy in the immediacy of the encounter as "renouncing all that the mind may conceive," accepting the total inexplicability of God in the superabundant preserving presence that is all and beyond all in order to belong "completely to him...supremely united to the completely unknown by an inactivity of all knowledge, knowing beyond the mind by knowing nothing," seeing, in short, the mystery, and affirming it by the highest possible negation that abandons the negation![45] In this way we move from a contemplative place "where he dwells" standing "next to" God "free of every limitation," to a consuming assimilation with him.[46]

At the summit of contemplation there is a coincidence of all in God and vision with the One-All. There is no longer any competition. He wants his reader to internalize the corpus and carry it into the liturgy where, by it, ἕνωσις unfolds in ἀγνωσία (unknowing).[47] God, the "superfullness of all" is both beyond them all and super-immanent to them all. The divine ἔκστασις is, strictly, *identical* with its absolute interior reserve, its alterity.[48] Not only in God, whose unity does not negate his trinity, not only in creation, where what is is despite God's superabundant fullness of being, but also in redemption, for our very ἕνωσις is a share in God's own. A dazzling fullness has arrived. This is what Jesus is and what is experienced (however proleptically) in the liturgy. "Most novel of all," he says, "amid the things of our nature he remained supernatural and amid the things of being he remained beyond being."[49] Jesus is the signification of the eschaton, its symbol, the principle of the unification of all. Eschatologically speaking, that is, in their fullness, theurgy and θεωρία are one. There is no exception to ἕνωσις, which is a unity beyond the distinction between unity and multiplicity. It is thus beyond the contrast between God and man (in Jesus), heaven and earth (in the sacraments), matter and spirit, knowledge and ignorance, liturgical action and the rest of vision. God transcends all and is all in all in Christ Jesus. The name for this experience of participation in the more than non-dual, though anticipatory and incomplete (even for Pseudo-Dionysius), is ἀγνωσία. It is the experience of true divine transcendence, coincident with absolute immanence, the utter simplicity of leaving all behind in aspiration for God and gaining it, super-redundantly, all at once. It is ineffably hidden from the understanding, just like its exemplar and cause, the unfathomable unification of God and humanity in the Incarnation. The point, then, of the entire intellectual acrobatics of the Dionysian corpus is to strain into the experience of participation in the ἕνωσις of God through the ἕνωσις of God and humanity (and world) in Jesus. Negation (un-saying) is not a rejection of the created (for that would be a rejection of the Creator) but rather an acknowledgment of the true alterity of God beyond every contrast as the supreme ground of them all, the super-fullness, hyper-identically containing all and yet the nothing of all that is. The fullness beyond all seeing and saying is equally incomprehensible and as plain as the man standing before you speaking parables (for the disciples) and the bread and wine raised above the altar (for the Christian initiates). As dark as night and as plain as day. A dazzling darkness. It cannot be taught (except as untaught) and cannot be seen (except as unseen) because it is too intelligible, too visible. Dionysian ἀγνωσία is the experience of ἕνωσις, the participation of creation in God and thus the experience of the total coalescence of love and vision, of intellect and will, of soul and body,[50] the union of creation and God, beyond all, preserving all in its gifted order, perfecting all in a "unifying power" (δύναμις ἑνοποιός),[51] which is itself experienced as an immersion in the enriching unification of the drawing love of return with the original creative love (ἔρως ἐκστατικός) that is itself a "yearning" for the creation that originally brought forth all things.[52] This yearning is a "unifying and commingling power" that springs forth from God, is shared with his creatures, making them what they are in themselves, whether angels or humans, all expressions in both their going forth and return of the one divine ἔρως that God is. Hence, the cataphatic, symbolic and apophatic moments of intellectual ἀναγωγή, however "critical" of one another, are, at the same time, deepening extensions of one another, necessarily undertaken as the creature strives with all its gifted ἔρως to trace the emergence and return of all things to the Divine Mystery. For this vision, the apophatic modes of ἔννοια and σύμβολον are mutually reinforcing and complementary, though *only if* speculation finds itself determined by the symbolic and thereby finds its power precisely in it. Aidan Nichols, following Balthasar's revision of the apophatic tradition in *Theo-Logic* II, noted above, articulates the reciprocity of the symbolic and conceptual in the following way, which I would like to quote in full:

> I find the mystery aspect of the revelation-in-transmission that is Tradition—a trait signifying not a deficiency in meaning but a superabundance thereof— to be best expressed through the combining of abstractly conceptual with concretely imagistic description. The uniqueness and personally self-involving character of the divine action, grounding as it does the mysteric in Tradition, points to a primacy for metaphorical description over conceptual. Yet the intelligibility of the declarations which accompany and interpret the divine action and which are passed down as such, and further refined, in the Church's traditioning process counterindicates a primacy for conceptual description over imagistic. A corrective complementary of the two is called for within a wider acknowledgement that the event of revelation is precisely disclosure, and thus chiefly cataphatic, while the overflowing plenitude of the content thus disclosed calls for an apophatic check on cataphasis. And this, of its own nature, issues in adoration and praise: "O the depths of the riches and wisdom and knowledge of God!" (Rom. 11:33). Habitual tact for combining cataphasis and apophasis also belongs with the "proper ethos" in approaching Tradition.[53]

This could only come across as prosaic after the Pseudo-Dionysius, but it validly expresses something of the Christian sensibility that he remains an unsurpassable master. Tradition, at its simplest (and most profound), bears through history the "good news" of a "resurrection of the dead and the life everlasting." We are beginning, in this study, to see how much eschatological vision, teleology, the ends to which we think, must control, and suffuse our understanding of reason. And again we return to the core of my argument. The Pseudo-Dionysius exemplifies the conviction that only an eschatological vision of an immaterial beatitude of disembodied bliss could be satisfied with the *lifeless* abstractions of speculative dialectic alone, which, given the mortal condition, can never reach cognitive vision but by a gracious descent of God that fills all things in that descent, a descent that is equally the ascent of his creature. Symbolic apophasis is squarely on the side of "eschatological realism," since, for it, the images of eschatology are more profound *transpositions* of transcendent truth by which the projects of discursive reason are always unravelled. Finally, because transcendent spiritual reality itself, for Christianity, is not a set of abstract concepts, even in an unthinkable transcendent unity, but a living and personal divinity, the biblical anthropomorphisms are in themselves *more apt* at expressing ultimate reality than the alternative mode of apophaticism on its own, which alone has governed theological reason in the West since the rise of Scholasticism, a turn in Latin thought marked by the extraction of reason from the theological context of apocalyptic eschatology altogether. If I could float a genealogical thesis, then, not to demonstrate it but to close this step in the argument: The separation of symbolical and conceptual apophaticisms, the marginalization of the former into the realm of subjective "mysticism," and the attempt of the latter to stand on its own as normative for theology, was perhaps the crucial moment in the separation of reason from faith that has been determinative of the history of Western (and now global) thought to this day, not only because such a primary separation within theology creates the conditions for the latter (since theology becomes here *only* a process of discursive reason) but also because speculative reason, on its own (and without the critical self-consciousness afforded it by revelation), can only tend to consider the historical event, symbol, image, myth, narrative, and parable of divine revelation by way of the external mode of mere conceptual *allegoresis*.

6

Anthropomorphism and Realism

"Thou didst walk through the sea with Thine horses."... Such anthropomorphisms have a truth, which men's favourite abstractions have not.[1]

Anthropomorphism, as the attribution of human characteristics to nonhuman entities, is—I have been bold enough to assume—an essential problem for human reasoning in its quest for understanding, and a common point of interest for philosophy and theology. I have endeavored to suggest that philosophy since Kant in particular has considered with great acuity that anthropomorphism is an unavoidable part of human thinking, for it calls into question traditional assumptions about the scope of reason to transcend the limitations of embodied finitude. Yet post-Kantian philosophy, I have argued, can be understood to be guilty of an even greater anthropomorphism by virtue of the transcendental character by which it sought to be reconciled with the problem. Negative theology, the classic response to the problem of anthropomorphism, has been, with the Pseudo-Dionysius as its proximate font and summit, (partially) represented as the means toward negotiating it successfully: it is neither a matter of surpassing the intrinsic limits of human finitude, nor of a full reconciliation with them by means of a priori strictures, but rather a reasoned immersion in incarnate experience that finds there the wisdom to discern the mystery of God.

The following set of reflections, coming rather swiftly on the heels of that representation, are only the initial soundings of a renewed orientation for theoretical research. Sometimes it is good to take a step back and a deep breath, to comprehend more carefully where one is. The concept may very well be a valid way of defining the problematic of Western thought and, if so, it may have

---

This chapter is an expanded version of my Hans O. Tieffel Memorial Lecture, delivered at the College of William and Mary on 29 November 2012, under the title: "Anthropomorphism and Negative Theology: Moral Reasoning and Religious Problems."

similar validity in relation to all human thought, when and wherever it becomes philosophical enough. It is surely valid, therefore, to think that anthropomorphism can be understood to lie at the origin of philosophical reflection in ancient Greece and, at the other end of Western history, remains the determining principle motivating our most contemporary "secular" modes of reasoning. If mortals are immortals, as the Mysteries whispered (and as Plato, Aristotle, and Plotinus would come rather emphatically to assert), the primary mortal mode of cognition—myth, narrative intelligence—must be *seen through* and in this trans-vision, its account of gods—immortals—and humans—mortals—must be re-conceived. The avowed Axial-era accomplishment of conceptual cognition, or theoretical intelligence is the apparent discernment of the stable within change, the immortal within the mortal, the permanent within and as the root of the whole cycle of instability that is the cosmos. If cosmos was the mortal frame, the immortals, which, in the theogonies, were "birthed" as the principles destined (by some unknowable ordering principle) to rule it, enforcing its fundamental law of order, justice (δίκη), when contemplated as such, came to be seen as expressive emanations of that "Unknown" power. One can see here the lineaments of Neoplatonic philosophy and thus how remarkably continuous the Greek tradition was, from root to stem to flower. Here the vision of the stability is itself participant in what it sees, necessarily involving a kinship of "like to like." The movement away from ignorance to knowledge through conceptual dialectic to an ultimate contemplation (θεωρία) of the immortal principles it presupposes is recognized as an awakening to a forgotten or obfuscated divine character. It is to find one's place in the cosmos. This is how the anthropomorphic problematic was negotiated in a classical sense. For the Christians, things were genuinely different. Revelation was not an epistemic awakening to what was already the case, as for their pagan interlocutors (that mortals are, really, immortals, at least some of them, namely, those who respond to the message positively; others are the refuse of the worlds), but rather a divine act that accomplishes a purpose hidden in the Creator's mind/word/λόγος from the beginning. The anthropomorphic problematic, here, has been steadily seen through the present study, for the Christians, not as an obstacle of illusion, the purest expression of the universal tragic mechanism of blinding for fallen immortals, but as a liberation of the mortal to itself, *as itself*. Rather, it is, itself, a vehicle of immortality, and even the centerpiece of such wherein the One-All (ἓν καὶ πᾶν) of divinity is fully descended into the one-all of humanity as function-principle of the one-all of the cosmos, and thereby in Jesus Christ eschatologically reconciles, through humanity, the sophianic one-all of the cosmos with God, wherein God becomes "all in all" (τὰ πάντα ἐν πᾶσιν).[2]

Continuing the engagement with some aspects of modern thought begun in the second part of movement two (chapter four), I would like to categorize, broadly, some basic movements in contemporary Continental philosophy as they negotiate the anthropomorphic problematic by reference to the classic philosophical theme of "realism." In this, I am concerned to situate the philosophical problem on its most appropriate ground—even if, as the argumentation laid down heretofore comes to suggest, the problematic itself becomes the ground on which philosophy itself rests. In light of what we have come to understand vis-à-vis the Areopagite, our terminus will again be what is commonly called "negative theology" (properly conceived as the "apophatics of the sensible") which, I believe I have sufficient reason to say at this stage of investigation, still provides the most sensitive if also penetrating treatment of the problem, a problem which we are (are we not?) bound to follow wherever it leads us.

Taking this religious *and* philosophical path places, of course, a difficult demand on us. At the beginning, I would suggest that this demand specifically requires us to introduce, or *reintroduce* two concepts, first, that of "apocalypse" and, second, of "Personality," into the sphere of our cognition. By the end of this chapter's discussion, I think, we will come to see the irreplaceable value of these terms.

(1) *Apocalypse*, ἀποκάλυψις will stand for the possibility and actuality of an "event" for human reason. By "event" I mean that which wholly transfigures what we have heretofore conceived as possible. An event is the first articulation of the possible. It discloses the world, allowing one to see it, providing a perspective on it. For an example, let us take the paradigm case, *divine revelation*: revelation is a (fully) historical phenomenon (though not merely) by which reason finds itself wholly transfigured, and ultimately therefore so does our understanding of our very humanity. A document from the Second Vatican Council, the "pastoral constitution" on the relation of the Church to the modern world (Gaudium et Spes) famously asserted that by revealing the depths of who he is in Jesus Christ, God also at the same time reveals to us the deepest meaning of our humanity. In this mutual disclosure of the divine and human in Jesus Christ, there is involved an *apocalypse of truth* for us, an ultimate disclosure of the meaning of human being that is a new beginning *for thought* (among other human kinds of things).

If historical, localizable, particularizable, apocalypse is at the same time universal—there is, *finally*, no exception to the reign of its influence. Jesus, as the Pseudo-Areopagite said, is the source (as creative principle) and end (as recreative principle), of every hierarchy, every order. He is the one, absolute hierarch that embodies in himself the whole fullness of every hierarchy, angelic, human, and divine (which, too, has its own order). As Jesus is to the *mon-archia* of the Father, so humans are to the angelic, noetic hierarchy that causes their own onto-noetic emergence. Analogous to the way in which *philosophia* glimpsed, through the power of theoretical intelligence, the intelligible conditions implicitly structuring the mytho-cosmic order, there is discerned, in the *philosophia Christiana*, a deeper pattern, then, that frames the whole hierarchical order of creation, the significance of which the Incarnation, even as an act in history (though not merely), revealed. ἀποκάλυψις would signify the fulfillment, in a proleptic manner at least, the required reconciliation of oneness and allness, unity, and multiplicity. Here lies the node of its particularly intellectual difficulty, its "infinity," or insolubility as a problem: How does our reasoning come to deal with an "apocalypse"—that which it cannot anticipate or grasp by its own power, but which has transfigured everything, even reason itself?

(2) By *Personality*, πρόσωπον, I mean the implications of an original transgression of philosophical principle, the affirmation of an unconditional *anthropomorphism*, that of reading reality at its most absolute *in personal, not* (merely) *abstract terms*. Being has an—and here we must borrow a term from Schelling—"unanticipatible" (*unvordenklich*) character: reality, by the bare fact of its "thatness," its sheer being there that precedes and invokes but always eludes rational reflection that is always too late for it, can only satisfy reason in its quest for the real if reason posits a Personal Source of being. Here there is no "proof" but only the path of reasoned reflection itself that becomes a "witness" to the shape of the transcendent. This is, so to speak, the apocalyptic character of being that echoes or calls back to religious revelation by corresponding to its assumptions about the personal character of the Absolute. The disclosure or apocalypse of truth demands, in other words, that reality is not, in its ultimate contours, a set of abstract principles, a dead mechanism, but is instead alive, indeed Life itself. The question of the basic intelligible principle of reality, philosophy's first question (if we are to take the so-called pre-Socratics as our guides), is finally inseparable from the question of God. This is still the case today.

The reintroduction of these guiding concepts means, in other words, that the question of God, the majestic cliff on which the breakers of metaphysical or theological inquiry never cease to crash, is a question that in its impenetrability, radicalizes intellectual questioning, raises its stakes, threatens it, challenges it— making it, then, *more philosophical*, if, as Simone Weil said in *La Connaissance Surnaturelle*, the very task of philosophy is to find and to extend, to develop, the most insoluble questions that we humans ask: "The proper method in philosophy consists in clearly conceiving insoluble problems in their insolubility, then to contemplate them, adding nothing, fixedly, tirelessly, for years, without any hope, in the waiting."³ God is the final insoluble question, that ultimate horizon, even beyond mortality (for if God exists, then death is a relative absolute, even if it were the case that this relativization had no ultimate meaning for us). We must comprehend *Unvordenklichkeit* as an element of ἄρρητος (ineffability).

If I may repeat the definition, anthropomorphism, generally speaking, is the ascription of human attributes or behaviors to nonhuman entities, both *above* human nature, such as to gods, spirits, angels and finally the monotheistic God, and *below* human nature, such as to wind, animals, trees, rocks, the earth, the universe in its totality, and so on. For perspective, I would add here (if only for the record) that "anthropomorphism," and its verbal form, "anthropomorphize," appear in English only in the eighteenth and nineteenth centuries. The word "anthropomorphite," the designation of a religious sect which seemed to ascribe to God, literally, a human body, appears in English in the mid-fifteenth century, but refers to a much older sect among Egyptian monks of the fifth and sixth centuries, discussed in prevalent literature of the Greek and Latin Christian traditions.⁴ To say, for example, that, precipitating (!) the flood, the Creator God "regretted" creating the world (Gen. 6:6: "And it repented the Lord that he made man on the earth, and he was grieved to his heart.")—perhaps the most commented upon "anthropomorphism" in the Bible—is to ascribe to God human-like feelings. Likewise, to call the earth "mother earth," or to imagine time as a "father," and the like is to "anthropomorphize," to give an essentially human shape to nonhuman realities. We do this today: we give hurricanes human names; we treat pets like members of the family, we pay to have an AI version "girlfriend" of a famous social media "influencer"—at least, there are apparently many who do. Human beings irreparably tend to consider the world of their experience in human terms; we "humanize" the world not only in order, it seems, to make it familiar and intelligible, to make the world our home, but also in order to be free over against it, and, often, to assert control over it, to be, in however a limited sense, a god. It would seem to be an essential aspect of human knowing to understand what is foreign, what is nonhuman, by analogy to itself. We make gains in knowledge by metaphor, the transfer of meaning through discernment of likeness between two otherwise unlike things. To ascribe to the sea a "wine-dark," οἶνοψ quality is to discern in it features of intoxication, disorientation, but also vibrancy and life, traits readily experienced with wine. Aristotle's principle regarding "scientific" knowledge (ἐπιστήμη), that the "lesser known" is reached by way of the "better known," can be brought into play here, if we remember (1) that "science" for the ancients (ἐπιστήμη of the Greeks and even the *scientia* of the Latins) is far indeed from the modern use of the term and (2) that for Aristotle the principle was concerned with grounding specific acts of knowledge on apodictic or self-evident and necessary principles, what he called the "naturally more intelligible." (As I have partially indicated, it was not until the modern period, and is perhaps a defining element of it—if the historians of ideas are to be believed—that the "better known" came to be identified with knowledge internal to the mind, "subjective" knowledge, and the "lesser known" with the objective world beyond the mind.) Knowledge of the latter came to be grounded in the self-evidence of the former. This transformation, and indeed a clear pathmark on the passage from "ἐπιστήμη" to modern "science," we see made explicit in the Baroque scholastic philosophy of Suárez in his 1597 *Metaphysical Disputations* noted previously— the first treatise, by the way, treating "metaphysics" as an autonomous discipline. His is a thesis that is simply developed rigorously by Descartes.[5] The fact that scientific knowledge, in the modern sense, as absolute, objective knowledge, propositional knowledge, and objective knowledge that can be grounded in the self-transparency of the finite subject is one of the basic paradoxes of modern thought. Objective knowledge, in the modern sense, requires the eradication of transcendent and divine participatory illumination as an ever-greater expansive condition for knowledge, as the tradition had held. For Descartes (who still holds on to the traditional expansive account, through the uncreated idea of divine infinity at the base of the mind), by contrast to Galileo (who has no interest in metaphysics, despite his revolutionary metaphysical presupposition, equating reality with measurable quantity, specifically geometric quantities, and making the entire qualitative dimension of human experience wholly irreal), the metaphysical foundations of physical knowledge are achieved by realizing the "clarity and distinctness" of ideas, first of the soul and then of God and of the universe. The paradox is established in evidence with Descartes avowed "dualism." Yet it remains that he central point of difference between classical and modern conceptions of science is that the latter can be characterized as *more anthropomorphic* than the former since for it the measure that man gives is the measure of truth. The attempt to found objective knowledge on the reduction of the subject to nil, in a pure self-transparency that permits the emergence of universal objective forms to be measured, abstractly, in the purity of calculative rationality is only to establish all the more strongly the anthropomorphism. We have noted this previously, by an explication of Heidegger, and we will make recourse to it again, further in the text.

If *philosophy* is the attempt to discern, to articulate, and to live by some truths or even by *the* universal, all-defining or definitive truth of humanity, and if *theology* is the attempt to articulate God's word or words as universal, all-defining or definitive in order better to live by them, then both philosophy and theology share the specific concern with the capacity of humans to know the truth and therefore with the limits and conditions of specifically human knowledge. It would seem banal to observe that philosophy and theology are concerned with specifically human knowledge—and, Socrates *included*—are both concerned with what the human can and cannot know beyond the avowed limits that appear to overshadow his mortality (Socrates' unique and specific concern, unlike his predecessor φυσικοί, was with the human being alone, who can only know *that* he does not know, which is the greatest knowledge).[6] Socrates, culminating the entirety of his received tradition in himself, established the anthropomorphic problematic in a renewed and fundamental way. In order to find the limits or conditions of human knowledge, we are dealing then, invariably, with the question of anthropomorphism: if all our knowledge is essentially shaped by our delimiting human conditions, then how do we truly know anything beyond ourselves? It is not marginal that the critique of anthropomorphism lies at the origin of philosophy in ancient Greece (in the *critique of the myths*, the emergence of *logos* from *mythos*, etc.), but we should also recognize that it is a critique that essentially marks the prophetic impulse at the heart of the Jewish tradition (in its *critique of idolatry*: "God is not a man that he should lie nor a son of man that he should repent," said Moses in Num. 23:19. Already, within the Pentateuch, we have a critical, and it seems quite sophisticated "debate" regarding the divine nature).

This philosophical-theological *sense* of anthropomorphism—definitive of Greek philosophy, the ancient Jewish religion, and therefore of Christianity, which considers itself, at least historically, at least in its attempt, then, at self-understanding, an awkward and ever-revising "synthesis" of the two—is intensified radically in the modern West. Non-religious or "secular" thought—thinking that self-consciously attempts to exclude the hypothesis of God from its quest for the world's intelligibility for the sake of a *self-conscious self-determining self-assertion*—lies in deep continuity with and builds directly upon this Jewish-Greek-Christian legacy. *Selbstbewusst selbstbestimmt Selbstbehauptung* is, by the way, my best attempt at a conceptual determination of modernity as "secular": it wants to define its own ends and accomplish them itself, and it knows it.[7] One could even argue that the *critical* impulse of modern philosophy—the recognition of the necessity that to justify claims to truth we must give *human* thinking a *human* scope and *human* limitations, that we must understand the particularly *human* conditions for human thought—is an impulse motivated and determined by a startling intensification of the awareness of the presence of anthropomorphism enshrined at the heart of the Greek and Jewish traditions, except that it thinks that it itself is, as Heidegger helped us see, this "hominization" of the world that assures our productive grip (our scientific knowing) on it. From Kant to Heidegger to Derrida, from the Enlightenment to the present, philosophy, one can argue, is defined by an intensification of this concern. In this sense, modern philosophy is no less "religious" than classical thought. As is commonly observed, there is a peculiar "prophetic" religiosity that is the hallmark of modern atheism, which finds the "god" of contemporary religious thought and practice to be inadequate, facile and unworthy of belief.[8]

Our particularly modern intensification of the "religious" problematic of the West, definitive of contemporary philosophy, can be expressed, for our purposes, in the form of a tautology: human thoughts are *human* thoughts. All truth is truth *for us*; any truth to which we are privy is, and as the high price of our access to it, merely human truth. And we would have to understand the human, for the sake of our tautology, in a specific way, that is, as *nothing more than human*. We are *merely* human, *only* human. Nietzsche said our thinking is "all too human." I would have to say that it is "but human." Human truths are *human* truths. Contemporary Western philosophy can be understood simply as a development of Kant's amplified awareness of the anthropomorphic form, that we humans are radically finite, tied to the conditions of historicity and the body (and hence temporality and spatiality): we can only know things as they are filtered through these elements that define our human being; the potentially known becomes actually known only as it becomes humanized, translated or transposed into the human sphere. Again, this is a problematic for modern science, which it methodologically resolves by bracketing (subjective) meaning from (objective, empirically measurable) truth. Modern science can be understood as the (useful) program of angelizing our knowledge. We spiritualize it in order to gain a grip of control over the world. And yet this "spiritualization" only recognizes the transcendence of the material and its laws. to make ourselves angels, we reduce everything to the material domain below us and become lords of its meaning.

As Husserl has shown, for us, intellectual knowledge is founded in the first place on the experience of the body in its world. *We are not angels*: we can only know reality in specifically anthropomorphic terms which are our own. And this hominization of man is the condition for the security of scientific grip, the hominization of the cosmos, knowledge that can be utilized. Utilizability, knowledge with a function that serves, not least by, through its productive power to reveal to us our ends, is a condition for the truth. Everything becomes all the more anthropomorphic.

Of course, our claims to knowledge, in philosophy and religion, must take into account these fundamental conditioning factors that define our humanity. Philosophy, modern and contemporary, can be properly understood to be motivated by an avowed commitment to a single intuition: we must finally be reconciled with our limits, our conditions, our human frailty, in order to reach the definitive truth—both of the cosmos, which is objectively utilizable and therefore empty of any meaning but what we give to it, and of ourselves, reaffirmed as master of meaning with every technological success, although with every greater success, the fragility of our mastery of our own knowledge, is simultaneously disclosed.

Philosophical anthropomorphism, in this radicalized sense that I have presented, would seem to be incompatible with realism, at least in what we take to be the classical sense, which holds that realities "outside" the mind exist independently of the mind and are knowable as such. Even Kant, on this account was a realist, inasmuch as he posited, with seemingly blatant inconsistency, the real existence of those "noumenal" entities, existing behind their manifestation in human experience. Kant's realism, of course, was a *critical* realism, for these real entities, the source of the phenomena that populate human experience, are strictly unknowable as they exist in themselves, apart from our encounter with them. Kant's lasting insight could be reduced to a commonplace of the tradition: the grasp of finite knowledge always implies a more to be grasped. As the American philosopher Lee Braver has argued in *A Thing of This World* (2007), twentieth-century Continental philosophy, developing the legacy of Kant, from phenomenology to Derrida, can be read in the main as a tradition of "anti-realism." This "anti-realism," as the name suggests, proposes that what is real is unknowable in itself, since all knowledge is fundamentally conditioned by the knower. Even the perceiver, as Thomas Aquinas already averred, is known only by way of the mediation of the world of experience as it reflects facets of our subjectivity back to us through our encounter with it. We know ourselves through knowing, which is our own divine like doing (*actus*). We can only *know*, therefore, *our experience* of the real world: our epistemic and linguistic structures, if they make it possible to know, also fundamentally shape and delimit the content of our knowledge.

Anti-realism's two main currents in Europe were phenomenology and post-structuralism. Phenomenology followed the German idealists by cutting off completely Kant's "noumenal" realm from philosophical inquiry in order to concentrate solely on the phenomena of lived experience, identifying the phenomena of experience, for all intents and purposes, with the unsurpassable realm of human truth. If we cannot know the tree as it exists in itself, apart from our experience, then that which is knowable, the tree as we experience it, the tree-for-us, is the sole object of philosophy. Incidentally, this is precisely what Husserl meant by his famous call for a return "to the things themselves." Post-structuralism and deconstruction, like phenomenology, asserted the impossibility of knowledge of transcendent realities as they are in themselves, since the structures of language and reason form a system of meaning that is always incomplete, always coming up short of the realities that it seeks. The dialectical or binary system within which reason and language work only refers to itself in an infinite pattern of deferral. Signs only point to other signs; transcendent reality vanishes at every turn from the grasp of the mind: *il n'y a pas de hors-texte*, "there is no outside to the text," or "there is no meta-text." For both phenomenology and deconstruction, specific, determining conditions are always already in place that define our knowledge—the material structures of human subjectivity for the former, and the system of language for the latter. These conditions fundamentally delimit our access to what Kant called the things in themselves and make all our knowledge specifically human, transcendentally shaped by our humanity. Again, this aspect of twentieth-century European thought stands in a remarkable continuity with the tradition as a whole. Its large difference, here, is an aspect of what makes it modern, the metaphysical skepticism of this "anti-realist" tradition. The "notior" of Suárez, having flowered into a subjectively grounded transcendentalism with Kant, has produced the fruit of an endless deferral of meaning in Derrida, who saw that the subject is given itself through language, to which there is no outside.

This anti-realism that defined the twentieth century has given birth in the twenty-first century to two counter currents, "speculative realism," on the one hand and what Braver, again, has termed "transgressive realism," on the other.[9] For speculative realism, also called speculative materialism, the anti-realism from Kant to Wittgenstein to Derrida has reached its terminus in a philosophical anemia far from the original ambitions of philosophy to know universal truth; it must give way to a new metaphysics that can undergird the claims of scientific materialism to know things as they really are, without remainder. The anthropomorphic conviction of post-Kantian philosophy, which asserts the human shape of all possible knowledge, is rejected and replaced, in an endeavor to undergird science, by some kind of absolute realism, for which what is known is what exists as it exists *independently of the knowing subject*. In Alain Badiou, for example, the godfather of this movement, mathematical set theory provides the metaphysical logic that maps the shape of reality in itself. This claim to know the real in itself without reference to merely human conditions or to the hypothesis of God, sets the foundation, for Badiou, for a new revolutionary, atheist politics after the faltering of the communisms of the twentieth century.

Transgressive realism, on the other hand, attempts to overcome the anti-realism of the last century, not setting it aside but by, paradoxically, developing its most basic insights and questioning its most fundamental presuppositions to the point that it turns, as it were, *inside out*. Braver traces this tradition back to the nineteenth-century Dane, Soren Kierkegaard, the so-called father of existentialism, for whom the Christian revelation, in which God enters history and simultaneously remains wholly beyond it, becomes the model for a philosophical program– according to which God becomes the most unique and anomalous "object" in experience, wholly reconfiguring our understanding of the nature of experience itself, and therefore becomes the most important element for our understanding of human subjectivity, precisely because it transgresses and refigures everything we thought our humanity to mean. For such transgressive realism, contact with the "impossible," that which exceeds the limitations of our rationality, or, I should say, *our conception* of our rationality, becomes paradigmatic *for* reason and the rest of human experience. Beyond Braver's analyses, I must mention—because it is perhaps the crucial key to Kierkegaard's thought—that the Christian thinker's transgressive realism promotes a radically distinctive account according to which *living Personality*, not abstract concept(s), becomes the apex of reality and its most intense and important modality.

The astute observer who is also a critical thinker will no doubt by now have become tired of my use of the term "reality." Its signification, and even the clarity or vagueness of such, will vary at each instance of its appearance. This is, I suggest, necessary. Generally speaking, and in a properly vague manner, let "reality" for the most part, mean "intelligibility" as such, the fundamental intelligibility of what is. At any rate, we must not allow the "all too modern" desire for abstract, grippable precision of the scientific sort get in the way of truth, which, as we will see, may or may not be precise, depending, again, on the variances of each instance of its appearing.

To understand transgressive realism, one must see the influence of the enigmatic Idealist Friedrich W. J. von Schelling (gestured to above) on Kierkegaard, for it was (the later) Schelling who saw *through* the foundational Western thesis of the correlation of the real with conceptual rationality culminate in Hegel's total equation of these two dimensions, an equation which hermetically seals reason from anything but itself, and it was Schelling who was perhaps the first modern philosopher to propose what Kierkegaard saw as a fundamental choice, introducing the will and freedom into the heart of philosophy, as its most recalcitrant problem, understanding them as those aspects of reality the most impenetrable to rational reflection, and thereby as the most crucial, and even, finally, as the primary condition or ground of human reason itself. We can articulate for ourselves such an intellectual starting point with a less than satisfying question, though one that is perhaps necessary, as long as we understand it as a permanent, insoluble question, a starting point for or goad to reflection: can there be reason, intelligibility, in an ultimate sense, without One who reasons? Is the concept of intelligibility itself intelligible apart from reference to the will and therefore, ultimately, to Personality?

Now the main proponents of transgressive realism in our time have likely been Emmanuel Levinas (one of the earliest figures through whom Husserlian phenomenology entered French thought) and especially Jean-Luc Marion (left undiscussed by Braver), both of whom mark a radical development in phenomenology, in continuity, it seems to me, with the Kierkegaardian line.[10] Transgressive realism, as these thinkers elaborate it, is built on the observation that the most basic human experiences, even the most banal or everyday ones, "saturate" or even explode the very structures or categories of our reasoning and experience. For Levinas, this means that the indestructible otherness or strangeness of other persons enters our experience as an all-determining force, which cannot be reduced to our own categories in which we always attempt to ensnare it. From this vantage, Heidegger's notion of the "ontological difference," his proposal for the all-determining, fundamental category of reality (to which God must submit in order to appear or not appear at all, as an ontic reality, which is theology's concern, as one among many ontic modes of investigation), is only yet another attempt to "overcome" the primacy of the personal for our final understanding of reality. "The primacy of the personal" is, for example, precisely what Levinas means by asserting "ethics as first philosophy." For Levinas, by contrast, the "ethical" relation, the predominance of alterity over sameness, and our beholdenness to the "face" of the other, our infinite duty toward the good of others, is inscribed, from the beginning, as the very structure of our own consciousness, and the structure of the real that is present "beyond" or, in his terms, "otherwise than," Being (or at least, Heidegger's account thereof).

Marion, it could be said, expands Levinas' core insights into a general phenomenological theory. For Marion, phenomenology seeks to allow whatever appears to give itself just as it is and attempts to articulate the intelligibility that it gives. Phenomenology only desires to describe things faithfully; here the paradigm of knowing that marks modern philosophy, that of the objectivity of the sciences, the exhaustive grasp of inert objects, is less dissolved than transformed. Rather, what matters is the "given," the phenomenological data of experience. Marion's conviction is that if, out of fidelity to experience, we seek to allow it to undo our preconceptions about the humanly possible, we find a logic to this experience that richly expands our concept of reason and ultimately of our humanity. If anti-realism is built on the *critical* articulation of what is and is not possible for human experience and knowledge by its determination in advance, then for transgressive realism, the content of experience again and again calls into question these rules that anti-realism has laid out in order to determine the meaning of human being. What is and is not possible ought to come from a study of experience and not be proposed as a procrustean bed that determines what counts as knowable and even real.

The "transcendental" mode of reflection begins with the question: What are the necessary conditions that what I already know require in order to be the case? Necessarily, then, such thinking can only establish or justify what it already knows. Transcendental thinking claims to know in themselves, as necessities for reason, the limits and conditions that define human finitude. By contrast, Kierkegaard's transgressive realism, and the counter-current that it spawned, is founded upon the possibility that these conditions can be disrupted, changed, transformed by means of an encounter with an alterity that may even suspend or nullify them. In this way, transgressive realism makes a wager for a more radical conception of finitude, which is, by contrast to the *mere finitude* of transcendental thinking, open to its own transgression, open to the radically new and "totally other."

Kant's secret, egregious anthropomorphism is found in the fact that he requires God, in order to appear, to appear under the general conditions of reason and experience that are staked out in advance, before God has any chance to make himself known—or to disclose to us the character of our humanity. And yet this hegemonic rationality, for Kant, is a specific kind of reason: the merely human kind. God, for him, in order to pass the test of human intelligibility, therefore must and *can only be* a "concept," evacuated of the dignity of any real content, reduced to the barest grip (of our own) on the world in the mode of the practical "as if" for humanity that guides practical reason—nothing more. God cannot appear in any other way for us.

In the context of transgressive realism, we may fill out a little more previous discussion. What happens, asks the phenomenology of transgression, if, faithful to the phenomenological principle, we endeavor to give the phenomenon, any phenomenon, *even* revelation, its full scope, *even* if it has implications for human reason, *even* if it is the place where human reason finds itself stretched, broken and transformed? For Marion two fundamental conclusions emerge here: (1) God is neither an object nor a "concept," he is not submitted to the general conditions of the possibility of experience. And, *it follows, therefore*, that (2) we are not that kind of creature for which the general conditions of possibility of experience determine our finitude.[11] For Marion this situation, uncovered by radical advances in phenomenology, requires nothing less than what he calls a double "exodus," of Western intellectual reflection from its current circumstances; first, an exodus of the question of God and second, an exodus of the question of the human. More fully: (1) An exodus of the question of God from the "finite territory of our experience and its a priori conditions" and (2), an exodus of the question of ourselves from this "territory that is delineated, closed, known in advance" that the "transcendental attitude secures for us by enclosing us there."[12] Apart from this double exodus, philosophy is enslaved to what Marion terms "metaphysics" (and Kant here is no exception, but in fact a paradigm case): a "metaphysics" for which what is possible is laid out in advance by our understanding of human reason, a rationality determined primarily by the "hard" sciences, and therefore where what counts as real is reduced to what is potentially knowable according to the paradigm of scientific knowledge, that can be termed "objectivity." Such "metaphysics," at best, he says, only "pretends to be purged from all anthropomorphism." Here we see Marion's fundamental debt to the Pseudo-Dionysius, for he repeats in a new key the Areopagite's observation of a secret anthropomorphism, what we could call *the real or foundational anthropomorphism*, within our purified or even "critical" concepts. (In other words, in the attempt to acknowledge and circumscribe the humanly possible, by excluding the divine, or worse, letting the divine into our systems in a regulated manner, we invariably *cast the divine in our own image*. We will return to this below.) Marion concludes:

Under the title of anthropomorphism, metaphysics, in order to describe the essence of God, denounces the use of determinations drawn from the sensible world and from the imaginations of poets and from human passions; but it denounces them only to substitute the most formal, universal and a priori concepts, without which its own transcendental posture would become untenable. It re-establishes an *anthropomorphism of the second degree*, which pretends to think God as principle, Supreme Being, last truth, moral author of the world, value of values, or as the human to come, etc.[13]

An "anthropomorphism of the second degree": God cannot be himself *and* appear to humans; he must submit to the hegemony of *our* limits and conditions *articulated in a supreme concept*, and in fact, here, he becomes, at least negatively, as a reverse image, the highest expression of human reason. It is not too much to say that we remain, in the Western intellectual tradition, in the same situation that exegete Albert Schweitzer denounced in his *Quest for the Historical Jesus* over a century ago: the liberal "lives" of the historical Jesus only invariably give us a picture of the author's moral and political ideals.[14] For this doubled anthropomorphism, even the Almighty is no exception to the law that delimits every claim to knowledge and the truth, and yet it only delimits God to a humanly conceived form. God, the Living God, disappears.

For the transgressive realist tradition, by contrast, what is most real is precisely what is most paradoxical, most transformative and elusive, for it unravels and deconstructs our preconceived limitations about our humanity, and in doing so comes, paradoxically, to define our humanity in a new way. For these thinkers—I have mentioned Kierkegaard, Levinas, and Marion—it is religious revelation, which I would summarize here in the terms introduced earlier as an "apocalypse of Personality," inasmuch as it gives the most radical limit-cases of phenomena, and that becomes the paradigm determining phenomenological intelligibility, the basic structures of experience and therefore of human rationality as such. This is why, finally, despite what could be said perhaps, I do not think Marion can be classified as an anti-realist: it is precisely for him the question of what realism really is. We do not know until what is given appears. If it appears as given beyond the capacity of finite reception, beyond the possibility of appearing, then that can either be interpreted as unreal or as giving, for the first time and as the paradigmatic case, the meaning of the real.

I would like now to reinitiate my earlier gesture toward a fuller explication of the first concept that I have wanted to reintroduce in this context, and with which we can articulate this paradigmatic status of revelation for reason and experience, precisely as, in the Kierkegaardian sense, the most transgressive idea—*apocalypse*. Following, of course, the general indications outlined by Marion in *D'Ailleurs, La Revelation* (2021, discussed, to an extent, in chapter 2) and, before him, Jean Vioulac, in *Apocalypse de la verité* (2014), for whom apocalypse is disclosed in its indubitable significance, either, to use Marion's terms, as a possibility, "*r*evelation," promoting an eclipse of the transcendental construction of reason, or as a phenomenal actuality, "Revelation," that enacts the eclipse, grounding, even unifying phenomenological intelligibility as such and therefore reason itself as its insurpassable paradigm.[15]

For the ancients, of course, apocalypse (ἀποκάλυψις, which means, simply, "unveiling") signified the disclosure of heavenly realities on the earthly plane, the revelation of the hidden secret to history and experience, the missing and inconceivable truth regarding the riddle of human existence that could only be given as "wisdom from above," and therefore as the highest wisdom. As for apocalyptic, so for these "transgressive realists," the ἀποκάλυψις τοῦ θεοῦ, "revelation of God" provides the essential human truth, inasmuch as it paradoxically transcends and "transgresses" every human possibility and every preconception of our humanity, requiring that our every philosophical conception of the world, of humanity and of God be refigured from out of its appearing. Can God, even God, propose a word in history that is definitive? Is the essential truth of our humanity knowable, even if it must be revealed to us? Or is it even that our philosophies are built on the premise of erasing this last word as a possibility? With this knot of questions, we return, in a way, to the beginning of this book and arrive at the point where we can introduce, or rather recall, another term, that of *nihilism*. By nihilism, we must mean, after Nietzsche, the situation in which the highest values are now meaningless, when the will, the human will, is unmasked as the desire to control the truth, even to make the truth for oneself. We exist, said Nietzsche, then Heidegger, and Marion today, in the age for which the truth is not the transcendent *term* of human desire and to which we are called, beyond ourselves, to conform, thereby realizing our apocalyptic truth, but, rather, its *product*. This "production of the truth" is the end or goal of the reduction of being, said Heidegger, to *Bestand*, "standing reserve": that which can be exhaustively known and utilized for human ends. Only that which can be exploited counts as knowable and as true. This is what Heidegger means by "technology": the mode of knowing correlates to nihilism. Lacoste has furnished us with a definition of nihilism that is perhaps even more precise: *l'affirmation de l'impossibilité du dernier mot*; nihilism affirms "the impossibility of a final word," that we, we humans, are incapable of reaching the last truth, and even that a last truth is incapable of reaching us. Nihilism is the assertion that any last or definitive word, even any ἀποκάλυψις of wisdom from above, any absolute truth is strictly impossible given the conditions of our finitude.[16] The obvious question proposes itself: Why is such a refusal nihilism?

Answer: Because for it the tribunal of human reason is absolute, indeed, and this is a human reason that possesses a specific character: *unbelief*. No truth is possible in the era of nihilism because nothing is believable any more. Not only the philosophical nihilist, but the person, the culture, the civilization under the sway of nihilism no longer believes anything, no longer lives for anything requiring total self-consecration, except, I suppose, self-gratification itself. To state it positively: *nihilism believes nothing*; it affirms that only *nothing* is possible. This unbelief is an abyss that ultimately swallows up reason, leaving only the gratification of instrumentalization as real.

Is there a link between nihilism and the philosophical problematic of anthropomorphism? Let us say that there is, if anthropomorphism is defined to the second degree, as transcendentally, that is, if the anthropomorphic form of all human knowing, itself impossible to deny, is articulated *as* the impossibility of the last word, and indeed, implicates itself *as* the last word. As the *impossibility* of the last word, anthropomorphism would consider that there is a truth that may or may not exist but is *essentially* beyond the human capacity to know it. As the last word, anthropomorphism would understand the human form as exhaustive of the truth itself. If the French and German philosophers we have referenced earlier are correct, these two seemingly contradictory "affirmations of nothing" are simply two faces of the same thing, which I have chosen to articulate in terms of (1) the denial of apocalypse, even as possibility, that the truth, the essential truth can be disclosed to us and (2) as the refusal or even marginalization of Personality (in the Absolute sense) from philosophical relevance, thereby reducing the truth to that which can be mastered by human reasoning, even and especially if it is mastered by our reason in a specific modality, *the negative*, where the highest reality can only be abstraction. Here reason's exhaustive mastery becomes the criterion of truth. One can only say that if apocalypse and Personality are valid concepts for philosophy, then the dismissal of these concepts from the field may very well be *idolatry*, a concept which I have sought to clarify in relation to Marion's reference to two "degrees" of anthropomorphism, the *naïve* kind, for example, of the ancient myths or of modern fundamentalism, and the *rational* kind, for example, of Kant (for whom what is possible for experience and knowledge are determined by an a priori conception of human reason) or even Heidegger (for whom the distinction between Being and beings conditions every human possibility, even, and especially, a divine revelation). Here, with reference to idolatry, we return to what I described earlier as the original, shared impulse of philosophy and theology, the sounding, we could say, of idols. The debt of the apophatics of the sensible to phenomenology is found in the latter's aspiration to bring the intelligibility of the given, phenomenality, to speech, to the way it wants to permit the obscurity of transcendence to shine, or to let the last word speak beyond the (merely) human grasp as a defining human possibility.

Let me now propose what might be considered an immodest conclusion. With the concepts of apocalypse and Personality (along with some corollary concepts, like idolatry and nihilism), Western thought would seem at least to be, if I am not mistaken, given some conceptual tools by which reason may be capable of belief worthy of Christianity, of seeing the intelligibility of that which proposes itself as the truth, and as the truth that is inexhaustibly more than what humanity can assimilate, conquer and know, but which apophatically grounds the μορφὴ τοῦ ἀνθρώπου in such a way that the human form that in-forms what it sees with human form (like cows and horses would if they had gods, and perhaps angels and dolphins do with theirs) is itself an expression of the (ἄμορφος καὶ ὑπερμορφος) μορφὴ τοῦ θεοῦ. It is offered the resources, then, to consider that this truth that transgresses our humanity and which is too much for us, *is* the human truth, the truth for us. And with this conquest of humanity by the apocalypse of the truth, humanity is given an exodus, and we would be in the situation to negotiatethe nihilism that reigns over us, a situation which Nietzsche himself—of course for fundamentally different reasons—called the "twilight of the idols"—and if a twilight for idols then a new dawn for reason, though of course it would seem to require a religious-like commitment to the invisible because hyper-intelligible truth that (for belief) sits hiding in the material world. The question that distinguishes us from Nietzsche is the provenance of these concepts, their appropriate horizon.

Revelation furnishes concrete data that requires philosophy to respond with concepts, concepts that, paradoxically, give us a philosophy at its most, well, philosophical. We see the great inaugural moment of this conception of philosophy, which I have proposed as a subtext in the "transgressive realists" mentioned earlier, and what I would call, more broadly, a "philosophy of revelation," in the sixth-century pseudonymous author who took his *nom de plume* from the philosopher convert to St. Paul's teaching in Athens mentioned in Acts 17, to whom we sought to listen in the previous chapter. According to this author, not only does revelation demand that philosophy be transformed in the light of revelation, but it also possesses a number of paradoxes, the logic of which we have come, after him, to call "negative theology." It is his unilateral commitment to hierarchical paradox, to the hyper-apophatic, that appears so utterly compelling.

"The history of Christ," to return to Simone Weil and her *La Connaissance Surnaturelle*, "is a symbol, a metaphor, but in the past they could believe that metaphors happen as events in the world."[17] It is the measure of the distance between the historical and the symbolic that provides an index for us regarding the intelligibility of the religious domain. This is the problem that anthropomorphism poses to theoretical reflection and that negative theology, brought to completion, to immersion in the human-world beyond purified abstraction, to an eclipse of the merely human by the fully human, is meant to span.

Fourth

7. The Priority of the Image in Christology (Cyril of Alexandria)
8. Anthropomorphism and Transcendence

7

The Priority of the Image in Christology (Cyril of Alexandria)[1]

> [T]here is much more in [Patristic theology] than a mere question of the meaning of words. It brings us close to a whole habit of mind and thought about the relation of this world and things in this world to the "world to come."[2]

The Christian anthropomorphism par excellence is Jesus Christ. With this, we reach the inner sanctum. He contains within the entire "principle of the uniqueness of things" for Christianity and any attempt, therefore, to sketch the lineaments of an apophatics of the sensible will show forth his outline. The upshot of our discussion to this point involves, abstractly speaking, the inseparability, from the logic of an apophatics of the sensible, of the constructive anthropomorphism demanded by the cosmological structure of our rationality. It is a commonplace, especially in light of Patristic thinking, to say that Christology, in order to be understood, must be experienced. For believers, to whom this commonplace matters, this experience normatively occurs in the liturgical act called "Eucharist." For them, thinking *about* God can only be a product of a lived encounter *with* God. Theo-logy is rooted in doxa-logy. Bultmann, as we have seen earlier, in his own Lutheran manner, set this in relief by a famous distinction: though humans may speak by divine authorization—"of/from" God (*von Gott*), in our necessary theoretical objectifications we inevitably speak beyond our authority—"about/over" God (*über Gott*).[3] In our day of hyper-instrumentalized ratiocinations, it is all the more important to recall and examine the particular exigencies of the Christian task of speaking about God. The Pseudo-Dionysius has introduced us to negative theology, which we have sought to wrest back from basic misunderstandings that ultimately deny the theo-logos they aim to comprehend and cloud over any possible comprehension of the particular Christian account of the principle uniqueness of the world. Cyril of Alexandria, formidably set beside the Areopagite, now throws in our face a prioritization in divine signification, the apophatics of the sensible that is our aim.

I will proceed in three essential steps, expressed here in the form of theses:

(1) For Cyril, theology—the penetration of human intelligence into the disclosure of the divine glory—finds its first condition in a participation in the sacrificial act of divine self-exegesis, which is the liturgy of the Church.
(2) Cyril's Christology is based on a Eucharistic "reduction" that enacts a mode of seeing that focuses by means of two nodes of dense intelligibility, *enfleshment* and *self-emptying*.
(3) Cyrilline orthodoxy is based on an experiential mode of vision that gives rise to proper theoretical reflection through a kenotic incarnation of reason in the textured opacity of images.

Against this background, we will foreground a fourth demonstration:

(4) The intellectual practice that corresponds to the sensible manifestation of divine glory in Christ is less one of classical philosophical *allegoresis* than of using Scriptural images to give flesh to thought.

An examination of this exemplary patristic intellectual practice outlines a Christological account of reason, reason as *the image of* "the Image of the Invisible God" (Col. 1:15).[4] This paradoxical reason involves a material habituation of intellect that corresponds to the peculiar exigency of theological speech identified by Bultmann. The concrete events of revelation, meditated on in faith, break open finite, world-bound rationality from within, drawing it into the divine sphere, not through a flight from this world but rather by immersion in the image.

Step (1)

In his *Commentary on the Gospel of John*, Cyril raises a profound question about the relation of Eucharistic and ecclesial unity: "We are still seeking to understand how to discover that we also are one, both corporally and spiritually, among ourselves as well as with God. . . . By means of a single body, his own, he blesses those who believe in him thanks to the mystic communion and thus make themselves con-corporal (Eph. 3:6) with him and each other."[5] In the Eucharist, Christians share in the life-giving flesh of Christ through the power of the Holy Spirit, who joins them to the Father in a liturgical exchange of the heavenly (glorified body/blood) and earthly (sanctified bread/wine). As God and mortals are made one, so is the primordial rift of heaven and earth healed and a "New Heavens and New Earth" is inaugurated where the created flesh of the resurrected Christ communicates the divine life. The "mystic communion" communicates to the human community the divine unity by reconciling human persons to the one God through the flesh of Christ.

In this context, Cyril's famous development of the Pauline Adam/Christ typology that forms a major thematic expression of his conception of deifying flesh by ἕνωσις is an elaboration of what he sees in the Gospel of John: a paradoxically glorifying kenotic incarnation that reaches its apogee-nadir in the Cross.[6] For Cyril, Christ, the Second Adam, is the Great High Priest who offers himself as a spotless sacrifice. The meaning of the Incarnation, he says, is unintelligible apart from the sacrifice of the Cross, the origin of humanity's great thanksgiving (εὐχαριστία) to God on the altar of the world.

Commentator L. Welch observes that for Cyril "the sacrifice offered by the second Adam is the apex of the κένωσις and hence the high point of the Incarnation."[7] He suggests that the most important passage of the entire commentary is that pertaining to Jn 19:30 ("When Jesus had received the sour wine, he said 'It is finished', and he bowed his head, giving up the spirit."). Here Cyril explains that the depths of the divine mysteries are fully revealed only at Christ's death. This passage makes clear that this sacrifice, eucharistically experienced, is the key to Cyril's mode of approach to the interpretation of Scripture. The events of sacred history, culminating in the full revelation of God's love unto death on the Cross, manifest the ultimate exegesis of *who* God is, as in Exod. 3:23: "I am/will be who I am/will be": "I will *show you* who I am."[8] For the bishop of Alexandria, the divine self-showing in sacred history is brought to culmination in the Church's "unbloody worship," sharing in the "life-giving blessings" of Christ's sacrificial flesh.[9]

Let us confirm with Welch Cyril's concrete theological starting point: the believer's liturgical participation in the glorifying κένωσις of the divine Son into a historical death culminating in the resurrection of his flesh. Divine κένωσις is the condition for human ἕνωσις. This starting point requires an articulation of the Incarnation in which the eternal Logos unites with flesh in order to restore all people to unity with each other and with God.[10] The fruit of this soteriological starting point in a community of bodies ripens into theological expression in Cyril's famous phrase, "*one* incarnate nature of God the Word."[11] Any deviation from this simple conviction puts salvation, an act of divinizing ἕνωσις, in jeopardy.

Step (2)

N. Russell observes that "enfleshment and κένωσις are fundamental concepts underlying Cyril's Christology."[12] We have seen earlier that θέωσις and ἕνωσις ought truly to be added to this list—soteriological and sacramental terms that are intrinsic to his account of Christ. Divinizing ἕνωσις through enfleshing κένωσις would be the appropriate phrase. If the flesh is, indeed, the "hinge of salvation,"[13] it is also the hinge of theological reason. We must try to make this clear.

The eleventh of Cyril's twelve anathemas against Nestorius demonstrates his conviction that a rational division of the natures results in the separation of Christ's flesh from the life-giving divinity:

> If anyone does not confess that the Lord's flesh is life-giving and the very-own flesh of the Word of God the Father, but says it is the flesh of someone else, different from him, and joined to him in terms of dignity, or indeed only having a divine indwelling, *rather than being life-giving*, as we have said, because it has become the personal flesh of the Word who has the power to bring all things to life, let him be anathema.[14]

For the flesh to be "life-giving," it *must simply be* the flesh of one divine Person who is "given in a material fashion."[15] Otherwise the Eucharist is non-salvific for it is communion with a *mere* human nature. Hence, the question of the body of Christ in the Eucharist becomes central to understanding Cyril's theoretical Christology. Crucially, Cyril grounds this conception of incarnate mediation of divinity in biblical terms, the "high priestly" activity of Christ, in which the *unity* of his humanity with the divinity in his one Person makes his sacrifice acceptable to the Father. As Cyril expresses it, investing reason with Scriptural images: Christ is "vested in the robes of divinity as God and offering priestly service as man."[16]

Believers' understanding of both the "unfathomable" unity of Christ and the *communicatio idiomatum* flow directly from this Eucharistic "reduction" (to use an apt term from a contemporary philosophical lexicon to which I have made plentiful recourse in these pages) of their thetic comprehension of the kenotic enfleshment of God. Reflecting on Cyril's first substantial response to Nestorius, *De Recta Fide*, in which he explicitly connects the Incarnation with the Eucharist, A. McGuckin comments:

> [The book's] two great consecutive ideas are firstly that if it is not God who personally effects our salvation as the subject of the incarnation then salvation is rendered ineffectual and the whole point of Christianity is lost; and secondly that

a double-subject Christology which divorces the man from the God in Christ makes void the church's hope and experience of redemption in and through the Eucharist, since the Eucharist is a life-giving sacrament precisely because it is the very flesh of God himself.[17]

These two points, a soteriological, kenotic Christology and a Eucharistic extension of the Incarnation-sacrifice of God, are inseparable for Cyril.[18] The inscrutability of the ἕνωσις is a sign of its divine provenance. This union is, first, participated in through a Eucharistic communion and, second, witnessed to in theological speech.[19]

Faith therefore has the character of a kind of vision that must mature from an experiential encounter with the ineffable on the human plane of materiality into fitting theoretical expression. But how?

Step (3)

A Eucharistic or sacrifice Christology is the condition for Cyril's key distinction between, on the one hand, the *perception of Christ in faith*, in which Christ is irreducibly "one incarnate nature after the union," and, on the other, *theoretical abstraction*, a recognition of two natures, which, however true (as in the Antiochene language of "association" to describe the relation), is merely the finite mind's attempt to reach the dazzlingly marvelous divinizing union of God and man in the flesh of Christ.[20] Cyril makes the distinction at least as early as 420, a number of years before the Nestorian controversy. In his paschal homily for that year, Cyril already rails against those who divide the natures of Christ.[21] He says that it is μόναις ταῖς ἐννοίαις, "only in the mind," that we can consider the natures divided. The *mere* mind cannot "grasp" God, much less the Word made flesh. For this, the mediation of a material body is needed.

Appealing to John 1 ("the Word was made flesh"), Cyril demands that Christians believe that the λόγος, in the act of incarnation, truly made human flesh his own. Most importantly, as a divine act, the manner of the union is wholly beyond conceiving, only perceptible in the phenomenology of faith named earlier. Any rational *division* of two natures is only an *epistemological abstraction* from the concrete encounter with the incarnate λόγος. The acknowledgment of the diversity of natures, if made the starting point in Christology, veils the Eucharistic, kenotic-henotic truth of the Incarnation. In other words, it is a *step away* from the living, present and saving Christ, a rationalizing attempt to grasp the divinity, to circumscribe God by human power and finally, therefore, a sort of demonic parody of the incarnation in which—as performed in the Eucharist—God paradoxically *makes himself* graspable (to the body), though in a wholly ungraspable way (to the mind).[22]

Cyril's thinking seems acutely redolent of Tertullian's famous claim that the irreducibility to human cogitation of the divine assumption of flesh is a sign of its divine truthfulness.[23] The vision afforded by this perspective makes further sense of Cyril's constant and seemingly anachronistic attribution of Arianism to Nestorius. The latter *de facto* makes the same *religious* error as Arius did previously by *not* allowing the concrete events of revelation to break open human rationality from within. What we can see in Cyril (which reverberates throughout the Patristic tradition) is the new intellectual horizon opened by divine revelation. It transforms human reason from within, not by means of abstract speculation in a dizzying ascent to a divine stripped of any signification but rather by kenotic immersion in the symbols of Scripture, an intellectual *imitatio Christi*.[24]

The Eucharistic reduction of visible material elements to invisible divine flesh imparts new vision. As we will now examine more carefully, the images of Scripture impart new speech to a tongue otherwise mute with religious awe at the mystery of this union.

Step (4)

Cyril's Christology attests powerfully to an evidently crucial dimension of Patristic exegetical practice with nominal similarity to pagan philosophical methods of interpretation: Christian *allegoresis*, the interpretation of the Hebrew text through the principle of Christ, is only an upshot of a more primary operation of using the text to *interpret* the lived encounter with Christ in ecclesial existence. We will see this through three controlling images that govern what can only be called Cyril's "sacrifice hermeneutic."

The image of the soul and body often follows Cyril's discussion of the unity of Christ with the Eucharistic elements, as well as that of the intrinsic unity of the two natures in Christ.[25] When we perceive a man we see before us one living creature: we do not *see* a being in two parts, body and soul; this division is a product of rational abstraction. The same is true with Christ: when believers read about his crucifixion in the Gospel, they see there, on the cross, God in the flesh; and when they taste the bread and wine, they unite with the same incarnate Son.

This common philosophical image, in Cyril's case, can be traced back to Plotinus, although it was virtually ubiquitous in antiquity to describe the relation between the divine and material elements of the cosmos.[26] For Plotinus, the "undescended" soul cannot share in the sufferings of the body, although it perceives the sufferings of the body; hence it suffers in an unsuffering way: it is ἀπάθη πάθη. Cyril's application of this philosophical image to Christ pushes it to the breaking point: the "suffering unsufferingly" of the divine Word *is* the suffering of God in the flesh. No abstraction will reach the truth: neither, on the one hand, the truth that divinity is impassible, nor, on the other hand, the truth that the flesh that suffered is the fully human flesh of Jesus of Nazareth. Rather, the revealed truth terminates conceptually in an antinomy. In the words of the (Cyrilline) fifth ecumenical council: "One of the Trinity has suffered for us" in his flesh.[27]

Cyril transforms other images as well.[28] The image of the iron and fire, for example, can be traced back to the Stoics and enters the Christian tradition through Origen. Cyril, and Apollinaris before him, make it central.[29] In his treatise *On the Unity of Christ*, Cyril begins with a programmatic philosophical statement on the priority of "feeble images" over mental cerebrations to signify divine things:

> He suffers in his own flesh, and not in the nature of the Godhead. The method of these things is altogether ineffable, and there is no mind that can attain to such subtle and transcendent ideas.... The force of any comparison falters and here falls short of the truth, although I can bring to mind a feeble image of this reality which might lead us from something tangible, as it were, to the very heights and to what is beyond speech.

Confronted by this utterly new datum, conceptual reason becomes wholly inept to its usual task and must give way to the newly discovered power of images, which are found to contain a metaphysical density that the abstractive process of conceptualization, in its pursuit of transcendent mastery of its object, loses. Cyril recenters his discussion of divine impassibility by introducing the image that promises to remain where conceptual reason collapses into contradiction:

> It is like iron, or other such material, when it is put in contact with a raging fire. It receives the fire into itself, and when it is in the very heart of the fire, if someone should beat it, then the material itself takes the battering but the nature of the fire is in no way injured by the one who strikes.

The image helps us understand, to a degree, the paradox that God suffers unsufferingly—like the fire in red-hot iron struck by the blacksmith's hammer. "*This is how you should understand*," Cyril continues, the way in which the Son is said both to suffer in the flesh and not to suffer in the Godhead. Although, as I have said, the force of any comparison is feeble, this brings us somewhere near the truth if we have not deliberately chosen to disbelieve the holy scriptures.[30]

Reason may explicate the image, but it can never surpass its power to carry the mind to the truth of revelation. The revelation of impossibility, that of the incarnate God who remains God, of the God who suffers without suffering, of the God whose flesh becomes bread on the altar, reveals conceptual reason's profound weakness. Reason cannot grasp what the image manifests. Conceptual reason may be expanded by tarrying with God in a kenotic descent that forges a new union with material images in order to bring the mind into the dazzling regions "somewhere near the truth." And yet it never outstrips the image. Just as God is made visible, tangible, in the flesh of Christ, so also does the image 'contain the uncontainable' fullness of the truth. The exercise of Christian intelligence on revelation must shatter on the shores of the image. In this shattering, rationality recognizes both its finitude and the wonder of God's acts. As God took on flesh, so reason must plunge itself into images in order to be awoken to a theological kind of seeing that will share, to some degree, in the eclipse of the distinctions that it both transgresses and upholds. And now, I think, one should perceive the distinctive character of a sacred hermeneutics, how far removed, indeed, it is from an epistemological account of revelation and, ultimately also, of reason.

Cyril's preferred image, even more than the iron and fire, is that of the coal and fire, which is derived directly from his exegesis of Isa. 6:6-7. In the second part of *Against Nestorius*, Cyril uses this image "to discern the mystery" of the union, an intellectual task sanctified by the kenotic submission of reason to the priority of images, in imitation of the divinity's kenotic submission to the flesh. The work of theology, as far as Cyril is concerned, is precisely this practice of clothing reason in the garment of Scripture in order to approach the region of divine truth. In the famous commissioning scene from the opening section of the Book of the Prophet Isaiah, the prophet has a theophanic vision of God on his heavenly throne:

> In the year that King Uzziah died, I saw the Lord seated on a throne, high and lifted up, and the train of his robe filled the temple (v. 1). . . . I said, "Woe is me! For I am lost; for I am a man of unclean lips; and I dwell in the midst of a people of unclean lips; for my eyes have seen the King, the LORD of hosts" (v. 5)!

In response to his lament at his own destruction upon seeing Uncreated Life, a seraph took "a coal that was burning" from the altar in heaven and touched it to the prophet's mouth, declaring that now his sins were forgiven. For Cyril this coal set within the human mouth that makes it pure is Christ himself: "He is compared to a coal because he is conceived as being from two things which are unlike each other and yet by a real combination are all but bound together in unity. For when fire has entered wood, it transforms it by some means into its own glory and power, while remaining what it was."[31] The fire engrosses and transforms the coal completely without changing itself at all. The coal is consumed by an unchanging living fire, incorporating its properties, and thereby comes to realize its very coal-nature, which only its union with the fire can bring about. Just like the heat-emitting coal, the flesh of Christ communicates the divine life-giving energies. The image of course is Eucharistic: the symbols of bread and wine, under liturgical conditions, are engulfed by their new signification of the Body and Blood of God.

Cyril also expounded this image in his earlier *Commentary on Isaiah*: "Now the coal is by nature wood, only it is entirely filled with fire and acquires its power and energy."[32] In this context, Cyril adds that the relation between the coal and fire is fitting since the miracles in the Gospel demonstrate that Christ "has energies most appropriate to God operating through his own flesh." Just as the coal has taken on the properties of the fire, and so can communicate the purifying properties of the fire to the prophet, so also the flesh of Christ has received the capacity to communicate the life-giving powers of the divine nature.

Just as in the modality of image does the divine truth paradigmatically reach our understanding, so also do life-giving powers of the divinized *humanity* of God reach us in our humanity. In Isaiah's *hekhalot* theophany, the angel touched the coal to the prophet's lips. Cyril's Christian interpretation asks in response: "Then how will he touch our lips?" He answers: "When we acknowledge belief in him."[33] Or, as he puts it in *Against Nestorius*, quoted earlier, when we "choose not to disbelieve the Scriptures," allowing, instead, their images to clothe our naked reason.[34] The coal touched to the prophet's mouth foreshadows the life-giving flesh of Christ, and thereby becomes the divinely given words in which to enrobe the human reason that seeks to peer through the kenotic sacrifice upon the majesty of God whose robe of glory fills the heavens.

> The kenotic ἕνωσις of the divine Word with flesh reverses the relation of flesh to the source of life: naturally and normally, flesh is made alive by being ensouled through the breath of God. And consequently the flesh could be conceived merely as a medium, an instrument of spiritual communication even to be discarded, instead of, for Cyril's Christian intelligence, a primary

site of union. In Christ, it is the flesh that gives life to the communicant's soul, for it takes on the properties of divinity for the sake of humanity. This Christological principle is the key to understanding the cosmic sacramentality of orthodoxy after Cyril. The kenotic ἕνωσις also reverses the normal ascent of reason "from better known to lesser known,"[35] from particular to universal, stretching reason precisely through a self-emptying κένωσις in the image. The Eucharistic "conversion of the gaze" that allows reason to approach the mystery of God's ineffable union with believers, in their humanity, is a way of seeing that anticipates the vision of the Last Day when the material world of flesh will no longer veil the invisible God, but like the coal, alive with fire, is replete with divine *doxa*.

What M.-O. Boulnois has said, therefore, about Cyril's Trinitarian theology applies to his sacrifice Christology: "More fundamentally, it is often found that he prefers the universe of images, always open to multiple significations, to that of the concept, which encloses reflection in a definition." She continues: "Very often therefore words with image-value replace more abstract concepts, even outside any metaphorical context. The image is no longer then only the rhetorical form making possible the establishment of a comparison with a second term but instead becomes the substitute for a concept."[36] It is as if, under the supreme intellectual pressure of revelation, Cyril must find another solution to the paradox of scientific knowledge than the one proposed by Aristotle: what is clear and primary in itself is posterior and lesser known to us (the ineffable union of God with humanity) while what is lesser known and posterior in itself is prior and more clear to us (our worldly rationality, joined to material experience, incompetent to penetrate the mystery of the union). To reach the better known in itself from the vantage of the better known to us, Cyril follows the direction that divine revelation has indicated, in a glorifying κένωσις of reason that receives eyes from tasting the Eucharistic sacrifice and a tongue from seeing the images of Scripture as divine words. In this synesthetic participation of the whole person in the living revelation of Christ are found the principles of the hermeneutics of Christian intelligence.

To summarize the preceding in a phrase, Cyril's fundamental distinction between abstract and concrete intellective visions deriving from out of his debate with Nestorius responds (as it were) to Bultmann's acknowledgment of the crucial ambiguity found in thinking "about" *God* with which we began. If the work of the *logos*, theoretical conceptualization, is to trade in concepts, this profession nevertheless requires the skill or *habit* of ceaselessly returning our conceptuality to that religious origin from which it springs, which is the revolving hermeneutic between Scripture and Eucharist that is the restless site of faith's encounter with Christ.

To conclude, there is a biblical background complementary to this intellectual procedure of Cyril in St. Paul's concept of λογικὴ λατρεία, "rational worship." The λογικὴ λατρεία of Rom. 12:1 is tied to the doxology that concludes the previous chapter, 11:33-36, in praise of the σοφίας καὶ γνώσεως θεοῦ, "wisdom and knowledge of God." What ties this "rational worship" to the doxology of divine wisdom is paradoxical: the "offering" of the believer's "body" as a "living, holy and well-pleasing sacrifice" to God (12:1). The Eucharistic overtones are hard to miss. It forms the liturgical milieu of intellectual service to the divine mystery. As a whole, this intellectual service of the *logos* that begins and ends in doxology takes a kenotic form for St. Paul as the famous hymn of Phil. 2:5-11 suggests. "Let the same [habit of] mind (φρονείσθω) be in you that was in Christ Jesus,"

> who, though he was in the form of God (ἐν μορφῇ θεοῦ),
> did not regard equality with God
> as something to be exploited,
> but emptied himself (ἑαυτὸν ἐκένωσε μορφὴν),
> taking the form of a slave,
> being born in human likeness.[37]

As I have had occasion, earlier, to discuss, St. Paul also speaks of "the mind of Christ" (νοῆν Χριστοῦ) elsewhere (1 Cor. 2:16) as a habit of thinking correlated to true "wisdom" (σοφία: possessed by God alone, and those to whom God discloses it), the principle of which is the capacity to discern the final unveiling (ἀποκάλυψις) of the Creator's will in the paradoxical glorification of the Messiah in the crucifixion (v. 7-8). Cyril's hermeneutic of revelation picks up here, so to speak, attempting to define the paradoxical contours of Christian intelligence.

Readers of the entire hymn know that the κατάβασις of the divine Word, which goes all the way through death, is revealed, by means of an *unforeseeable* act of salvation from the invisible Father, to be the initial disclosure of a continuous, deepening expression of a glorifying *anabasis* that manifests what St. Paul calls elsewhere "the glory of God in the face of Christ Jesus" (2 Cor. 4:6). The "habit of mind" orienting a total human disposition—expressed in the verbal φρονείσθω—is tied to the revelation of divine glory: it is a way of thinking that perceives the disclosure of divine glory (*kabod*/δόξα) *in* the evacuated (or kenotic) form of the Cross and which thinks *from* it, and in thinking from it, "sees" *within* and *through* it, passing, as he says elsewhere, "from one degree of glory to another" (2 Cor. 3:18): "And all of us, with unveiled faces, seeing the glory of the Lord as though reflected in a mirror are being transformed into the same image" (2 Cor. 3:18). Here St. Paul is speaking of the discernment of the glory of God manifest in Jesus Christ *through* the proleptic witness of the Pentateuch, which involves a transforming vision of the principally, though hidden, Christological form of the Scriptures. This glorification through the image reflected in the mirror of Scripture involves a redemption of the mind (see vv. 14-15). The Cyrilline hermeneutics of the image we have examined earlier may be understood as an explication of this principle.

Paul, we could say, is sketching a philosophical program for attaining the wisdom of God—which, if he had used the word, he would perhaps have called "theology."[38] A full elaboration would include 1 Corinthians 1-3 (on the wisdom of God in the foolishness of the Cross coincident with the foolishness of man), 2 Cor. 10:3-4 (on waging intellectual warfare), as well as the prologues of Ephesians and Colossians (exemplifying distinctively Pauline γνῶσις). This Pauline porch opens onto the wide panorama of what has been called the "philosophy of the Church Fathers,"[39] of which the thought of Cyril of Alexandria is a particular case.

Allow me give the last word to a complementary witness to a similar "kenotic" conversion of rational praise, now from the Latin tradition. I am thinking of St. Augustine from the end of his treatise *On the Trinity*. The theory should be familiar, but what does the North African philosopher leave us to contemplate? "This trinity of the mind," he says,

> is not really the image of God because the mind remembers and understands and loves itself, but because it is also able to remember and understand and love him by whom it was made. And when it does this it becomes wise.... To put it in a word, let it worship the uncreated God. It is after all written, *Behold the worship of God is wisdom* (Jb 28.28).... For this is called man's wisdom in such a way that it is also God's. Only then is it true wisdom; if it is merely human it is hollow.[40]

In a similar vein, the Pseudo-Dionysius said that those who do not understand the Scriptures "do not understand our way of doing philosophy."[41] For his part, Cyril says: "when people have come to believe, the power of learning naturally follows."[42]

The kenotic *doxa*-logical turn of "theo-logy" designates the aftermath of a bomb placed within history by the hands of a man come from the eschatological beyond (cf. Jn 3:13). Like a Trojan horse the Image that visibilizes the invisible Father destructs from within the human search for wisdom. Its blueprint for the reconstruction involves a long-term project. Its instrument: a reason informed by revelation for which image englobes concept and flesh communicates the life of God. The aim of this imperial conquest of earth by heaven is just as radical: to make some poor thinking-flesh on the far material fringe of the spiritual cosmos fit for the δόξα of the resurrection of the dead and the life of the world to come.

8

Anthropomorphism and Transcendence

This late, recapitulatory chapter wants to respond, from out of the intellectual perspective that has developed, to a concept of perennial interest to religious reflection: transcendence. We have seen facets of an intellectual account in four different ways of four different thinkers (Balthasar, Bultmann, Pseudo-Dionysius, and Cyril) that one may hope has provided a progressive immersion into the apophatics of the sensible. In light of the ground we have covered, I want to make a final go at theoretical reflection on the whole thing. I proceed in three steps. (1) Through an analysis of the concept of "phenomenological" transcendence, we discover that transcendence must possess certain fundamental features: "unanticipatability," "irreducibility," and "impossibility." (2) This analysis of the phenomenon of transcendence in the religious domain raises a second question, which is answered by recourse to what has been called, earlier, "transposition": How does transcendence express itself immanently? (3) In light of the phenomenon of transposition, a third question is raised, which brings the path to its conclusion: our guiding question of "anthropomorphism." A positive assessment of this topic discloses a thesis I have assumed earlier, but which requires final articulation, the elucidation of which becomes our terminus: in order to conceive the human experience of divine transcendence appropriately, anthropomorphism is both inevitable and a means toward its accomplishment. I will try to extend this insight, initiated earlier, a little more by the end of this chapter.

(1) The irreducibility of transcendence: From the purely immanent to the unassimilable

Is the human mind capable of transcendence? According to Hegel, transcendence is only a moment within an ever-expanding immanence, in the same way as the ripples of a rock dropped into a pool soon overtake the whole. To begin with, Hegel assumes the wholly traditional axiom as *phenomenologically* true—*quidquid recipitur ad modum recipientis recipitur*—that the subjective experience of an object, its appearance *für-mich*, "for me," is clearly distinct from the object, *an-sich*, "as it is in itself": our knowledge is first marked by its partial and incomplete character. Yet this self-evident character of the limitations of the finite mind before its object is not what it is in Aquinas, the sober recognition of the fundamental status of creaturehood, but rather a lack to be overcome, a terrible, vertiginous void that cries out to be spanned. The transcendence of the *an-sich* to the *für-mich* can be bridged by a "real self-appearance," an object *an-und-für-sich*: the mind can completely exhaust reality through the process of speculative dialectic. I am risking here, of course, a clarification of Hegel's terminology. Between his categories of the in-itself and for-itself, I have interpolated the for-me, in order to take account of the observing mind, the appearing-to, that brings out the potential of the in-itself, although it is an appearing that determines the *essence* of the thing itself, and is only contingent on the recipient in a secondary sense: to be something is to "self-shine," to appear. "The appearance," says Hegel, "is in general the truth of being and a richer determination than the latter insofar as appearance contains united in itself the moments of reflection-in-itself and reflection-in-another."[1] Ultimately, this dialectic plays out at the broadest possible level between thought and being. Thought and Being are finally one in "absolute knowing" at the far end of a divine odyssey, the "phenomenology of Spirit" wherein the finite spirit realizes that it itself in its process of knowing is the Absolute coming to complete knowledge, the identity of Being and Thought, but the possibility of this accomplishment depends on their implicit identity in the first place, which the process makes explicit. Thought, or consciousness, has no need to go beyond itself in order to discover its truth, which is ultimately the truth with a capital T: the Absolute *is* the immanent truth of consciousness, and the movement of consciousness itself is the attempt of the Absolute to come to consciousness in and for consciousness itself.

Transcendence, the alterity of Being to thinking, is only a moment in the process of thinking's realization of its identity with Being. Transcendence, then, is reduced to a moment of immanence. Hegel's answer to the question is therefore positive: the human mind is indeed capable of transcendence with a capital T but only at the cost of dissolving transcendence itself. Schelling, of course, would have none of this: the coincidence of Being and thinking is only an illusion of thought, which, if it thinks it can master Being, is only in immanent conversation with itself. The dissolving of transcendence does *not* create the real coincidence of Being and consciousness but rather lets go of transcendent Being by reducing it to a vapid concept immanent to consciousness, and even more, shows itself to have never grasped it in the first place by virtue of Being's identification with an abstract concept internal to thought. Yet, on the other hand, the very fact of thinking presupposes Being, and presupposes it in a specific way: namely, as something that thinking cannot exhaust without destroying itself. Being, for Schelling, is always (as I noted previously) *unvordenklich*, "immemorial," or better "unanticipated." Thought itself, for Schelling, therefore requires this ever-transcendent and free character of Being to it, as its "unanticipatable ground," in order for itself to arise as thought in the first place.² And yet both Thought and Being, in their relation, are expressions of the *Ungrund*, that precontains in an inarticulate way both in its unfathomable, hyper-potential unity. Being mediates the ineffable to the Thought that is elicited or awoken by it. Thought engages with the *Ungrund* through Being, and their end, together is an enriching reconciliation with it that completes its possibility for reconciliation with what it is not as what it is. It is true that Schelling is concerned to eschew anthropomorphism by conceptualizing an abstract principle. The apophatics of the sensible, which, as we have seen, promotes (and stems from) an identification of Principle and Personality in the Absolute (as—to be precise—the ground of a fully-but-not-merely non-dual conceptuality that *conceives* itself as a moment within an ever-greater figuration of meaning), could harness the implications of Schelling's proximate position on Thought and Being: thought must *receive* Being, and receive it in a particular way: as having its source in a will, in a freedom that is absolute, in the mode of subjective personality. The truth of Being is found in the self-revelation of the Absolute, which is a temporal repetition or unfolding of an eternal event in God. As the late German philosopher Robert Spaemann has put it: "Thought, with its aspiration to truth and to the disclosure of Being, is doomed to frustration at the unanticipated nature of being, except on one condition: it must think of the Unanticipated itself as subjective personality."³ Philosophical truth, thought's real encounter with that which transcends it, and even more, the activity of thought itself, depends on the free revelation of the divine, a wisdom from above.

We see in Schelling's critique of Hegel the beginning of the possibility of the introduction of novelty as philosophically intelligible, which Kierkegaard will take up with mad abandon: the highest knowledge, the knowledge of God, is not realized by means of the working out of that which is already implicit within consciousness or knowledge as its *condition of possibility* (as is the case from Plato's concept of "recollection" of the Forms to Kant's transcendental idealism and to Hegel's absolute idealism), but rather by means of a fundamental *impossibility*: thought must contain more than it can possibly contain in order to be true.

According to the late Hungarian philosopher, Miklos Vetö, it is worth noting, the possibility of novelty and uniqueness as thinkable in metaphysics opens onto a new chapter with Kant, and particularly the concept of the a priori synthesis (which in the wake of German Idealism is understood as the intelligible structure of subjective freedom itself), though it can be traced back to the revolution for thought implied by Christian revelation. This sets the stage for Kierkegaard.[4] Kant, that *Lumèire*, does not, therefore, take us completely off course. If for Kant the world of noumena is always out of reach, and if Hegel simply excises the noumenal realm altogether, Kierkegaard, following Schelling, rediscovers the necessity of the unanticipatable for knowledge, which, again, requires the mind's encounter with that which transcends it, which is paradigmatically an encounter of two freedoms. Kierkegaard's intellectual model is a stripped-down form of Christian revelation, for which God does something impossible, something completely new and unforeseen, namely, entering history in order to deliver truth (himself) to a humanity that is otherwise fundamentally incapable of it. The "absolutely different"[5] that God brings in the incarnation is only comprehensible *inasmuch as*—I risk the anachronism—it "transgresses" (to use Lee Braver's term)[6] or "saturates" (to use Marion's term)[7] our normal categories that we must erect in order to perceive and to know (however we articulate them). These are, to be sure, perpetually and expansively self-transcending forms of intentional desire, something Marion, after Schelling and Kierkegaard, will see as a response, an elicitation by the excessive data of intuition, a desire that is ever only infinitely expansive lack of the finite, only fulfilled by way of a free descent of the infinite to which it is invariably ordered. In Kierkegaard's language, this "transgression" is explained in the following way: the degree of our subjective passion for the Absolute, wholly internal to ourselves, becomes the measure by which the Absolute is made "objective" in experience: the intensity of immanent passion, the pathos of subjectivity, manifests the peculiar objectivity, or transcendence that pertains to the Absolute. The "inwardness" of the receiver manifests the transcendence of the communicator. This paradoxical "relation" with the Absolute is "truth"—that is, the kind of truth that pertains to such an "object." Knowledge in this case therefore requires a reorientation from the starting point of the event of revelation itself, which provides along with its appearing the very conditions for its reception: it converts the receiver, elevating the receiver into its sphere, making the receiver capable of it (to use Balthasar's language from the first volume of *The Glory of the Lord*).[8] Kierkegaard's answer to the question is, like Hegel, also affirmative, but the affirmation comes at a marvelous cost: it rests on the fundamental *impossibility* of the human capacity for divine transcendence, for which it really is ever striving for, but only ever in proportion to its own finitude, and thereby ever only equally distant (and proximate) to the infinite. This capacity instead comes from a free act of the Transcendent itself, its absolute power to transgress its own transcendence by becoming immanent, an act which disrupts but then, through our fidelity to it, expands our rational grasp of the intelligible, is a real "crucifixion of reason." And yet it is nevertheless intelligible to love.

Like Hegel, the phenomenology deriving from Husserl offers a positive assessment to our question: the human mind is indeed capable of transcendence, for it is only transcendence: the passage from interior to exterior, an openness to alterity, defines the human in a dynamic movement called intentionality. Here the mind, or consciousness, is what it is by means of its encounter with an "object." Yet, this encounter with transcendence is discovered only through the phenomenological method which requires in the first place that the question of the real existence of objects of conscious experience be ruled out of play. The phenomenology of Husserl is only concerned with immanence, the world of meaning, the world of consciousness itself. Its object is the "phenomenon" that composes the totality of consciousness' content. The fact that this phenomenon is the result of an event of "correlation" between *noesis* and *noema*, between the act of intending, which contributes meaning, and the intended object, which receives the meaning through the act of noetic intention, and is as such an irreducibly complex act of "constitution," does not change but expresses the pure immanence of phenomenological intentionality.[9] Phenomenological transcendence, at least in its classical expression, is reduced therefore to the movement, within immanence, of *transcending* alone, which defines phenomenological consciousness. In this way, Husserl's phenomenology stands on the side of Hegel's phenomenology. Heidegger does nothing to change this fundamental transformation of the concept of transcendence accomplished by his early master. It could be said that he simply carries it even closer to Hegel by equating this immanent movement of transcendence (reserved to consciousness by Husserl) with being itself, which is considered as a finite movement from out of nothing and into nothing. Being itself is an ecstatic passage of transcending that defines temporality: it is finite, finitude itself, with nothing beyond it: there is no transcendent, only the transcending passage within the immanence of being, inexhaustibly finite, without contrast and without remainder.

In a way that has gone virtually unnoticed, Jean Wahl, influenced by Kierkegaard and Schelling, has called into question this phenomenological conception of transcendence as a mere passage of immanence. As early as his *Existence humaine et transcendance* (1944), Wahl criticizes Heidegger for collapsing transcendence into immanence, arguing for the impossibility of a pure concept of human finitude that erases alterity (although he wants to see in the concept of transcendence multiple modalities, and in particular proposes that "existential" transcendence, that which creates human subjectivity, can be found outside of religion).[10] Subjectivity, says Wahl, acknowledging Kierkegaard as his source, is constituted by its presence to an unassimilable transcendence. Yet Wahl's critique of the contemporary, phenomenological notion of transcendence, focused on Heidegger, reached its clearest point in his massive *Traité de métaphysique* (1968). Here Wahl observes that the concept of transcendence, in order to be intelligible, requires two parts: a movement of transcendence, *transcending*, and the goal or term of the movement, the *transcendent*. Of course, the term or goal, if it is wholly graspable, is no longer transcendent, so it must remain ungraspable, but not so as to dissolve into nothing—it must be relevant, that which elicits the movement of transcending, which requires it in order to move in an intelligible manner. Transcendence is thus an irreducibly complex phenomenon that requires a metaphysical approach. The tension between the ecstatic movement of transcendence and the ever-elusive transcendent toward which it moves constitutes the whole existential drama of human subjectivity. To use Heideggerian language, the Kierkegaardian phenomenon of the Absolute, Wahl's paradigm for the concept of transcendence, fundamentally transgresses the ontological difference, exposing it to be an abstraction of human making that requires reality to be squeezed into it in an a priori way: whatever does not fit into its iron law does not count as possible. By contrast, in Kierkegaard's portrayal of Christian revelation upon which Wahl leans, we have the impossible itself as founding phenomenon, the condition of intelligibility for Christian experience. The Absolute reveals itself by becoming that which it is not, a player on the ontic field, one among other beings in the person of Jesus of Nazareth. Yet this ontic being among other beings is *at the same time* the Absolute, the ontological reality par excellence, existing beyond the domain of beings, but existing freely *for* it, and ultimately therefore, by virtue of this freedom with regard to being itself, ἐπέκεινα τῆς οὐσίας, as the good "beyond being"—that by which being gains its ultimate intelligibility. To be all the more "beyond being" is to be, freely, all the more immersed in being as the beyond being. Clearly, here Schelling's conception of God as "Herr des Seins," Lord of Being, is a valid description. The ontico-ontological distinction articulated by Heidegger disallows from the beginning the possibility of religious transcendence as experienced in Christianity: God as the Infinite, who in becoming finite reveals the true nature of his infinity, which is not merely the obverse of finitude. The onto-theology therefore that Heidegger so castigated remains present in his thought in a negative mode: God is a prisoner to the ontological difference for Heidegger much like he is, say, to the transcendental conditions of reason for Kant. This reading of Heidegger is further justified in the later Heidegger where, after the pagan "turn," divinity is conceived as subordinate to the "fourfold" of earth, sky, gods, and mortals that composes the basic intelligibility of the sacred.

If it is indeed the case that the phenomenon of religious transcendence exceeds the capacity of phenomenology to describe it, then we will have to ask how we can properly approach it.[11] The attempts of Schelling and Kierkegaard have been briefly noted earlier. But let us turn here to another thinker who lies outside of the canon of philosophy, properly so called, in order to magnify the chorus.

(2) The concept of transposition was introduced by Nietzsche previously. I would like now to examine it as a phenomenon. As such we find it in a sermon preached in 1944 by the British scholar of Renaissance literature, children's author and Christian apologist C. S. Lewis, revised for publication in 1961, entitled "Transposition."[12] In this text, Lewis attempts to answer the problem of immanence in intelligibility: that all of religion and indeed all of the data of revelation itself contains nothing in its expression that is not simply borrowed from natural human experience. If immanent explanations suffice for our description of the intelligibility of the phenomenon, then why appeal to transcendence? For example, just as, on the face of it, justice and revenge, or love and lust, can consummate in the very same act, so it goes also, it seems, for the supernatural aspects of our experience and our faith, which can apparently be made fully intelligible wholly within an immanent frame. Why, Lewis asks, is the Apocalypse of St. John itself simply filled with elements of terrestrial experience, albeit imaginatively and fantastically dramatized, such as crowns, thrones, swords, music, and so forth? Why, we could also ask, are the Gospels themselves capable of being read so fruitfully and insightfully by exegetes concerned methodologically *only* within their context in the Second Temple Judaism of the first century? How, in other words, can the Christian confession of the presence of "higher" reality, in the case of Christianity, heavenly truth and at its most intense summit, God himself, in the "lower" region of the earth make sense? What is the relation between these two realms, heaven and earth? How can heaven be expressed in earthly terms and be a true revelation of transcendent reality? How do we differentiate the supernatural "more" within the natural, cosmic frame? How does one separate the voice of God from

thunder?[13] How to tell the angel from the stranger?[14] How does one see Jesus as God? Lewis finds the beginning of an answer by recourse to an analogy: his own emotional experience and its relation to his senses. Lewis first observes that two opposite emotional experiences, dread and aesthetic rapture, have the very same neurological response when abstracted from the emotion and considered solely in themselves. Dread and rapturous delight both manifest physically in the very same twinge in his stomach. The physical reaction that occurs as an immediate reflex to waking in the night to the screams of a child in the room next to yours, and that of answering the phone to find out that a spouse's cancer has miraculously disappeared is, disconcertingly, one and the same. It is the very same wrench in the chest that manifests, on the one hand, that aching longing, that *Sehnsucht* or spiritual desire that only an infinite plenitude can fill, as well as, on the other hand, the horror of experiencing a great personal loss. It is the presence of the emotion itself, desire or dread, that makes one and the same physical experience pleasurable or painful. Another example: the physical experience of what the French call *jouissance* can be the manifestation of the most intense spiritual experience of union with God and of the most animalistic physical pleasure between strangers behind the dumpster. The equality, at a sensory level, of mystical rapture and what is so wolfishly called today "good sex" is the genius of Bernini's "St Teresa in Ecstasy" to display.

According to Lewis the emotions, compared to simple physiological response to stimuli, belong to an irreducibly richer, more varied, higher domain, are *manifest* in the sensory sphere necessarily at a more simplistic level since the resources and possible variations of the latter are far more constrained—despite the fact that the emotional experience is crowned or consummated precisely in its "overflowing" into the sensory domain of the body's self-experience. If you have ever seen a youngster turn a hose on full blast with his mouth over the nozzle, you know what I mean. There is no one-to-one correspondence between the emotional domain and the sensory. They relate in a similar way, Lewis observes, to the relation between a drawing of a tree on a two-dimensional plane and the real three-dimensional thing under the artist's gaze. To supplement his example, let us observe that the relation between a theoretical description of the molecule H_2O and the water spilling over your hand from the tap requires a translation of the richer system into the logic of the poorer, where any point of the poorer system must be made to bear multiple significations which in the richer system are distinct. Think of this process in reverse in Stokowski's famous transcription of Bach's Toccata and Fugue in D minor for orchestra where the single notes of the organ piece spread out so deeply over brass, percussion, strings and reeds.

This passage from a higher level to a lower Lewis terms "transposition." He notes further that the phenomenon of transposition can only be understood when one already possesses knowledge of the higher world, which is present in the realm below in the modality of faith. Therefore the higher cannot be approached solely from below, since the categories of the lower sphere are in themselves *only* of the lower sphere. For example, the materialist who sees, according to the material given, only the "twitchings of grey matter" that correspond to thought, would conclude that such twitchings are *all* that thought "really" is; or the imaginary two-dimensional person, sliding along the surface of a drawing will never be able to understand that lines emerging from a point represented depth, that the slim triangle shape is a transposition of a country lane into two dimensions. At the same time, we must recognize that our knowledge of the higher domain, in terms even of the Christian revelation, is quite small, and fundamentally attached to the symbolic action of transposition itself, for which the higher becomes expressed in the lower, and the lower therefore raised into the higher (in a similar way, again, to the neurological expression of the emotions). Only faith in the higher reality allows one to see the material event as a symbol, as the incarnation or expression of the higher in the lower.

Our paradigm case of this action of transposition, as far as revelation is concerned, is the sacraments, which are a continuation through time and space of their source, the incarnation of God in Christ. We are, for Lewis, in our normal, "earthly," that is, embodied, historical experience, like two-dimensional creatures who know at least enough of the three-dimensional world to know that their world is flat, that is, that our world, even in its unspeakable lushness and the infinite folds of its dense intelligibilities, is a radical impoverished image of the higher, angelic world, whose solidity, density and reality exceeds *this* world, much like the performance of Tavener's meditation on the Annunciation, "Thunder Entered Her," relates to its specifically ordered notes on the score sitting flat and silent before the musicians who almost magically transpose it through their instruments into lived experience of the music. And think of the title: "Thunder Entered Her" is an expression taken from earthly experience of thunder, on the one hand, and the physical passage of "entering," alluding to an experience of sexual intimacy, in order most *properly* to express the mystery of the Annunciation where Mary of Nazareth, like the Temple of old, was "overshadowed" by the Spirit and found to be with child (Lk. 1:35). Here we find that the symbolic character of the expression, utilizing aspects of the material and temporal dimension proper to human experience, *best* approaches the transcendent reality itself.

In light of the phenomenon of transposition, it is tempting to articulate a dictum: *So much materiality, so much transcendence*—since the former, lower domain, in its *explicit* inadequacy so much more clearly expresses the alterity of transcendence than any extrapolation from it to abstraction. The symbolic, metaphorical, and figurative domain is in this way more appropriate to the kind of divine transcendence that Christianity demands. I quote a theologian to remind us of this: "A purely transcendent God (if there could be such) would be an abstract, purely negative mystery." The God of revelation is unique, his immanence is not in conflict with his transcendence but only the apogee of its expression. Hence, the theologian continues: inasmuch "as [God] draws near to us, we begin to realize how high he is above us; and as he unveils himself to us in truth, we begin to grasp how far he is beyond our understanding."[15] If transcendent reality is, at its height of intensity, that of abstract principle, as in classical philosophy, then "the Form of the Good," "thought thinking itself," the One, The Ineffable beyond the One, the Nothing, *Idipsum*, *Ipse actus essendi subsistens*, "that than which nothing greater can be thought," *Posse ipsum*, and so forth would be *the most appropriate* expressions of which we are capable to refer to divine transcendence, full stop. But, bearing a relative and important validity, these are all shattered as limitations and constraints by the Christian revelation of the Triune God, whose transcendence is marked first by the freedom of God to manifest himself in truth, by the freedom of sovereign personality, by *the appearing of the Living God*. Our greatest conceptualizations of God serve an explication of the pregiven mystery.

Taking the eschatological structure of the phenomenon of Christian transposition into account, we can perhaps express it this way: the truth of this, lower world, "earth," in its final consummation with the higher one, "heaven," when "liberated from its bondage at ἡ ἀποκάλυψις τῶν υἱῶν τοῦ θεοῦ, "the revelation of the sons of God,"[16] is itself one of passage *from* the limitations of the present state that requires transposition, a passage that, at best, even our greatest mystics only sense in moments of sublime beauty and stillness, and a passage *to* the unleashing of this lower world's inherent fittingness with heaven and the vision of God in the resurrection of the body, a world and a body transvalued beyond their natural capacities, but in this way precisely brought to fulfilment—these very same senses that see the fire and feel the heat, smell the crackling wood, will likewise see and feel and smell the "Consuming Fire" of God himself by means of their unimaginable flooding with truth of heaven, of which the image of fire is the most adequate in our experience. Besides reference to the requisite passages in Augustine's *City of God*, XXII, I refer also to Aquinas, who, in his *Commentary on the Sentences* and in great to debt to Augustine, considers the role of the senses and the material world, both transfigured, in the vision of God:

> In beatitude the essence of God will be seen like an object of indirect vision, because on the one hand bodily sight will see so great a glory of God in bodies, especially in the bodies of the glorified—and most of all in the body of Christ—and, on the other hand, the intellect will see God so clearly, that God will be perceived in things seen with the eye of the body, even as life is perceived in speech. For although our intellect will not then see God from seeing His creatures, yet it will see God in His creatures seen corporeally.[17]

The central point, as the Pseudo-Dionysius already observed, and in doing so made it the principle difference between his thought and that of the Platonism of late Antiquity with which he was in deep conversation (through Proclus), is that the symbolic domain is not the figurative projection of that which can be more authentically expressed by conceptual reason. The human experience of transcendence is human inasmuch as it places the symbolic dimension at the center and at the apex, as the condition for the experience of divine transcendence in human terms. I recall here again a quotation referenced earlier, from the *Ecclesiastical Hierarchies*: "The heavenly beings, because of their intelligence, have their own permitted conceptions of God. For us, on the other hand, it is by way of the perceptible images that we are uplifted as far as we can be to the contemplation of what is divine" (I, 2, 373B). In the sense that Christianity gives to what is called "negative theology" (more broadly, the Areopagite speaks of "our philosophy"), it functions by reference to and never escapes from embodied experience, which is what the "denial of denial" (what Aquinas, developing it in his own system, will call the "way of excess") is meant to signify, for it is "beyond assertion/affirmation/predication and denial/negation/abstraction."[18] The eclipse of every contrast, of every hierarchy is accomplished by the God who does not destroy them or set them aside, but in his goodness sustains them, revealing himself through them as in eclipse of them in an ultimate, eschatological *henōsis* with humanity that is the new beginning of all things.

Before the divine reality, the human, however far the reach of his speculative powers, is fundamentally impotent. With our thoughts about God we are shooting arrows at the sun. For this path of thinking, in the final account the simplest images of human experience with which Holy Scripture is replete, are, to quote Louis Bouyer, "less of an obstacle to a deep intuition of God's transcendence than the most refined concepts."[19] The recognition of the priority of images in theological vision is rooted in the deepening awareness of the religious mystery that we can state with another aphorism: *personality is higher than possibility*. Personality, at the absolute, contains an identification of replete actuality and brimming, infinite potential. To reach in an adequate manner, the divine kind of transcendence, our anthropomorphisms must be deliberate—otherwise they are merely masked by lifeless abstraction.

(3) Taking a step back from what I have now concluded would allow us to make a penultimate observation. The meaning and end of philosophical reflection, and therefore, the measure by which it is judged, is found in its fidelity to the native profundity that marks, if I can put it this way, the *humanity* of human experience from end to end: I am speaking of love, of evil, of freedom, of joy, loss, sadness, novelty, creativity, the meaningfulness of the affective dimension, and so on. These are the greatest realities of human experience and they are the objects of human intellectual aspiration that are the most important and at the same time the most difficult. We could encapsulate this field of questioning under the broader rubric of the question of the human as such (*Was ist der Mensch?*) and finally, ultimately of the question of God (*Was ist der Gott?*), of the human relation to God, an intertwining of questioning, which, at the end of the day, is always meant when we ask the abstract question about divine transcendence.

We are not capable of any experience that is not (fully) human—theologians and philosophers included. Our experience, as an intellectual experience, is therefore determined the perennial enigmatic dimensions of our humanity. "All humans by nature desire to know" the final value of our humanity, its definitive meaning, which is tied to both God and the world. Our desire for the definitive, known in such a way as not to destroy but perfect our worldly being, must be understood as a key that unlocks, for us, reality itself. It is the holy grail, which we have possessed all along. And yet the grail is intended for a specific use. If it is not filled it is perhaps good for the museum and not much else. At the museum it is not realizing itself, the end to which, as a product of human culture, it, like the cello, mute on a stand in the darkened concert hall, objectively aches for. The Christian thinker, whose thought is being described here, intuitively senses it to be an indication of the most important aspect of reality and the ungraspable essence of transcendence itself: personality. Transposition into a conceptualization drained of blood takes us farther away from these certain perennial realities—sacrificing proximity, experiential knowledge, for the sake of a distance that can "grasp" the totality (but which is a grasping that only grasps the idea of the reality reproduced within the mental domain as a concept)— whereas the images and figures received and formed in the everyday give us an inexhaustibly richer "taste" and "touch" of these realities themselves.

"The Cause of all," said the Pseudo-Areopagite, "is above all and is not inexistent, lifeless, speechless, mindless."[20] From this perspective, Thomas Aquinas was right to demand that knowledge, if to be realized, must enact a *conversio ad phantasmata*, a return from abstraction to the experiential encounter with the image provided by the senses, which is itself the means of the personal encounter with the reality that transcends our experience of it, irreducible to our knowledge of it. Our objects of knowledge (whether natural or divine) are inevitably situated as frontiers of the human domain, and the paradox of human knowledge is that only immersive recourse to the domain of human experience allows us to transcend it. This paradox is one of the most important keys to any rearticulation of metaphysics, the wonder of being, as both a Christian and intellectual enterprise. We can summarize its paradoxicality by reference to some of the basic principles of reason, intensified, as we have found them to be in "negative theology." Reason must move in stages. First, it must recognize the limitations of the "affirmations" that it in some cases receives or in other cases, proposes: what we say about reality always falls short of the things themselves. Hegel rightly saw this as the fundamental starting point for our understanding of human knowledge. Yet we have found them to be a certain and substantial pricetag on precision and clarity: distance from the reality with which we are concerned. By distance, of course, in the intellectual sphere, I am appealing to the metaphorical analog of physical vision (an analog that underwrites much of the tradition of Western philosophy) to signify the generalization, the fading out of the irreducible and essential particularity, the "thisness," let us say, of realities, that ancient terms like the Neoplatonic ὑπάρχις and ὑπόστασις, and the post-hierarchical *haecceitas* (for that matter) were forged to help us see. This distance, requisite for vision, implicitly recognizes the inevitable and infinite transcendence of things themselves to our thoughts, which only begin by means of the elicitation of experience by that which transcends thought. This implicit recognition of the infinite transcendence of the objects of our thinking to our thinking therefore leads to a critical negation of our concepts, the recognition of the fundamental insufficiency and provisionality of our conceptual achievements, even if and especially because the greatest of these are necessary *by virtue of their utility*. They say something true, but on the other hand, they are not that which they signify. It is ultimately the irreducible meaningfulness that we sense in this experience, in its humanity, that must become the judge of our thinking: our concepts (usefully) pull us back from this native meaningfulness of experience and on their own they attempt to master it, which they can have some success at doing inasmuch as they provide results, as Bergson observed, whether or not they correspond to real ideas that transcend our minds. And yet we recognize simultaneously that these material images at the root of our concepts are the first bearers of this meaningfulness. In them the affective and intelligible are irreducibly intertwined in a way that corresponds to our total humanity. The figurative dimension prepossesses the truthfulness that concepts seek to grasp more adequately and make some costly but necessary progress in reaching. The purification of our idols by concepts, necessary when we naively equate these images with the transcendent things themselves, only allows us to see this all the more. Yet we must keep moving toward the higher things. We can see anew, through the critique of our concepts, that the world of images, replete with the basest anthropomorphisms, *is already in contact with* that which we were compelled to seek by means of the path of conceptual purification.

There is no escape from our humanity. Return to it allows us to enter the knowledge of the ever-greater surplus of experience over itself, of the excess of intelligibility that marks the human from the beginning. In short, the appeal to anthropomorphisms, once one recognizes both their necessity and essential limitations, itself bears within the passage to the more than human, to immersive transcendence, the experience of the coincidence of opposites.

At the heart of human experience is the more than human. The human is (like God) a surplus, a paradox, an excess, an unknowable infinity, but (unlike God) qualified by an "infinite" finitude. The deeper we receive our humanity as it is, the more we are liberated to exceed it. The human does not need to leave his humanity in order to encounter divine transcendence, even less so to understand it (in the appropriately more-than-epistemic, participatory way). This passage, articulated by allusion to the terms of Dionysian negative theology, proffers the necessary elements of intellectual reflection on God that takes the data of revelation into account, that is, the antinomic identity of personality and being for our understanding of divine transcendence. The Dionysian answer to our question (Is the human mind capable of transcendence?) is perhaps the most humanly satisfying one. Its answer is: yes, but only in a fully human way, which revelation turns out to privilege above all: "Things into which angels long to look" (1 Pet. 1:12).

But what does the human see?

The human creature, straining to see God, is blind. One sees nothing. There is no thing to see. And one *only* sees things. Things emerge through proportion, by seeing one thing in light of another, and, then, by the original proportion giving act of world itself. One's vision must be reduced to thingliness *by reason*, which grasps, through proportionate contrast, this or that. But the Absolute, the

One-All, the Origin and End is "not this, not that." If this were the whole story, it would be remarkable enough, for, in recognizing it, we would de facto stand beyond it; we would be its *Weltspielers* or even capable of simply awakening to our identity with the Unqualified Absolute. Many venerable spiritual masters, east and west, seem to have done so and to have taught it. And yet, perhaps there is more. Thought with *God* in mind, the *world*, the limitless whole that gives original proportion and this or that within it, is not the last master of what appears. God, who exceeds the proportion, is master of it. God's difference with the proportion is that there is no proportion between him and it. No proportion means both absence and negation, "purified" presence beyond affirmation as beyond denial.[21] Already reflection demands a movement beyond negation into a silence of adoration at the presence-in-absence, the self-excess of God. Beyond negation, human speech, the management of the order of differentiations of the world loses its mastery, its pertinence. This line of thought may be called, as I have suggested, "non-dual": to think world means to think contrast and duality.

To think God's distinction with world, to think *creation* therefore, means to think beyond duality. But there is more. No proportion does not and cannot shut down a further and more stupefying possibility, that God is *free* in relation to the world.[22] We may come to find out, after the fact, that God may speak. God may act. And in either case, he acts and speaks as the master of world. The first thing God says is that he has chosen to create. The world did not have to be. By bringing it into being God has actualized a possibility, has realized a decision. Christianity, premised on the appearing of God as word and as actor is a more than non-dualism. It is fully non-dual, but not merely. For if God chooses to act and speak, he may do so *through* the world, taking it up as his instrument, as the means of his communication and as the end of his action. God may take up the world as his object. As its master, he may have a purpose with it. And we cannot slight him if that purpose is the world's total glorification through privileged partnership with his human creature in an endless collaboration from out of the finally completed beginning established in (and promised by) Jesus Christ. The aim of the beginning is called by Christ the kingdom, which means the reign of God on earth as in heaven, the conformation of earth to God in proportion to the way heaven is. It means heaven-on-earth, which means earth as the place of heaven, materiality and spatiality and temporality unlocked as the bearers of spirit and eternity, just as the sacraments anticipate from within the form of this world, a form established through the differentiation of heaven and earth, of spirit and matter, of disincarnation. The descent of God in Jesus Christ is the reversal of disincarnation. It is the final establishment of the beginning, of a new heavens and new earth, the setting of the table, the deep breath of the player before the bow runs across the string.

Already in the metaphysical mode of reflection of traditional negative theology, the reduction of impossible vision (beyond proportion) to rational comprehension (within proportion) takes the form of a contrast that is illegitimate inasmuch as it names two in comparison in order to signify the incomparable, that which is wholly beyond proportion. The *concepts* that it forms only articulate, in the final analysis, an innerworldly contrast that is understood as significative of that which is beyond the world. This contrast may be called antinomy, an appearance of conceptual irreconcilability. It is the form the world takes in attempting signify that which is beyond it. Take the concept of *creation*. God is free. God chooses. Freedom and choice, and the will and reason inherent within the act of decision are concepts that name things we only understand as temporal and even historical. In any event worldly. And when we apply the necessary qualifications (God is not constrained by time, he is eternal; he is not constrained at all, and so his freedom, his will and his reason are infinite, etc.), then we must affirm that we are knowing what is beyond world by means of world, beyond history, the sphere of human action, by means of it. We are knowing what is beyond us by reference to us, as temporal, finite, historical knowers and doers. God alone *is*, properly speaking. The world is only by "participation" in *being*, which God is. The world receives being from God (who freely gives it), and *only* God can give being, which God is, to that which is *not* God.

God and world make two; God and world do not make two. If we continued to think this way, we can say that God is being, the fullness of being, the unqualified act of existence, and yet also the one whose wholly unqualified transcendence (even by "being") allows him to be *a* being among other beings, allows, in other words, the beings that are to have a place in relation to him. We are in all of this, stuttering. We are using qualifications that do not fit. They hide more than they reveal. We are knowing in a qualified sense, then. *Through* these worldly forms one may perceive intellectually, but that one does not perceive anything except by means of an image that unites the two in one as vehicle. This image is called *symbol*. Symbolization is the enfleshment of conceptual antinomization. Our knowledge is our own. Anthropomorph. Here, sticking with the concept of creation, our controlling image handed to us is that of the God who speaks and in speaking gives forth the primordial distinctions, like sky and earth, light and dark, chaos and order (though it does not control by the negation of all others, like that of the wise craftsman, which has its own venerable history both inside and outside the biblical canon). These are distinctions that place the world (out of nothing) in relation to the Creator. One tradition of conceiving the symbol (σύμβολον: the joining of two) thinks of it according to the Neoplatonic logic of the cause (αἴτια) for which the lower is itself and is also the effect, the "influence," ἐπίδρεσις, and "result," ἀποτέλεσμα, the manifestation of the higher. It is both other and not other to the explanation (αἴτια) for its being. And the cause itself is *precisely as cause* only the effect of that which is higher than it, which it is in stretching out for it, manifesting it, which it enacts *by* producing its effect. The ἐνέργεια of God are (pl.) God; God is (s.) not his ἐνέργεια. The lower *is* the higher, disclosing its "precontaining" plenitude in its multiplicity; the higher *is not* the lower, but its unifying ἀρχή.

However much the tradition has utilized the Neoplatonic lexicon of cause (and to great effect), the biblical horizon must master it by the image of the divine creative word. The world is God's speech; God's speech is not the world but its principle. The world is because of the divine principle, the Word, that gives it being, and it accomplishes itself through a free collaboration with this Word who has called it forth from nothing and now calls it forth to an "ever-greater" fullness united with it in human flesh. The conceptual serves the narrative by explicating it, by pinpointing and articulating its inherent intelligibility. The conceptual in no way escapes the anthropomorphism, but is, in fact, subordinated to the lower, more metaphysically "crude" modes. This prioritization at the human level in the comprehension of revelation, reflects (as all does) the greater mystery of God's "election" of humanity. The shockwaves running through the (to us) barely utterable celestial hierarchies at the "crowning" creation with humanity, first made "a little lower" than the angels (Ps 8:5), should still be registered, all the more when the eschatological implications of that ordering have been disclosed. Since negative theology prioritizes the epistemological (for obvious reasons), let us stay with that. The ancients had an apothegm that may serve as a starting point here: the known is known according to the mode of the knower. Angels know God angelically, aliens, in an alien fashion—at least to us. In every case, God is known by a creature, through the creature, and according to the specific distinctives of that creature. The anthropomorphic mode of knowledge—embodied, "participatory" precisely as knowledge-in-the-flesh, is fully worldly, but not merely. In fact, if we ponder the meaning of revelation, centered on Jesus Christ, on his Father's kingdom come, then we would have to allow that this anthropic mode of being (and knowing, and, let us add, doing) is normative, governing not only for us, but for all—even the angels, whose higher god-like modes of seeing and doing come to serve the prioritization of this new (that is, perfecting) "economy"—perhaps even (and we seem authorized to talk this way) including God himself, who assumed our flesh, its historicity, temporality, its world, in an everlasting fashion. Central to the Pauline testimony is the claim that (to use the subsequent Patristic lingo) this hominization of God and divinization of creation (through humanity) was his plan, from the beginning.

The angels are already gods. If humans are to become "judges of angels" (1 Cor 6:3), gods of gods, sharers of the divine throne with the Christ (Rev 3:21), it is first by accepting the *humility* of this prioritization of the human, which, in the first place, pulls down the "pretensions" of the angel-like humans (the wise, the powerful, the beautiful),whose glory belongs to that former "economy" and requires them to reorder their wisdom, power, and beauty by the revealed wisdom and power and beauty of God in Jesus Christ (1 Cor 1:18-31), who "humbled himself" to the point of death (Phil 2:8). Hierarchy (wisdom, power, beauty, being) remains, but it is liberated by love. Love reveals the hierarchy's ground; it brings being its true fullness; power becomes service and beauty the proportion of the disproportionate; wisdom ("from above") is made manifest in the foolishness of matter and flesh, which are shown to be the terminus of God: "Jesus is the source and perfection of every hierarchy."[23]

Fifth

9. Concluding Sign

9

Concluding Sign

Perhaps worse than a novel introducing new characters in the *dénouement*, it is a risk to end a book with the introduction of a new conceptuality. Here the risk is necessary. It is also valuable since it forces us to recognize the provisionality of this (as any) extended intellectual exercise. The theoretical line developed through the preceding chapters, seeking to understand the "principle of the uniqueness of things" on the Christian account, moved from an "anthropic principle" to a negated-and-properly-negative negative theology along the thread of a hyperbolic excess of signification that uniquely sustains the communion of materially "descended" intelligence with the Uncreated, disclosing, at least enigmatically—the apophatics of the sensible.

Now I will venture to tie the tether of such a λόγος to the current of a μῦθος that is (as I have argued) the permanent base of any conceptual rationality. The task is never to regionalize or homogenize the Christian account but always to diversify and pluralize it, a method of particularized universalization termed "right use" that will have to be the object of attention on another occasion.[1] Only then, in the vast, kaleidoscopic matrix of humanity's unfolding historical experience of world, would we have a chance to chase the proper signification of the unfathomable divine unity that is our ecstasy, beyond the difference between a one and a many, of an I and a Thou, but nevertheless founding it, sustaining it in the gratuity of love that calls it forth, through the fire of holiness, as beloved.

The second thinker I mentioned in the introduction to this essay was Pavel Florensky. In a recently translated collection called *Early Religious Writings: 1903-1909*, Florensky's dialogue, "The Empyrean and the Empirical," is placed.[2] In this piece, Florensky differentiates a Christian "supernatural worldview" from an ersatz imitation through a dialogue that explores analogies between the supernatural understanding of the natural as site of divine miracle and the natural (i.e., scientifically investigated) orders of mathematics and physics. The reduction of empirical experience to that which empirical investigation (science) allows on its own terms in the end only reduces the value of the empirical to self-referential sign without meaning. This sign may possess a coherent intelligibility, an intelligibility of coherence, but it also and precisely as such may be comprehended as a "symbol" (a key term, to be sure, in Florensky's lexicon) with referentiality beyond to the spiritual world. In his attempt to expound the worldview of "B" correctly, the interlocutor, "A" offers a coherent interpretation of the basic elements of Christianity that does not exceed the empirical: what Christians call revelation, "A" suggests, coherently, is only humanity's representation to itself of its own intrinsic possibilities, the conquest and mastery of nature. Evil, for example, is the symbol of a primordial "loss of psychopathic equilibrium" that causes disorder for humanity, particularly sickness and death. Jesus of Nazareth, "the self-healing man," realized the human potentiality to master nature and thus exhibited god-like powers. Resurrection signifies the possibility of the eradication of illness and the indefinite extension of life through advances in medicine and technology, and so forth.[3] "A" himself does not agree with this account but only interprets "B"'s Christianity through the lens of his scientific empiricism, a merely empirical approach. "B" responds with an extensive elaboration of his "worldview," the rational set of coherent possibilities in the world. His account reverses perspective (so to speak) on empirical experience, making a distinction between the empirical and the empyrean: "Divinity is not derived from the empirical. Just the opposite: the empirical is a manifestation of the divine."[4]

"B"'s "naturalistic" view of Christianity "A" later in the dialogue terms "planar": it is flattened out, unidimensional, "satisfied with one plane of reality."[5] By "naturalistic," Florensky refers in the first place to a certain aesthetic sensibility (if also, of course, to the set of philosophical convictions termed "naturalism"). This is a single-perspective viewpoint that strives for natural realism, for *accurate depiction*, realistic representation in painting and literature. Aesthetic and philosophical naturalism share an intellectual kinship, both involving a "planar" attitude one could call anti-metaphysical or rationalistic. Ironically, Florensky likens the scientific approach in art and philosophy to primitive, two-dimensional drawing, without perspective or "depth." "B" elaborates Florensky's alternative, which corresponds to a "symbolist" mentality in literature and an iconographic "reverse perspective" (as he develops elsewhere) in painting:

> We are not satisfied with this "planarity" of reality; we demand that perspective be recognized.... This depth of perspective means that we do not level the whole diversity of reality into one plane—the plane of sensuous perception. It means

that we do not squeeze and dry reality like a flower between the pages of the thick account book of positivism.[6]

The symbolist, iconographic, and empyreal perspective does nothing to restrict the activity of scientific exploration of the empirical with its methods. But it does allow this exploration to direct attention away from itself when such is suggested (to a consciousness that possesses an open perspective) by its findings. Here Florensky refers to some of his favorite mathematical and physical aporiae, set theory, non-algebraic numbers, and incommensurable quantities, coordinating them as examples that develop, after what we have seen earlier, a transgressive methodology of differentiation among objects within the empirical (by differentiation among sciences) and then beyond it as simply a logical extension of the process already undertaken. One can only reject this extension by an a priori commitment to a "planar" worldview that accepts only the impossibility of a difference between the known and not yet known, *not* by observation of the phenomena themselves, which are available for either interpretation.

I now present the major elements of "B"'s presentation. Differentiation between pieces of glass and ice of the same size and clarity cannot be undertaken by geometry, but by another method of investigation, (say) chemical analysis. Two discrete instances of slapping a man cannot be differentiated except by moral reflection and according to its laws (slapping an enemy out of greed or hatred or slapping a friend out of righteous indignation or to divert him from a path of self-destruction). The first case involves an apparent empirical identity according to one method, for which the introduction of another empirical method will discern the difference. The second case involves an empirical indistinguishability that conceals an essential distinction discovered non-empirically. A third and fourth case follow.

The third involves objects appearing "contemplatively" as identical but "speculatively" as distinct.[7] Mathematics is contemplation that becomes speculative when the properties of relations it discovers requires the rational construction of "new arithmetical schema" to make sense of them: irrational numbers. Here he introduces the "simplest" geometric observation of the properties of a square: the relation of a side of the square to its diagonal is incommensurable: there is a difference internal to the relation that is not measurable through observation of the segments themselves. Only a new kind of science and a concomitant kind of seeing must be developed in order to articulate and to analyze the new kind of phenomenon. The Pythagoreans, Florensky observes, understood this discovery of another order of geometrical properties to be mystical of the highest order, a direct and perilous contact with living roots of the world. Some mathematical objects cannot be expressed by (whole) number and thus manifest themselves as without essence at all, since number, according to Pythagorean doctrine, is identified with essence. After further explication of mathematical incommensurabilities in transcendental numbers and set theory, Florensky turns to the final type of object: "those only distinguishable by means of mystical perception."[8] In this category, Florensky introduces the Christian sacraments: empirically, they are indistinguishable from any other ritual or ceremony, but church doctrine teaches a distinction, just as geometry teaches a "speculative" distinction between two line segments, the side and diagonal of a square. The sacraments, manifesting the empirical world's "mystical potential," possess in themselves an essentially new essence, "like a new creation."[9] Florensky gives evidence for the validity of this distinction by reference to the ordinary religious experience of the simple believer, who "feels" God's forgiveness in the reception of Holy Communion or experiences the renewal of life and the purification of their soul in the act of baptism. That these are real experiences cannot be denied; their analogy with the previous forms of scientific methodological differentiation only widens the scope of the rational comprehension of human possibility. And they imply a further expansion of the character of rationality itself, although this is richly prepared for already in the physical, mathematical, and moral domains.

So far, Florensky's "A," in his account of his "worldview," his rational account of the world of human experience, has presented four types of object empirically available: the merely empirical, the moral, the speculative, and the mystical. Each requires, to be properly made manifest, its own kind of "science" (although Florensky does not use that term, even analogously, across the four categories) or rational method or methods for the intelligible differentiations within it. The empirical is the site of appearing of every kind of object and the game of intelligence is played by rightly responding to the contrasts given: at the purely empirical level, differentiation among objects requires appeal to different methods in order to find and articulate their differences. Similarly, the moral domain is not found except by differentiation from the merely empirical: measuring the electrical activity of the brain or performing a chemical analysis of the hormones in the bloodstream of the person who slaps another only measures the effects of the personal, moral sphere as it is transposed (we should say) into the material. The moral requires its own properly differentiated principles and methodology for investigation. Geometry, a branch of mathematics concerned with the properties of relations among shapes, is a science that requires a particular kind of abstraction called "contemplation" and yet within the very heart of it there are discovered properties ("objects") that demand a further differentiation in order to proceed into *their* level of reality, which corresponds to "speculation," within which a constructive or "fundamental" mathematics is employed that discovers properties within abstract models that paradoxically both exceed what is possible in the world but also found both empirical experiments that prove their veracity and advances in "applied" math with revolutionary consequences, that is, technological development.

Extending the differentiation by another degree—each of which is absolute, wholly differentiated from the other kind of object, but also each of which is fully immersed within the empirical domain and yet in excess of it in such a way as to suggest, rationally, that qualitative reaches are present beneath it—the "mystical" perception of the empirical likewise indicates that the planar view is reductive and restrictive. The "empyrean" view, by contrast, sees the empirical as "the given front plane" of reality. The distinctions made in order to be scientifically faithful to empirical experience again and again have suggested that there are further "layers" behind each level, "irreducible" to one another and yet related through "correspondences" that (by way of, for example, ritual action or prayer or already in mathematical speculation and even more mundanely in moral action) can be points of interchange between the levels. The planar approach and the depth approach fully share the empirical level in the same way as someone, observes Florensky, who cannot read could, sitting on a park bench one sunny afternoon, share a physical page of Goethe with someone who understands the poem written on it. Even more, the front planar level, for the empyrean view, becomes charged with special value: the empirical world becomes the "representative" and "bearer" of higher worlds, in other words a "symbol," defined as "an organically living unity of that which represents and that which is represented." Perceived symbolically, the empirical loses its independence and, Florensky says, playing with the etymology of the term *empyrean* "glows with the flame of another world" and ultimately expresses its transcendental union with the higher world, itself "mingled with fire" for religious ("mystical") perception. This perception proposes itself as the highest and most fundamental viewpoint, an expression of an "absolute worldview," the world, even the phenomenal world of measurement and rational differentiation, approached as a kaleidoscope of symbols, expressions of the noumenal in which its fullness resides.[10]

An extravagant appendix to the dialogue focuses further on the relation of the empyrean worldview to the sacraments, which in the preceding dialogue were the focus of the fourth type of object. It begins with an extensive catalogue of spiritual perception through the reception of the sacraments in devotional and hagiographic literature in the Catholic and Orthodox traditions: visions of fire falling on the gifts of the altar or of angels officiating at the service, fragrance emerging from consecrated elements, and the like. One could include here of course more common contemporary fabalistic phenomena like incorrupt bodies of saints, weeping statues, or bleeding hosts which make up much of the bread and butter of popular Catholic culture (at least). Florensky's approach is to take these common stories "tautegorically," as true on their own terms (repeating Schelling's approach to myths), as demonstrations of breakthroughs into the "experience of the empyrean" in our otherwise outward-facing empirical viewpoint. After a brief theoretical reflection on the mystical character of sacraments (which I set aside here), Florensky catalogues a second set of tales and legends about extraordinary empirical phenomena accompanying sacramental experience with which the popular and traditional spiritual literature of Christianity is, again, so replete. This catalogue of data again sets the basis for a theoretical sketch that serves as the content of a final brief section of the text, locating, I think, what is probably most purposeful in all this for an apophatics of the sensible.

Florensky first explains why he attributes "such great significance" to literature so clearly hagiographical and hyperbolic, embellished and idealized. The significance Florensky places in tales and legends, myths and folk tradition in fact can hardly be overstated. Imagine someone putting the same kind of ultimate credence to legend and fable as is common today regarding modern science, and you begin to approach Florensky's point of view. His credence, by contrast, is intelligent. I will represent his "fragmentary theoretical considerations" that justify his position in short form.[11]

There is, begins Florensky, a "scientific-philosophical worldview." Its attitude is that of the "bookkeeper" who "calculates every side" of reality, attempting to hold in consciousness "every detail" in order to "split" apart the "elements" of the world of experience into rationally ordered relations, and to "underscore" and "highlight" those parts that come forward for this or that particular method of calculative separation and ordering. This fragmentation through abstractive representation may be exemplified by the fourfold differentiation of objects and method explicated in the dialogue. Florensky himself, an eminent inventor, scientist, and mathematician, may be taken as an eminent representative of this perspective, which, however, in him, a little like Pascal in another time and place, is not closed in on itself. As a whole, the scientific approach is founded on a basis, a human basis, a pre-given, cohesive and coherent, meaningful sphere of experience, *a world*. In relation to this base, the scientific conception of experience is artificial inasmuch as it purposefully blinds itself to this base through a procedure of abstraction from it, as is basic to its methodological form. "In order to perform this labor of splitting, this fragmentation, the consciousness *must have* that on which it operates, and this thing on which it operates is *something that is given to the spirit*."[12] What is given to the spirit, an already preformed value-laden horizon of meaning, may be called "popular experience," whereas the adjudicating calculative representation may be called "scientific experience" of the world. Both modes of experience are human and inhabited daily and to differing degrees by the same people. The first type of scientific experience comes to the fore of consciousness and "dominates" when reflective rationality is at work as "the foremost factor," whereas the second type rules consciousness when "contemplation and activity" are at work. To use the later Husserl's language, the "lifeworld" first gives the context of meanings where I am self-conscious; my awareness is correlate to the world as an ordered whole where I enact my entire business of living. It is out of this world, the lifeworld, that the "data" of science, merely through methodological self-delimitation, can be drawn. "The task of scientific experience," says Florensky, "is to underscore and separate. The task of popular experience," on the other hand, "is to provide the most full-bodied experiences, to provide material that, as much as possible, is not underscored and separated."[13] Continuing the analogy with Husserl, we could contrast the "natural attitude" behind the scientific way of viewing the world (a world of objective things, ready and waiting for a schematic representation) and the "personalistic attitude" that sees the world as a human and lived place. Both scientific experience and popular experience are representations. The latter possesses characteristics that do in fact make possible its schematic representation by scientific consciousness, but this abstractive schematic representation is anticipated or pre-schematized by a kind of holistic schematism of the intelligence that does not underscore and separate. This kind of formalization of human experience is found in dreams, in works of art, in myth, in folk wisdom, and in legend. It is a process of the discovery of an envisioning of reality, an "induction" of truth "by a thousand generations and millions of experiences," offering, he says, an "undistorted (though often symbolic and even conventional) drawing of reality."[14]

Science must therefore eschew the temptation "to see only good or bad science," approximations to its own abstractive rationalizations, in the mythic, narrative intelligence of popular wisdom and legend: "science must delve dispassionately into popular wisdom, which because of its integral unity, is always ahead of science."[15] Myth really *is* bad science, inasmuch as its words are conceived as quasi-conceptual or half-baked terms, a child's attempt to produce scientific concepts, "instruments for calling forth a schema . . . a primordial, half-meaningless philosophy [within] primitive thought."[16] But it is not *merely* bad science. It is myth. Much more than science, it is the translation of "direct" experience, which abstractive objectification can only make opaque and indirect. Legend and folktale, hagiography of saints are all manners of concretizing "mystical" experience in story and symbol; science can only catch the "concomitant processes" of the mystical (by analogy, again, to the way the lines on the polygraph page *correspond* to the moral domain of the lie). The "mystical" experience is human and has a world, involving the transposition of contact with the "other" world into the hieroglyphs of the mundane, a contact that emblazons this world with its own, intrinsic and most proper otherworldliness, its naturally supernatural, empyrean character.

Florensky offers a definition: "Myth is the symbolism of the profoundest experience projected onto the empirical . . . the foundation of all knowledge of reality." Myth directly offers the world in its most paradoxically objective; it is the truest vision of the world, offering abstractive rationality its original coordinates (through mythic intelligence's primary differentiations, such as chaos and order, that immanently structure human moral consciousness, giving a world as a place of lived action, of meaning, of significance). Legend is analogous, a lighter, but no less serious form of comprehension of the world: It is "the projection of mystical perceptions on concomitant empirical phenomena." Legend sees the world as a place of signs and draws forth the signs from out of its supra-theoretical or hyper-intelligible experience of the world. An "authentic legend (which is always religious in character) is a narrative about a miracle whose specialness is highlighted by signs."[17] The elusive but evident peculiar uniformity or core paradigms of intelligibility across traditions and cultures that structural anthropologists or phenomenologists of religion were always chasing evince a "connection between that which is symbolized and that which symbolizes."[18] The content of the stories are "projections of experiences corresponding to them," the perception of the fantastical or miraculous in the consciousness open to the empyrean gradations, represented by "certain empirical particularities" in the stories that crystalize as symbols, operation points for powers in their freedom outside of our *control*—and the system of representation that justifies, enacts and extends it, science and the enframing instrumentalization that eschews the *poetic* constructions of popular experience on which it stands, preventing the ὑπεράρχειν, the self-presencing of what is, in its allure and charm, to come forth as it is.

I have proposed, in the preceding pages, a reading of the tradition of negative theology that prioritizes symbol over concept, material immersion over abstraction, in knowing. The perspective I intended to develop sees the entire apophatic exercise as a preparation for sacramental encounter and that as an exercise in anticipation of the glorification of creation. Descent as end over ascent. Or, to say it in a more Dionysian, and Christian-theurgical way, descent as end of ascent. This approach, I tried to indicate, does the most justice to the whole scope of the tradition's material, in its ordered prioritization, Scripture, the Fathers, the Medievals and us. Beyond what I have been able to do here, this articulation of the apophatic program, insofar as it is a valid and even preferred intellectual expression of the Christian "way," in aspiration for harmony with its revealed sources, would more adequately prepare, I think, the Christian tradition for encounter with the wisdom traditions of the world that, through transforming emergence of understanding, deepens the Christian account rather than conforming it to a perceived understanding of σοφία ἀνθρώπων, "human wisdom." It would employ, then, on ever-again frontier territory, the tradition's classic method of *iusus iustus*/ὀρθὴ χρῆσις, as best I understand it.[19] From this vantage, I have tried to defend (if that is the right word) the axial age accomplishment of the recognition of the critical priority of narrative comprehension for human understanding (both for theoretical intelligence itself and a full understanding of ourselves). I have written, therefore, as a student of Plato and St. Paul (and both in the Pseudo-Dionysius and Cyril), all of whom, in their fidelity to myth and to symbol and to sacrament (whether philosophical or prophetic or both) have sought they key to the human mystery. I have only wanted to think in the light—to the utmost of my marginal ability—of the ἀποκάλυψις τοῦ Χριστοῦ as the disclosure of the σοφία τοῦ θεοῦ.[20] I think this wisdom has more to say. And we will only hear it by submerging ourselves, in its wake, into all the intellectual promenades, corridors and labyrinths of the human cultural world and—who can say—even beyond, into interdimensional or extraterrestrial worlds. It is at least imaginable. Theological ground is always virgin territory. And virgin territory is always theological ground.

Ἰδοὺ καίνα ποιῶ πάντα, "Behold, I am making all things new," says Jesus Christ in history from beyond it.[21] It is one simple believer's obscure and still-dawning hope of what that finally and fully renewed beginning promises for the world (τὰ πάντα, "all things," says St. Paul),[22] that I have offered this to any reader both patient and intrepid enough to have made it to the final pages, for it is that hope, and nothing else, that I have tried to understand a little better through the present labor, —and not without the help of many historical sources I respect, those I agree with or disagree with, all of whom I love for the gift of helping me better see. Perhaps there was something here that helped you see the Christian vision, and perhaps, as the Apostle urged, νοῦν Χριστοῦ ἔχειν, "to put on the intellect of Christ."²³

The "highest task of art," said Soloviev in his 1890, "The Universal Meaning of Art, "is the perfected incarnation of this spiritual fullness in our reality, a realization in it of absolute beauty . . . to give" [same thing] a true presentiment "of the life of the world to come."²⁴ By "this spiritual fullness," the philosopher meant "the metamorphosis of physical life into spiritual life," which, he explains, entails nothing less than that it "contains within itself," in descended, incarnate form "its Logos, or revelation . . . a life" therefore, "that has the capacity to inwardly convert or animate matter, or truly being incarnate in it," and, finally, a life that is ultimately "free from the material process [ruled by death] and therefore remains eternal." If we may be permitted to strike "art" from the first phrase and interpolate "all human things," then I think we have a way of conceiving the Christian thing fully in harmony with Soloviev's vision and that which I have tried to articulate here.

The concept serves the figure. λόγος explicates the myth. Reason functions against a mythic horizon. Narrative implicitly situates reason, permitting it an ordered milieu of distinctions that it goes to work on, seeing them and drawing out their structural significance. When a mythic milieu is challenged (perhaps by another, competing one, perhaps by the analytics of reason within it, perhaps by cultural exhaustion or some other cause), reason itself suffers challenge too. Reason loses its place when the myth falters. The myth must be refigured, repaired, perhaps even replaced. The question of reason's role in the work of repair, refigurement, or replacement is a large one. Let us only note here that reason has a role and perhaps even a significant one. Plato proposed this, as did Augustine, or Thomas Aquinas, Descartes, anyone working in the time of meaning crisis. (If there ever is a time that is not a time of meaning crisis is an interesting question. There are, surely, greater and lesser times. Our own time seems to be among the greater.) If Plato is our model, or St. Paul (or both, among many others, perhaps), it would seem that intellectual work serves, let us say, the refiguring repair of the received myth. For St. Paul, of course, it was revelation that goaded conceptual activity in a form that we may be right to call "theology." (By revelation, I mean divine action, historical event read as divine act, even definitive, or rather penultimate, which brings the story of Israel's election to its climax.) For Plato, it was intellectual vision, a spiritual perception, inchoate but real, goaded by a master (or set of masters: Socrates and some unknown

Pythagoreans) and pursued with every ounce of energy as a way of life, taught a skill of perception *through* the received myths, which purified and refigured them in forms that framed his rational activity and served as veiling revelations of our origin and end in the invisible world, similar to the way the body reveals the soul while also veiling it. Intellectual fidelity to an event, for example, the resurrection of Jesus of Nazareth on the third day, will certainly call on all one's intellectual resources to make a response. And one of the aspects of this response will involve reckoning with the way that this event requires a (hermeneutical) refiguring of the received stories of one's people, one's faith, and yet understood in a way that is consistent with them, that understands this event as light on this tradition's deepest meaning. And if a thinker or writer aspires to fidelity to that event and its meaning in today's crisis of meaning, that one writes as a Christian. If he believes in that event and trusts the apostolic witness to communicate the meaningfulness of it, he is in some sense (if there is any sense to it) "Christian." A minimalist definition, but one that works well enough for here. The (Pseudo-Dionysian) symbol, I have said, joins two. It joins, to make it plain, concept and image, or, at the widest, λόγος and μῦθος. Symbol is the specifically human achievement (as the Pseudo-Dionysius said), because of its mediating position between the angel and the beast, between the intellect and the sensory, between the spiritual and the material. The specific "function" of the human in the cosmic hierarchy is to join the two, two worlds, two orders, heaven and earth, ultimately and most profoundly, God and matter. The sacraments are enactive anticipations of this function, but so too, in a lesser but meaningfully anticipative mode still, is anything human, from art to technology to speech or the simplest act, even a gesture. The utterance "book" interweaves the intellectual and material domains, visibilizing the invisible and carrying up the visible into the invisible. All of this is classic Christian speculative reflection utilizing the *microcosmos* motif. Humans materialize the higher in the lower, elevating the lower to its hidden purpose, exposing its peculiar "principle of uniqueness" on the Christian account of things.

The argued for prioritization of incarnate symbolization over the concept, of the necessity and validity of anthropomorphism or the apophatics of the sensible, retains, despite the critique, the validity of the concept. Let no one accuse me, in these pages, of anti-intellectualism, I who used concepts, developed a theory, and made arguments throughout this work in order to show their subservience (activity that made it an intellectual work, a work of philosophy and/or theology, it makes little difference to me). The time has come, then, finally, for me to say something at least about the place of the concept. I will do so by reference to an epistemological distinction between propositional knowledge and factual truth, on the one hand, and personal knowledge and meaningful truth, on the other. Everyone knows the distinction, in French, between *savoir* and *connaissance*.[25] Propositional knowledge is abstract truth. Underwriting, at least in some of the least profound theories, by logical coherence, is all that it requires. To absence of error we can also add a correspondence with the facts. Propositional knowledge is belief about facts that is justified (by coherence, correspondence and/or verificational checks). "It is raining" either corresponds with the situation outside my window or it does not. Check. It either avoids absurdity or fallacy or does not. Check. It is falsifiable. Check. And so on. Personal knowledge, by contrast, belongs to truth that is felt as such. (Propositional knowledge, of course, includes an experience of "cognitive rest," but the affective dimension serves as a sort of external cap, a final verification, to the rational activity, at least if truth is a proposition.) Personal knowledge is meaningful. It involves speech, oral or written, that is, human communication. Personal knowledge pertains to truth that matters; it is knowledge of truth that is human, human truth. When the act of speech foregrounds the meaning or becomes meaningful to a reader or hearer, it is an event of truth and involves knowledge of a prioritized kind. In disclosing itself, it discloses a world, and in disclosing *its* world, it discloses *the* world, which is *seen* from a particular vantage. The more meaningful the truth, the more profound the view of the world. Propositional knowledge is merely the presentation of facts. In order to perform its activity (however valid or useful) it suppresses the world, the world of meaning, the world of presences within which the statement, as a human statement, is made. It functions purely at the level of *langue* and not *parole*. The statement, "he is risen!," lying somewhere close to the beating center of Christian belief and life, can be examined from both propositional and personal vantages, as an item of *langue* or *parole*, and so on. In doing so we see the difference between the *presentation* of fact and the *presencing* of meaning. Within the witness' exclamation that "he is risen!," however inexplicable apart from time and patience for rational reflection, the hazy outlines of a fundamentally transformative view of the world can be perceived. We see, here, the difference between two kinds of knowledge and two kinds (or perhaps modes) of truth. And we should see the reasonableness of the prioritization of one over the other, as well as the capaciousness of one vis-à-vis the other. (Personal knowledge permits a place, perhaps regulatory or verificational, within its scope, for propositional analysis, in an analogous way, perhaps, that within the entire human order, the scientific activity of methodologically bracketing the empirically unverifiable, however incomplete, in order to foreground the world's intrinsic physical order is permissible, not to mention remarkably productive and epistemologically remarkable as a human capacity.) Personal knowledge gives the human in giving the world. At the level of religious knowledge (I could also say "theological"), it may give God, disclose his presence, in intellectual modes as much as affective, that is, non-objective modes, of course. Propositional knowledge can be personal. Consider a religious dogma, for example. But it can detach itself from the personal and participatory by taking its rational rigor for the (meaningful) truth (as opposed to its disclosure in propositional mode, and forgetting its place in a wider milieu of disclosure, such as the liturgy or prayer), as in the dogmatist, for example. Truth is supremely meaningful or it is not the truth.

The perception of this distinction between personal and propositional knowledge carries a large implication for the argument now reaching some kind of resolution. The implication is that both figure and concept, poetry and philosophy, myth and reason may serve to presence the meaningfulness of things. And yet these two domains do so in distinct ways. Λόγος may presence meaningful truth as much as μῦθος. And yet, if Plato and St. Paul are our guides, it only does so by reference to μῦθος (whether implicitly or explicitly), the *received* μῦθος that it respects for its divine origin, however distinctly these are conceived (as an event of primordial speech carried through yet marred by the sacred traditions, or as the *history* of a people personally covenanted with the Creator for the completion of his creation, who, despite their infidelity, justifies himself in their election). There is no correspondence to reality in myth except in a problematic way, but there is a communication of the meaning of the deepest enigmas of the human experience. And it is only in this "personal" context that, in the last analysis, the propositional has any value at all. It is only because the world is meaningful, or at least holds out the promise of meaningfulness, that logic matters. Figure and image and narrative disclose the truth, giving us sight in the world, on ourselves and before higher things in this phenomenological sense. Concept does too. Yet it discloses in its own manner. By way of classification, concepts disclose the intrinsic order of things. They name the fundamental distinctions that presence the world, and thereby they make things present. The concept "red" can be delineated on the chromatic spectrum as possessing a relatively long wavelength, or as a primary color with various cultural connotations (say, romantic "heat," when paired with black or navy blue, or "purity" when paired with white) and physiological effects (increased heart rate or appetite stimulation). When the poet tells me how much depends on the wet "red wheelbarrow" sitting in the yard beside the chickens, I learn nothing propositional, but I am stopped in my tracks. And reflection is provoked. I could, as scholars have, unfold or pursue the meaning (or meaningfulness) of the poem, and the view on the world (and on myself, and perhaps even God) that it elicits, possibly without ever coming to an end. I will use concept and theory to do so. When the concepts, in their grip on things, become opaque to them, then they will have lost their own significance, though I can continue to utilize them, enchanted by their coherence or grip, their classifying power, for God knows how long. But in doing so I will have lost something important, perhaps essential. This is not to say that this or that concept or image, or even the symbol that joins them enjoys a final or definitive meaningfulness. Truth (or rather our access to it) is historical and its meaning is "placed." This is what makes it human. But the promise and hope in the definitive presence (and therefore enjoyment) of a truth that totally incorporates the historical and worldly dimensions of meaning, that is, our full humanity, accomplishing the unification of God and world, of absolute and particular, of eternity and time, of unity and multiplicity, and, in and through humanity, all things, is what gives meaning, so to speak, to meaning on the Christian account. What else but such an unending vocation could truly beatify us, filling all our potential? If I cannot enjoy a nap in the shade of tree (or a glass of wine and good conversation) in the "vision of God," what kind of God is that? Of course, I expect the tree and the nap to be realities of which my experience of a pleasant moment at my grandfather's house to be only a shadow. There will be a reader (or two) who will find my attempt to embrace the eschatological (and its present implications) imprudent. And that reader will be right. With the eschatological we can only stammer and finally fall silent as the intellectual performs its task of opening our eyes to the divine things we suffer. And it is with the recognition of that silence that I wish to close, knowing that tomorrow (if it comes) I will have to return to the contemplation of "all things human and divine," first and finally in the body that I fully (but not merely) am, the body whose fullness I do not understand.

Appendix

Annotations to a Few *Loci Classici*

I annotate three texts, by Cassian, Aquinas, and Paul. The Cassian text is from his *Conferences*, number 10, where he discusses the "Anthropomorphite" heresy. In this context, prayer is understood as a deconstruction of mental images in order to transcend the world to God. I ask the question here about the status of "image" in a Christian context. I propose that Cassian is offering, not a rejection of "image" per se but an eschatological one. Aquinas: a text on the distinction between the will and intellect and their hierarchical relation vis-à-vis their ultimate "object" God. Paradoxically, for Thomas, the will has relative priority over the intellect since it is the "direct" path to God in acts of love, whereas the intellect is always indirect, since it must pass through the material domain first. Both Cassian and Aquinas imply a refigured conception of "image" whereby the anthropomorphic form comes from God: humans are "theomorph" first—even in the domain of the will—and this serves as the primary, pragmatic condition for valid anthropomorphic truths of reasoning. Knowledge grounded then in right practice. Paul's text is the Philippians hymn. Here we find the origin of this kind of theological reasoning.

John Cassian (d. 435)

Conferences, X, "The Second Conference of Abbot Isaac. On Prayer"
Chapter 3, "Of Abbot Serapion and the Heresy of the Anthropomorphites into Which He Fell in the Error of Simplicity"[1]

> When he [Photinus, "learned deacon" from Cappadocia] explained that the image and likeness of God was taken by all the leaders of the churches not according to the base sound of the letters, but spiritually, and supported this very fully and by many passages of Scripture, and showed that nothing of this sort could happen to that infinite and incomprehensible and invisible glory,[a] so that it could be

comprised in a human form and likeness, since its nature is incorporeal and uncompounded and simple, and what can neither be apprehended by the eyes nor conceived by the mind, at length, the old man [Serapion] was shaken by the numerous and very weighty assertions of this most learned man, and was drawn to the faith of the Catholic tradition.[b] And when Abbot Paphnutius and all of us were filled with intense delight at his adhesion, for this reason, namely, that the Lord had not permitted a man of such age and crowned with such virtues, and one who erred only from ignorance and rustic simplicity, to wander from the path of the right faith up to the very last, and when we arose to give thanks, and were all together offering up prayers to the Lord, the old man was so bewildered in mind during his prayer because he felt that the Anthropomorphic image of the Godhead, which he used to set before himself in prayer, was banished from his heart, that on a sudden he burst into a flood of bitter tears and continual sobs, and cast himself down on the ground and exclaimed with strong groaning: "Alas! Wretched man that I am![c] They have taken away my God from me, and I have now none to lay hold of; and whom to worship and address I know not." By which scene we were terribly disturbed, and moreover with the effect of the former Conference still remaining in our hearts, we returned to Abbot Isaac, whom when we saw close at hand, we addressed these words.[d]

[a]
The basic or perennial debate in Christian theology, like ancient philosophy, concerns the appropriate manner of conceiving God. Can we think God without misrepresenting God, without committing idolatry? Theophilus, patriarch of Alexandria, wrote his now lost festal letters of 399 on the "Anthropomorphite heresy." In these letters, he proposes that images are restricted to the visible domain and can only signify corporeal things like themselves. Images cannot therefore convey the invisible nature of God. For Cassian, partaking of the same theological tradition, prayer is an act of deconstructing our images, which are used as leaping off points to enter the divine presence in prayer.

[b]
The "Anthropomorphites," according to Isaac's definition, "maintained with obstinate perverseness that the infinite and simple substance of the Godhead is fashioned in our lineaments and human configuration" (X, 5). They pray with images, and thereby conceive of God as an image of man—in fact they identify the anthropomorphic form with God: there is a univocal relation between

the image (human form) and the archetype (the divine form). Consequently, God has a body, a face, hands, feet: these biblical images are not metaphors but descriptions of God. For Isaac, however, true prayer is wholly imageless, without mediation, a "looking upon the "glory of [Christ's] face and the image of his splendour" with the "pure eyes of the soul" (X, 6).

c
Commenting on this passage in a lecture, "The Image of the Invisible" (2009),[2] Olivier Boulnois notes that the great iconoclastic debates of Eastern Christianity were resolved only after three centuries by overcoming this concept of image represented by Egyptian monasticism that is the basis of the anthropomorphite theology and that of Isaac and John Cassian. The iconodules held that the humanity of Christ, his essentially anthropomorphic character, was a *unique* image, one in which the *identification* of the visible and invisible is achieved. Christ is the hypostatic union, where the human nature of Jesus *is* the human nature of a divine person, through which the invisible is made visible in a definitive but inexhaustible way. The anthropomorphic form of an icon, therefore, is a representation through which the invisible divinity is given; yet it is not a representation of the nature (οὐσία) of the invisible God, which is impossible, but is rather a representation of the humanity of Jesus, whose personal identity (ὑπόστασις) is both divine and human. Such a revised conception of the image is possible, even necessary, concludes, Boulnois, because the anthropomorphism is, in this singular case, the opposite of that which the iconoclasts castigated (passing from human form to God, "circumscribing" God by the anthropomorphic form by which one represents him); rather, here, the human form (assumed by the Son in Jesus) *comes from God*: the humanity assumed by the Son is, before the Incarnation, and as its condition, is an "anthropomorphosis," to quote Falque, see later) of the divine speech; the Incarnation is the self-"anthropomorphosis" of God. God gives the human form to us; he conceives us and caught up into that perfect conception of us that God has (the man Jesus Christ), we are elevated to him by the transformation of our humanity.

d
Is Cassian a straightforward iconoclast? In Cassian's vision, the goal of the monk's life of prayer is to achieve a heavenly state already within the earthly mode, to reach, as it were, further into the human destiny from the midst of

the present time. This is what Christ came to give us—the means to reach that universal human end, which can be anticipated in advance:

> still He retired into the mountain alone to pray, thus teaching us by the example of his retirement that if we too wish to approach God with a pure and spotless affection of heart [the only way, he says, to approach God], we should also retire from all the disturbances and confusion of crowds, so that while still living in the body we may manage in some degree to adapt ourselves to some likeness of that bliss which is promised hereafter to the saints. (X, 6)

The transfiguration of Christ on the mountain with his three most intimate disciples becomes the guiding image of monastic life:

> This then ought to be the destination of the solitary, this should be all his aim that it may be vouchsafed to him to possess even in the body an image of future bliss, and that he may begin in this world to have a foretaste of a sort of earnest [down payment] of that celestial life and glory. This . . . is the end of all perfection . . . the whole life and all the thoughts of the heart become one continuous prayer.(X, 7)

Here, for Isaac, through refusing every image, by transcending every concept, one, like Christ, becomes the image, *incarnates* the union with divine glory that is the singular human destiny. Hence, if anthropomorphism is rejected by the Cassian tradition, this is only for the sake of *a greater anthropomorphism*, where the "image and likeness of God" (Genesis 2) becomes fully so. The original biblical injunction against images is based on an affirmation of a divinely ordained image: the living human person. But it is the perfected human person, in unspeakable union with God, that is the true likeness of God. For the theology of the Egyptian deserts, we don't become less human by virtue of union with God, but all the more human the more like God we become, straining to place ourselves beyond the present order of the world from within its very heart. In the present, within the horizon of the world, this takes the form of radical asceticism, by which one can achieve at least an anticipation of the eternal life when all things are transfigured in God and God is "all in all."

Thomas Aquinas (d. 1274)

ST I, 82, 3, resp.³

"Whether the will is a higher power than the intellect?"

> The superiority of one thing over another can be considered in two ways: *absolutely* and *relatively*. Now a thing is considered to be such absolutely which is considered such in itself: but relatively as it is such with regard to something else. If therefore the intellect and will be considered with regard to themselves [i.e. absolutely], then the intellect is the higher power.... [the intellect possesses the idea of that which the will seeks, "the good"].... Therefore since the proper nature of a power is in its order to its object, it follows that the intellect in itself and absolutely is higher and nobler than the will. But relatively and by comparison with something else, we find that the will is sometimes higher than the intellect, from the fact that the object of the will occurs in something higher than that in which occurs the object of the intellect. Thus for instance, I might say that hearing is relatively nobler than sight, inasmuch as something in which there is sound is nobler than something in which there is color, though color is nobler and simpler than sound. For, as we have said above [q. 16, a. 1; q. 27, a. 4], the action of the intellect consists in this—that the idea of the thing understood is in the one who understands; while the act of the will consist in this—that the will is inclined to the thing itself as existing in itself. And therefore the philosopher says in *Metaph*. VI that *good and evil*, which are objects of the will, *are in things*, but *truth and error*, which are objects of the intellect, are *in the mind*.ᵃ When, therefore, the thing in which there is good is nobler than the soul itself, in which is the idea understood—by comparison with such a thing—the will is higher than the intellect. But when the thing which is good is less noble than the soul, then even in comparison with that thing the intellect is higher than the will. Wherefore the love of God is better than the knowledge of God; but on the contrary, the knowledge of corporeal things is better than the love thereof.ᵇ Absolutely, however, the intellect is nobler than the will.ᶜ

a

Anselm, echoing Augustine, said God is *that than which nothing greater can be conceived*: he is above and beyond conceiving; he is always greater than any idea we have of him. This separates Christianity, where God is (at best) living and personal, from (classical) philosophy, where God is (at worst) the highest and governing idea of a system of thought. At best, classical philosophy conceives of the highest idea, the Good, as the greatest intensity of being, indeed, as the paradigm (so to speak) of being, beyond being but that toward which being, insofar as it is being, aspires. At worst, Christian intellectual tradition (in the practice thereof) reduces the divine reality to one's idea of that reality, that is, the governing conception of a scheme of being—as the highest being by which the scheme of being in its totality makes final sense. Anselm, again echoing Augustine, also said, *if you can conceive it, it is not God*. Here, even between the classical and the Christian at their best, we have two fundamentally competing ideas of the nature of divine "transcendence": this turns on the idea of the Living God.

b

Pascal's *pensée* 298, *The heart has its order, the mind its own, which uses principles and demonstrations. The heart has a different one. We do not prove that we ought to be loved by setting out in order the causes of love; that would be absurd.* Commenting on this a contemporary philosopher refers to our passage in Aquinas. He says:

> St. Thomas says that it is better to know a stone than to love a stone but better to love God than to know God, because love conforms the lover to the beloved, while knowledge conforms the known object to the way-of-knowing of the knower. When we love a dog, we become more doggy, but when we know a dog, we raise it up to our own level: thought. When we know God, we drag him down to our anthropomorphic level, we make God more humanoid than he really is; but when we love God, we are raised up more loosely to his level, we become more God-like than we were (for "God is love").[4]

c

> Love, which is an act of the appetitive faculty, even in this life tends primarily to God and from him passes on to other things. Accordingly, charity loves God directly but other things through the mediation of God. In knowledge, however, the converse is true, since we know God through other things, either as cause through effects or by way of eminence or negation. (Thomas, ST II-II, 27, 4)

The intellect is "higher" than the will, when both are conceived "absolutely," that is, in themselves, or rather, in God. By "higher" the Dominican means "nobler" or "superior" in value. Conceived in themselves, in their truth, that is, in God, intellect and the order of knowledge is superior, for the reasons he gives. Relatively speaking, that is, within the domain of the relative—that is, from within the human relation to God—but also relative to one another, the will is nobler, for the reasons he gives. The will is "inclined to the thing as existing in itself" whereas the intellect has no inclination at all, for its object (knowledge) is within itself. Therefore: "love of God is better than the knowledge of God."

Paul of Tarsus (d. *c.* 67)

The Philippian Hymn (2.6–11)[5]

5. Let this mind be in you, which was also in Christ Jesus;[a]
6. Who, being in the form of God [μορφὴ θεοῦ], thought it not robbery to be equal with God;
7. But emptied himself, and took upon himself the form of a servant [μορφὴν δούλου], and having been born in the likeness of men [ὁμοιώματι ἀνθρώπων], and being found in the appearance of man [σχήματι ἄνθρωπος];[b]
8. He humbled himself, and became obedient unto death, even death on a cross;
9. Wherefore God also has highly exalted him, and given him a name which is above every name;
10. That at the name of Jesus every knee should bow, everything in heaven, and in earth, and under the earth;
11. And every tongue confess that Jesus Christ is Lord, to the glory of God the Father.[c]

a

There is much to say about this famous passage in the letters of Paul. As a way of sort of swallowing the whole pill, let us simply observe Paul's transformation of a passage from the prophets in vv. 10-11: "By myself I have sworn, my mouth has uttered in all integrity a word that will not be revoked: Before me every knee will bow; by me every tongue will swear" (Isa. 45:23; quoted by Paul also in Rom. 14:23). The earliest Christianity has inserted Christ into the heart of the picture of Jewish worship: now, by virtue of God's action in and through Christ, "confessing" Christ as Lord is the path of the "glorification" of the Father. Here we touch that which makes Christianity what it is, in all of its unsettling strangeness: the death and resurrection of God's "anointed," his appointed servant, which, paradoxically, means "world ruler," is precisely the means by which God's original intention for the creation is finally accomplished ("the kingdom of God"), and this human Image of the Father, Jesus of Nazareth stands at the center of it.

b

It is worth comparing this Christian vision of God, its metamorphosis of the Jewish vision, with one from the earliest days of Greek philosophy: that of

Xenophanes, the teacher of Parmenides (fifth century BC). Fragments of his critique of anthropomorphism are found in Clement of Alexandria's *Stromateis* [third century AD; lit. "patchwork quilt"]:

> Xenophanes of Colophon, teaching that god is one and incorporeal, rightly says, *There is one god, greatest among gods and men, similar to mortals neither in shape or thought* [B23]. And again: *But mortals think that gods are born, and have clothes and speech and shape like their own* [B14]. And again: *but if cows and horses or lions had hands and drew with their hands and made the things men make, then horses would draw the forms of gods like horses, cows like cows, and each would make their bodies similar in shape to their own* [B15]. (*Stromateis*, V, xiv, 109.1–3)

In book VII, iv, 22.1, Clement also refers to Xenophanes' critique of the mythical conception of the divinity: "The Greeks suppose that just as the gods have human shapes so they have human feelings; and just as each race depicts their shapes as similar to their own, as Xenophanes says, *the Ethiopians making them dark and snub-nosed, the Thracians red-haired and blue-eyed* [B16], so too they imagine that they are similar to themselves in their souls."[6] For Clement, of course, this critique of the base anthropomorphisms of the myths, the emergence of philosophy in Greece, is a step out of darkness into light: it is an anticipation of Christianity.

c

Commenting on Clement's full approval of Xenophanes' critique of pagan religion, Parisian philosopher Emmanuel Falque, perhaps uniquely, wants to move beyond such a view inasmuch as, he says, "the Christian accusation that the pagan practices of anthropomorphism is such that the flight of God into a nonhuman, even inhuman, world seems definitive." He does not, of course, want to return today to an original pagan naïveté or an anthropomorphite account of the divine nature. Instead, he says, Clement's full acceptance of the philosophical critique of myths was

> necessary at the time in order not to reduce God simply to the idol of man. Bearing in mind, however, the incarnation and resurrection, we note that such a gap between human beings and God ... was ill considered. Not that mankind ought to reduce God to mankind's image ... but that God himself, taking note, as it were, of these nuptials of human finitude [i.e. incarnation and resurrection], brings the wedding ceremony to its full conclusion.

"There is thus," Falque continues, "an appropriate kind of *anthropomorphism*, or perhaps an *anthropomorphosis* by God, that it has been a mistake for Christianity to forget." Quoting the Philippian hymn, Falque notes the difference between the *anthropomorphism* rightly critiqued in paganism, which constrained the divine by the shape of the human intellect, and the *anthropomorphosis* of Christianity, the transformation of the human condition by God's "nuptial" encounter with us:

> It was not the initiative of human beings, but of God, that he should become like mankind, adopt the human form, and be recognized as such. God does this by the incarnation and even more by the resurrection, which does not make him leave his body but allows him to live his body differently and so incorporates forever the form of man in the Trinitarian perichoresis. The God of the Christians is thus in some way "anthropomorph," whatever theology sometimes thinks.[7]

Here Christianity is neither inscribed within the mythic picture of the divine, nor the critique of μῦθος by a purified conceptual apparatus, "logos," but in some way incorporates both in an altogether different mode. The key to the whole picture can be found in the Christian conviction that (let us say) *Personality is higher than Abstraction*, that the divine Essence is not an abstract idea but living act, and that therefore Essence and Person are distinct rationally but equally absolute-as-one in reality, in God. Here anthropomorphism is finally required to transcend abstraction toward the mystery of the divine tri-hypostatic personality. The Essence of God is not dead, but alive, the Essence of the Tri-hypostatic Personality of the Uncreated One that Knows itself as infinite consciousness and Experiences itself as such as the pure bliss of infinite love. Abstract *negation* of images, symbols, narratives, if considered absolute, become a way, then, of pushing away the divine reality, the living God himself, the one to whom alone every negation must finally be negated, where, somehow, the experience of apophatic non-duality becomes preparation for the face-to-face encounter in the ἀποκάλυψις τῆς ἀποφάσεως τοῦ αἰσθητοῦ—the revelation of the apophasis of the sensible—the End that was always already present πρὸ καταβολῆς κόσμου, from the beginning of ourselves, awoken to as an invitation to unfathomable and eternal adventure.

Notes

Preface

1 I refer the reader to Whitehead's *Symbolism* (New York: Fordham University Press, 1985).
2 Christos Yannaras, *Elements of Faith: An Introduction to Orthodox Theology*, trans. Keith Schram (London: Continuum, 1991), 50–1.

Introduction

1 *The Pilgrim of the Absolute*, ed. Raissa Maritain (Tacoma: Cluny Media, 2017), 68.
2 Ibid., 89.
3 Ibid., xxiii.
4 Ibid., xxiii–xxiv.
5 For Schleiermacher's term, see §§ 4–5 of the introduction to the second edition of *The Christian Faith*.
6 *The Pilgrim of the Absolute*, 251.
7 See Jean-Yves Lacoste's lectures *From Theology to Theological Thinking* (Charlottesville: University of Virginia Press, 2014), to which I refer here and under the perpetual direction of which I labor.
8 *The Pilgrim of the Absolute*, xxiv.
9 Dei Verbum § 24. *The Documents of Vatican II*, ed. Walter M. Abbot, SJ (New York: American Publishers, 1966), 127.
10 Ibid., xxiv. (Italics mine).
11 Ibid., 88.
12 T. S. Eliot, *The Four Quartets* (New York: Harcourt Brace, 1971), 30.
13 Ibid., 31.

Chapter 1

1 "Theology: The Old Covenant" (IV.1; vol. 6 of the English translation).
2 Balthasar, *The Glory of the Lord, vol. 6, Theology: The Old Covenant*, trans. Brian McNeil (Edinburgh: T&T Clark, 1991), 31–2.

3 Ibid., 34.
4 Ibid., 34–5.
5 Ibid., 35.
6 "Theophany and Indication: Reconciling Augustinian and Palamite Aesthetics," *Modern Theology* 26, no. 1 (2010): 76–89.
7 For the essential discussion of indication, see Husserl, *Logical Investigations*, vol. 2, ch. 1, §§1–4 (in Findlay's English translation, it is found in vol. 1 [Abingdon: Routledge, 2001], 269–74).
8 Ibid., 270.
9 Balthasar, *The Glory of the Lord*, vol. 6, 34, 35. Emphasis added.
10 See Maurice Merleau-Ponty, *The Visible and the Invisible*, ch. 2 (Evanston: Northwestern University Press, 1968), 50–103.
11 Onomatodoxy, the intelligibility of which is based on this principle, was established as an important influence on advances in the mathematical ideas of the infinite in the early Moscow School. See Laren Graham and Jean-Michel Kantor, *Naming Infinity* (Cambridge: Belknap Press, 2009), and Sergius Bulgakov, *Icons and the Name of God*, trans. Boris Jakim (Grand Rapids: Eerdmans, 2012).
12 *Lost in the Cosmos: The Last Self-Help Book* (New York: Farrar, Straus and Giroux, 1983).
13 Ibid., 32–3.
14 Of course, this certainly strengthens Manoussakis' claim for an implicit reference to Husserl here.
15 Ibid., 12.
16 Ibid.
17 Roland Barthes' remark is pertinent here: "Thanks to what in the image is purely image (which is in fact very little), we do without language yet never cease to understand each other." See *Image-Music-Text*, trans. Stephen Heath (New York: Hill and Wang, 1978), 61.
18 Ibid., 11.
19 The notion of "sensory manifestation," named several times, may be taken as coincident with "theophanic indication." The empirical sign—"signs and wonders"—accompanying divine speech carries with it, precisely, the sense of absoluteness, the radically excessive character of the presence given to speech. The divine speech gives words to the sensible experience, interpreting it as indicative of itself, of the Absolute. To qualify this as "empiricism" is only true in the sense that it could contribute (and in fact has, historically) to the qualified empiricism that would require knowledge to move from the visible to the invisible, from the logic of the material order to its higher ground (as in, for example, Thomas Aquinas).
20 Husserl, *Logical Investigations*, vol. 2, Investigation 1, §4, 274. Emphasis original.
21 Ibid.

22 Ibid., 12. Verse locations are provided by Balthasar. I excise them here for the sake of concision since all Christian theologians, anyway, are intimately familiar with them through the constant meditation requisite for their assumption of the job title.
23 Ibid., 59. The God of Jesus Christ is one of limitless glory, an abyss of holiness that burns as an infinite fire of love. In other words, God is serious business. Even philosophers have to find a way to acknowledge this, to sense and be aware of it, letting it guide their intellectual-pragmatic tasks.
24 Ibid., 57.
25 The gift that is given is faith. Faith, which is the believer's own precisely as given from beyond him, allows him to see the invisible. The "eyes of faith" are not, therefore, a compensation for a deficit of intuition, as in: "I don't see the step before me in the darkness but I must step out into the void anyway." Rather, it is the response appropriate to an excess of phenomenological intuition over one's conceptual, theoretical grasp of what is given. One pledges one's believing trust to what appears, in the invisible revelation of glory that he is given eyes to see. A mundane example is the love between friends. One does not see that love itself but knows it perfectly well. Faith, its particular kind of seeing, and knowledge are not opposed. See Jean-Luc Marion, "The Recognition of the Gift," and "They Recognized Him, and He became Invisible to Them," chs. 10 and 11, respectively, of *Believing in Order to See*, trans. Crina Gschwandtner (New York: Fordham University Press, 2017), 125–43.
26 Bernard, *On Loving God*, trans. Robert Walton, OSB (Collegeville: Cistercian Publications, 2009).
27 Balthasar, The *Glory of the Lord*, vol. 6, 59.
28 Emmanuel Levinas, "Meaning and Sense," in *Collected Philosophical Papers*, ed. Alphonso Lingis (Dordrecht, Netherlands: Martinus Nijhoff, 1987), 106–7.
29 *Summa theologiae* I, 1, 1 resp. obj. 2.
30 Ratzinger, in *Truth and Tolerance*, 173, speaks of the "two apparently contradictory fundamental principles of Christianity—the link with metaphysics and the link with history."
31 For an elaboration of this fundamentally anti-Gnostic point, see Balthasar's introductory essay to his selections from Irenaeus' *Against Heresies*: *Scandal of the Incarnation*, trans. John Saward (San Francisco: Ignatius Press, 1990). The Patristic intellectual setting of any repossession of an apophatics of the sensible is most important. See Chapters 5 and 7 on Pseudo-Dionysius and Cyril of Alexandria.
32 H. Dielz and W. Kranz, *Die Fragmente der Vorsokratiker*, 10th edn (Berlin, 1952), B23–24. Englished by Jonathan Barnes, *Early Greek Philosophy* (New York: Penguin, 2001), 42–3, slightly amended.
33 See appendix for this critique and its significance.

34 To better understand the Eucharist as "paradigm of *theōsis*" the reader should pair what is said here with Augustine's reflection in *City of God* X.6. "Sacrifice," he says there, "is a divine thing." See also, of course, Jean-Luc Marion, "Sketch of a Phenomenological Concept of Sacrifice," in *Phenomenologies of Scripture*, ed. Adam Wells (New York: Fordham, 2017), 44–64.
35 Lacoste, *Experience and the Absolute*, 72.
36 Pseudo-Dionysius the Areopagite, *The Divine Names* 596A-C and 645C (*Complete Works*, 55–6 and 64).
37 Ibid. 640 A (*Complete Works*, 60): ὥσπερ τινὰ κανόνα κάλλιστον ἀληθείας. The entire line of thought developed here is essential.

Chapter 2

1 On this theme, the reader may wish to make a mental note regarding my *Eclipse of World*, presently being revised for publication.
2 I hope the text would profitably be read in concert with Study 5 of William C. Hackett, *Philosophy in Word and Name* (Brooklyn: Angelico Press, 2020), 174–208, which, around the Pauline concept of *apocalypsis*, elaborates comparatively between Marion and Lacoste.
3 *Quaest. Subt.*, q. 15, n. 16. Cited in Emmanuel Falque, *Dieu, la chair et l'autre*, 463.
4 See St. Augustine, *De genesi ad litteram*, IV, 32, 49: "And so the human mind first experiences through the senses of the body the things that have been made, and from there gains such knowledge of them as its human weakness allows; and next it looks for their causes, if by any manner of means it may attain them where they abide primordially and unchangingly in the Word of God. . . . The angelic mind, on the other hand, adhered in analloyed charity to the Word of God, after being created in due order before all the rest, and so it first saw in the Word of God the things to be made before they were made. . . . Once they were made like that, it also came to know them in themselves, with an inferior kind of knowledge of course, which was called evening" (*The Literal Meaning of Genesis*, trans. Edmund Hill [Hyde Park: New City Press, 2013], 270).
5 See ST I-II, q. 4, a. 3 and 5–6.
6 On the theme of metamorphosis, see Emmanuel Falque, *The Metamorphosis of Finitude*, trans. George Hughes (New York: Fordham University Press, 2012).
7 By "saecular," as opposed to the merely "secular," I mean to indicate the final priority of the theological account of history, which turns on perhaps the most basic distinction of common Christian apostolic witness (if there ever was one), the apocalyptic notion of the two ages as this developed out of a major strand of the Judaism of the Second Temple Era. The merely "secular" (as non-theological, non-

religious, merely natural) is only possible from within this primordial distinction of the West. From the theological point of view (and every point of view is finally theological), secularism must be conceived of as a Christian heresy, that is, a religious decision predicated on Christian assumptions.

8 This is important because it transposes the knowledge of God, now the paradigm of all knowledge, onto the mundane sphere. The exigency of this transposition explains, perhaps, Aquinas' specific developments of the Areopagite in the threefold way. I return to this in Chapter 4.

9 Parisian philosopher, Jean Wahl expressed this simultaneity of transcendence as upward movement exteriorily, which is elicited by the other, and also as a drive inward toward interiority. In Levinas, the simultaneity of this double movement, of transascendence and transdescendence, is found in the relation to an alterity that can never be reached becomes the condition of the possibility of the interior selfhood of the "subject" itself. In Henry, it is the opposite, the autoaffected interiority of the self is the condition for the construction of a movement outside of the self. For Wahl, this duality is irreducible in both directions, for one side is incomprehensible without the other. See Jean Wahl, *Existence humaine et transcendance* (1944).

10 In this vein, the reader may wish to consult Gregory Rocca, *Speaking the Incomprehensible God* (Washington, DC: Catholic University of America Press, 2002).

11 "Sin is that which removes the possibility of grounding, and, therefore, explanation, i.e., the possibility of reasonableness. In the chase after sinful *rationalism*, the consciousness is deprived of the reason inherent in all being. Because of over-intellectualization, the consciousness ceases to see intelligently. Sin itself is something wholly rational. It is wholly according to the measure of rationality. It is rationality in rationality, or devilry, for the Devil-Mephistopheles is naked rationality" (Pavel Florensky, *The Pillar and Ground of the Truth*, trans. Boris Jakim [Princeton: Princeton University Press, 1997], 133). For a profound meditation on the "dark face" of creation in the fall of man, its depravity and demonic self-absorption, see Sergei Bulgakov, *The Lamb of God*, trans. Boris Jakim (Eerdmans, 2008), 149–56.

12 *Hoc quod amant velint esse vertitatem*. Confessions X, 23, 34.

13 *Amant eam lucentem, oderun eam redarguentem*: "They love the truth when it enlightens them, but hate it when it reprehends them." Augustine, *Confessions*, X, 23, 34; Heidegger discusses this text in "Augustinianism and Neoplatonism," §10 c, *Phenomenology of Religious Life*, 147–8.

14 Heidegger, "Augustinianism and Neoplatonism," 148.

15 Ibid.

16 The concept of the "last word" and the framing of thought by the logos of the eschaton originates in Jean-Yves Lacoste. See, for example, the final pages of *Être en Danger* (Paris: Cerf, 2011), 358–70.

17 This is a thesis (or is it a quip?) of Stanislas Breton, developed in *Théorie des idéologies et la réponse de la foi*.
18 See Stanislas Breton's interview with Richard Kearney, appended to the English translation of *The Word and the Cross*, 137.
19 See *Being Given*, trans. Jeffrey Kosky (Stanford: Stanford University Press, 2002), 211–12. Here the saturated phenomenon is "absolute," that is, "without analogy" to anything in previous experience, and therefore "depends on no horizon." Marion calls it, therefore, an "unconditioned phenomenon."
20 See Marion, *Certitudes négatives* (Paris: Grassette and Fasquelle, 2010), conclusion.
21 "Débat," in *Dieu en tant que Dieu: La question philosophique*, ed. Philippe Capelle-Dumont (Paris: Cerf, 2012), 282.
22 *Being Given*, 265: "Only the impact of what gives itself brings about its arising, with one and the same shock, of the flash with which its first visibility bursts and the very screen on which it crashes." Shane Mackinlay, *Interpreting Excess* (New York: Fordham, 2009), highlights, for us, this ambivalence by arguing that Marion's conception of saturated phenomena implies an "active reception," a hermeneutical moment, which is always already in play.
23 "The given, issued from the process of givenness, appears but leaves concealed givenness itself, which becomes enigmatic"(*Being Given*, 68).
24 "The appearing . . . gives that which appears" (*Being Given*, 52); that is to say, the concept of givenness gives, or rather marks, phenomenology's access to the transcendent "thing itself," transcendence within immanence without constricting transcendence to the contents of consciousness, as in Husserl.
25 See Smadar Bustan, "Givenness and the Orthodox Jew: Aporias in Marion's Theory of Saturated Phenomena," *ThéoRèmes* [online], uploaded 12 July 2010, accessed October 8, 2012. http://theoremes.revues.org/63; doi: 10.4000/theoremes.63. "The term 'ungiven' does not appear in Marion's works."
26 See Lacoste, "La présence et la demeure," *L'intuition sacramentelle et autres essais* (Paris: Ad Solem, 2015), 29–57.
27 159–77, esp. 174–7.
28 Though not, of course, from anthropomorphic measure, since the category of event is supremely human.
29 See Denzinger, # 530 (Heinrich Denzinger, *Enchiridion Symbolorum*, 37th ed. [Freiburg: Herder, 1991], 216–17): Benedict XII "Benedictus Deus" (29 January 1366): "have seen and see the divine essence by intuitive vision, and even face to face, with no mediating creature, serving in the capacity of an object seen, but divine essence immediately revealing itself, plainly, clearly and openly to them."
30 The *comprehensor*, as far as beatitude goes, for Aquinas means not "the inclusion of the comprehended in the *comprehensor*," since "whatever is comprehended [in this way] by a finite creature is itself [merely] finite." Rather, "comprehension

means nothing but the holding of something already present and possessed: thus one who runs after another is said to comprehend him when he lays hold of him" (ST I-II, q. 4, a. 3, rep. 1). Comprehension in the beatific vision, therefore, means being finally present to the One that we seek, not exhaustively grasping his essence, which is impossible. For Aquinas, every revelation of God wholly reveals him but not fully, which is impossible given that God can only be exhaustively known by himself and we are only granted a share in that knowledge according to the maximum of our finite capabilities, which are themselves only known a posteriori, and therefore, in revelation, remain the most fully secured compared to any other act of knowledge.

31 *Apologia pro vita sua*, 18.
32 See, among a number of places in his oeuvre, Saint Thomas Aquinas, *Summa Theologiae* I, q. 75, a. 5.
33 *Omne enim quod cognoscitur non secundum sui vim sed secundum cognoscentium potius comprehenditur facultatem* (Boethius, *On the Consolation of Philosophy*, LCL 74, p. 410 lns. 75–77).
34 *Sed intellgentia quasi desuper spectans concepta forma quae subsunt etiam cuncta diiudicat, sed eo modo quo formam ipsam, quae nulli alii nota esse poterat, comprehendit* (410, lns 97–100; here I amend the English translation found *en face*.)
35 See David Bentley Hart's criticisms of Marion from this vantage in the second chapter of *You Are Gods* (South Bend: University of Notre Dame Press, 2022), esp. 27–30.
36 *D'Ailleurs, La Revelation* (Paris: Grasseet, 2020), 75.
37 For his definitive statement of this, see *D'Ailleurs, La Revelation*, part III, chs. 3–6.
38 See *D'Ailleurs, La Revelation*, 73–4.
39 Marion's comments on Suarez are critical here. For him, this propositionality of revealed truth detached from contemplative wonder at its manifestation founds one massive pillar of the modern age because it guides thought irreparably down tracks leading to the (absurd) possibility of a precisely scientific character of theology apart from the consent of faith. See *D'Ailleurs, La Revelation*, ch. 4, esp. 87–94.
40 I would only suggest A. N. Williams study, *The Divine Sense* (New York: Cambridge University Press, 2007), on the intellect in patristic thought, both Greek and Latin, for the substance of this claim.
41 *Metaphysics* 1072b20–25.
42 I follow Richard Seaford's thesis most fully presented in *The Origins of Philosophy in Ancient Greece and Ancient India* (New York: Cambridge University Press, 2020).
43 *De Anima* 420a20–26.
44 This phrase, and the account I indicate here, comes in the midst of Marion's discussion of St. Paul's "anticipation" of Nietzsche's well-known criticism of the concept of being in *D'Ailleurs, La Revelation*, 545–7.
45 See *D'Ailleurs, La Revelation*, ch. 17, 467–94.

46 The intrepid cybernaut may wish to compare the account I begin to sketch here with that of cognitive psychologist, John Vervaeke in his remarkable fifty-part lecture series, "Awakening from the Meaning Crisis," https://www.youtube.com/watch?v=54l8_ewcOlY, released from January to December, 2019.
47 Tertullian, *De Resurrectione Carnis*, ch. 8.
48 See, for example, chapter 4 of his later opus, *The Justification of the Good*, trans. Boris Jakim (Grand Rapids: Eerdmans, 2005).
49 *Summa Theologiae* Ia2ae. 91, 2, resp. A creative retelling of natural law theory in light of a fuller eschatology than Thomas could adumbrate must await the future, it seems to me.
50 See Louis Bouyer's "biblical and Eucharistic" view of the Trinity in *The Invisible Father*, trans. Hugh Gilbert, OSB (Petersham: Saint Bede, 1998), 230–3. This quotation comes from his analysis of the nature of the "progressive" revelation of God in the history of Israel, with which the revelation of Jesus Christ is in direct continuity; 142.

Chapter 3

1 "Welchen Sinn hat es, von Gott zu reden?" (1925) in *Glauben und Verstehen 1: Gesammelte Aufsätze* (Tubingen: J. C. B. Mohr, 1933), 26–37. "What Does It Mean to Speak of God?" (1925), in *Faith and Understanding*, vol. 1, trans. Robert Funk (London: SCM, 1969).
2 See Jean-Luc Marion, *The Erotic Phenomenon*, trans. Stephen E. Lewis (Chicago: University of Chicago Press, 2006); St. John of the Cross, *The Spiritual Canticle*, in *The Collected Works of Saint John of the Cross*, trans. Kieran Kavanaugh and Oscar Rodriguez (Washington D.C.: Institute of Carmelite Studies, 1991).
3 See Miklos Vetö, *The Expansion of Metaphysics,* trans. William C. Hackett (Eugene: Wipf and Stock, 2018).
4 The rational character of humanity is founded on this capacity to conceive of the world as a whole and oneself as distinct from it. The world is "my" world. I am also a "part" of the world, included in the whole. I see myself as both in the world and over against the world, as an actor that is immersed in the world. I can conceive of the world objectively, but this objectivity can never completely crystalize because I am entangled with the world, the world is part of me and I am part of the world, and it is, by definition, an inexhaustible place. This objectivity (necessarily qualified) is abstracted from the "foundation" of subjective experience within the world of ordinary life, the lifeworld. It is from here, and nowhere else, that our abstractions emerge. See Edmund Husserl, *The Crisis of European Sciences and Transcendental Phenomenology*, trans. David Carr (Evanston: Northwestern University Press, 1970).
5 To conscript (yet again) a distinction from Thomas V. Morris' *The Logic of God Incarnate* (Ithaca: Cornell University Press, 1986).

6   I quote here William Franke's translation from *Commentarium in Parmenidem*, Bk VII, 53k-76k, *On What Cannot Be Said*, vol. 1 (South Bend: Notre Dame Press, 2007), 90.
7   "On Not Three Gods: To Ablabius," in *Christology of the Later Fathers*, ed. Edward R. Hardy (Philadelphia: Westminster Press, 1954), 256–67.
8   See *Summa Theologiae*, I, 1, 7.
9   Nyssa, *Ad Ablabius* (emphasis added): "In the case of the Supreme and Divine nature, the word 'Godhead' is fitly adapted to that which it represents to us, as a kind of special name. We . . . following the suggestions of Scripture, have learned that that nature is unnameable and unspeakable and we say that every term either invented by the custom of men, or handed down to us by the Scriptures is indeed explanatory of our conceptions of the Divine nature, but does not include the signification of that nature itself."
10 Nyssa, *Ad Ablabius*.
11 Nyssa, *Ad Ablabius*.
12 See Jean-Yves Lacoste, *From Theology to Theological Thinking*, trans. William C. Hackett (Charlottesville: University of Virginia Press, 2012).
13 *The Ecclesiastical Hierarchy Hierarchies*, III, 3, 12, 444a (Complete Works, 222).
14 For the concept of theandric energies (θεανδρικὴ ἐνέργεια), see Pseudo-Dionysius the Areopagite, Letter Four, 1072C (*Complete Works*, 265).
15 "Our hidden tradition," says the Areopagite, is "one with sacred scripture": see *The Divine Names*, 592B (*Complete Works*, 52).
16 Ibid., 648A (*Complete Works*, 65).
17 Ibid.
18 An expansion of the concept I borrow, of course, from Jean-Yves Lacoste.
19 See *The Divine Names*, 592C (*Complete Works*, 52), for the eschatological prioritization.
20 1 Cor 13:12.
21 Eph 3:20.
22 Eph 3:20-21.
23 It is worth noting that St. Thomas Aquinas, for all of his classical prioritization of the universal over the particular, actually considered intellectual activity as the erection of a framework or setting for love. "Man approaches," he says, "nearer to God through love than through reason, because in love man does not act himself, but is in a manner of speaking drawn nearer to God himself" (*Summa Theologiae*, 26, 3, ad 4). Or again, "The movement of love reaches God more perfectly than the intellect does" (*De Veritate* 22, 11, ad 10). Or again, the end or purpose of knowledge is made complete in "desire, love or happiness" (*Summa Contra Gentiles* 3, 25.). In God, of course, knowledge and love, the act of intellect and will, are one. There is no real distinction between intellect and will in God. This suggests that Thomas is closer, in actuality, to Soloviev (and even, perhaps, Scotus) than at first seems possible.

Chapter 4

1. See Karl Rahner, "Devotion to the Sacred Heart Today," in *Theological Investigations vol. 23: Final Writings* (New York: Darton, Longman and Todd, 1992); "Some Theses for a Theology of Devotion to the Sacred Heart," *Theological Investigations* 3 (1974): 321–30; and "The Theological Meaning of the Veneration of the Sacred Heart," *Theological Investigations* 8 (1971): 217–28.
2. For Scripture as the "soul" of theology, see Dei Verbum (Vatican II), § 24.
3. Says Origen in critical response to Celsus, that in the "philosophy" of those who "believe in the Son" the "reason of everything is his Son" incarnate in Jesus—impossible for divinity on Celsus' conception. "And we would also hold," he says, transforming the meaning within Celsus' own words with the new Christian conception, "that God is not able to do anything contrary to his own character." *Contra Celsum*, V, 24, ed. Henry Chadwick (New York: Cambridge University Press, 1953), 282.
4. See, for example, Friedrich Nietzsche, *Thus Spake Zarathustra*, trans. Thomas Common (New York: Random House, 1946), prologue, 7–8.
5. See Daniel Cohen, *Formes théologiques et symbolisme sacré* (Paris: Ousia, 2010).
6. Marion, "Débat" (with Jean-Luc Nancy), 254.
7. The now-budding AI revolution is presently coming to be understood, especially by many of its initiators, as terrifyingly opening Pandora's box with potentially deleterious consequences for the human race.
8. Jas 3:15.
9. *Critique of Pure Reason*, Bxxx.
10. See Andrew Willard Jones, *The Two Cities: A History of Christian Politics* (Steubenville: Emmaus Road, 2021).
11. Kant, *Prolegomena to Any Future Metaphysic* (New York: Cambridge University Press, 2004), 108.
12. Ibid., 109. On the notion of analogy in Kant, see F. Marty's massive study: *La connaissance de la métaphysique chez Kant: une étude sur la notion kantienne d'analogie* (Paris: Beauchesne, 1980).
13. Immanuel Kant, *Anthropology from a Pragmatic Point of View*, trans. Victor Lyle Dowdell (Carbondale: Southern Illinois University Press, 1978), 83–4. An extended discussion is found in in Jean Borella, *La crise du symbolisme religieux* (Lausanne: l'Age d'Homme, 1990), 151–3.
14. See Francisco Suárez, *Disputationes Metaphysicae*, 8.
15. For this paragraph, see Nietzsche's "On Truth and Lies in a Non-moral Sense," in *Basic Writings*, trans. Walter Kaufmann (New York: Modern Library, 2000). See also Jüngel's discussion in section two of "Metaphorical Truth," in *Theological Essays*, vol. 1 (London: Bloomsbury, 2000).

16 *Ueber Wahrheit und Lüge im aussermoralischen Sinne*, Digitale Kritische Gesamtausgabe. http://www.nietzschesource.org/eKGWB/WL/print.
17 Ibid.
18 The following comes from *An Introduction to Metaphysics* (*Revue de Métaphysique et de Morale*, 1903), published in English in 1912, which also appeared as a chapter in *The Creative Mind*, 1965. References in parentheses are to the former, stand-alone version of Bergson's famous text.
19 For this image, which I use in the inverse way of Levinas, for whom, in continuity with the Greek tradition of metaphysics, concepts touch reality, whereas the image misses reality for its shadow, I would direct you to his early iconoclastic essay, "Reality and Its Shadow," in *The Levinas Reader* (Oxford: Wiley Blackwell, 2001).
20 Alfred North Whitehead, *Symbolism: Its Meaning and Effect* (New York: Fordham University Press, 1927).
21 St. Irenaeus, *Libros quinquos adversus haereses*, IV, 20, 7, ed. W. Wigan Harvey (S. T. B. Cantabrigiae, 1857), tome 2, 219.
22 Rom. 1:17; 3:21; Phil. 3:9, et al.
23 See Ps. 16:11, Mt. 7:23, 2 Thess. 1:9 for variations of the biblical trope that is traced back to the blessing of God's presence in the tabernacle and temple, and behind it, to the creation narrative itself.
24 Isa. 65:17, 2 Pet. 3:13, Rev. 21:1 (with heaven, *ouranos*, suddenly in the singular).
25 See Mt. 22:39 and parallels.
26 1 Jn 4:8.
27 *On the Essence of the Truth: Plato's Parable of the Cave and the Theaetetus* (London: Continuum, 2009).
28 *Schelling's Treatise: On the Essence of Human Freedom*, trans. Joan Stambaugh (Ohio University Press, 1985).
29 "On the Essence of Truth," in *Basic Writings*, ed. David Farrell Krell (New York: Harper Perennial, 1993), 111–38.
30 *Schelling's Treatise*, 163 [German text, 233].
31 *Mindfulness*, 131.
32 Ibid.
33 Ibid.
34 Ibid., 134.
35 Paul Ricoeur, "The Hermeneutics of Symbols and Philosophical Reflection II," in *The Conflict of Interpretations: Essays in Hermeneutics*, ed. Dan Ihde (London: Continuum, 2000), 329.
36 Lacoste, *Experience and the Absolute*, 32–4.
37 *Poetics*, 1457b, 6–9.
38 See *The Divine Names*, 592D (*Complete Works*, 53).

39 Even in Kant, or indeed, especially in Kant, this is true, inasmuch as he *dogmatically* determines in advance what is and is not knowable, in the first place by way of his *metaphysical* distinction between noumenal and phenomenal worlds.
40 See Ian McGilchrist, *The Matter of Things*, vol. 1: *The Ways of Truth* (London: Perspective Press, 2021), especially chapters 11–13, which, among other things, argue for the grounding of scientific knowledge in metaphorical language, embodied experience, and creative imagination—all stemming from a religious sensibility of the transcendent meaningfulness of the world.
41 See Michel Henry, *Barbarism*, trans. Scott Davidson (London: Continuum, 2012).
42 See Marion's concept of "negative certitude" for a view of the centrality of insoluble problems, like God, human nature, the gift, and so on, for philosophy, whose very insolubility for philosophy is a negative sign of their reality, and therefore a justification, infinitely greater than mere "positive certitude," for both religious faith and philosophical inquiry. Jean-Luc Marion, *Negative Certainties*, trans. Stephen E. Lewis (Chicago: University of Chicago Press, 2015).
43 Rémi Brague, *Du Dieu des chrétiens et d'un ou deux autres* (Paris: Flammarion, 2008).
44 Phil. 2:6-11.
45 This is called "areoelastic fluttering." The traditional explanation of the bridge's collapse, now debunked, is similar to "areoelastic flutter" thesis but distinct. According to the hypothesis of "resonance" due to externally applied force, the bridge failed as a result of environmental conditions that correlated with the tendency of the very structure-system of the bridge to oscillate at a precise frequency. The "torsional frequency" of this Tacoma Narrows Bridge structure happened to be keyed to the precise swirling pattern of the gusts of wind in the area due to the material structure of the countryside (the so-called von Kármán vortex). So at the right frequency, even minor periodic force can produce violently large vibrations, because the system (bridge) does not have time to release the energy that the force (wind) provides but rather keeps it within. Think of fly-fishing: one has to have the precise rhythm of swinging their arms with the length of the line in order to apply the correct force that will carry through their arms, the pole and line in order to whip the tiny "fly" tied to the end of the line through the air and set it down on the water across the stream. In the bridge's case, the external gusts of wind occurred at a specific rate that set the bridge-structure itself into a resonating rhythm.
46 In Plato, of course, the eschatological pertains to the worthy individual's ascent to the spiritual world. But the visionary trained in philosophy can come to see the highest in the world of experience become diaphanous to his gaze.
47 Besides the Incarnation itself, there is perhaps no better expression precisely of this paradoxical presence of God than in the revelation of the divine Name in Exodus 3. A new "metaphysics of exodus" would take its starting point here.
48 For this language of impossibility, finitude, paradox, see the conclusion to Marion's *Certitudes négatives*, esp. 316–18.

Chapter 5

1. *The Ecclesiastical Hierarchy*, II, 7, 404B.
2. *Epistle Nine*, 1104B.
3. *The Ecclesiastical Hierarchy* I, 2, 373B.
4. *Pseudo-Dionysius: The Complete Works*, trans. Colb Luibheid and Paul Rorem (Mahwah: Paulist Press, 1987), 197.
5. "Only-begotten son" is, first, a messianic title, and, according to the specific *theologia* of early Christian thought, a *symbol* eschatologically disclosive of the hypostatic *taxis* within God. What appears in the end (Omega) is the beginning (Alpha).
6. To call Jesus "intellect" (*nous*) in a Neoplatonic schema, of course, involves a statement of function analogous to Word in the Johannine parlance: in his natural activity he mediates the participation of the lower, the creaturely with the higher, the divine. For the Pseudo-Dionysius, in a Pauline way, this ascription implies a fitting hidden reference to the mediatorial role of the Incarnation, now revealed, that brings about the eschaton.
7. *The Ecclesiastical, Hierarchy*, I, 2, 373B. (*Complete Works*, 197).
8. See the *locus classicus* in St. Augustine, *City of God*, XXII, whose indecision regarding the bodily nature of the vision only stresses all the more powerfully the central place of the body itself: his eschatology, rightly, cuts against and undoes from within the Neoplatonic architectonic that shapes Augustine's conceptuality, as it ought to do for anyone's conceptual architectonic.
9. Daniel Cohen, *Formes Théologiques et Symbolisme Sacré*, III.1.2, 178–81.
10. Ibid., I.2.2, 40–52.
11. *The Divine Names*, 648A (*Complete Works*, 65).
12. "The Divine Essence, that Inaccessible *Kabod* Enthroned in Heaven: Nazianzen's *Oratio* 28.3 and the Tradition of Apophatic Theology from Symbols to Philosophical Concepts," *Numen* 57 (2010): 1–29.
13. Ibid., 1.
14. John Dillon and Mark Edwards, "God in Dionysius and later Neoplatonists," in *Oxford Handbook to Pseudo-Dionysius the Areopagite*, ed. Mark Edwards et al. (New York: Oxford University Press), 139.
15. Proclus, *In Parmeniden*, 1191.
16. See Damascius, *Doubts and Solutions Concerning First Principles*, I 21, 8–10. See *Traité des premiers principes, vol. 1, De l'Ineffable et d l'Un*, ed. Leendert Gerrit Westerink (Paris: Les Belles Lettres, 1966). For an English translation of some fragments of this text, see William Franke, *On What Cannot Be Said, vol. 1: Classical Formulations* (Notre Dame: University of Notre Dame Press, 2008), 91–107.

17 See Joseph Wolinski's contribution to the article "Dieu," "II. Théologie patristique," in *Dictionnaire critique de théologie*, dir. Jean-Yves Lacoste, 3rd edn (Paris: Presses Universitaires de France, 2007), 389.
18 See *The Cambridge History of Later Greek and Early Medieval Philosophy*, ed. A. H. Armstrong (NY: Cambridge University Press, 1967), 460.
19 See Letter Nine, *Complete Works*, 280–9.
20 On the Trinitarian *taxis*, see his comment on the Spirit as "within the shared unity of Father and Son." (*The Divine Names*, 637C, *Complete Works*, 59).
21 On the central "importance of the Fathers for the structure of faith," see the discussion in Joseph Ratzinger, *Principles of Catholic Theology* (San Francisco: Ignatius Press, 2009), 133–52.
22 See Jean Borella, *Guenonian Esotericism and Christian Mystery*, trans. G. John Champoux (Hillsdale: Sophia Perennis, 2017).
23 *The Ecclesiastical Hierarchy*, III, 1, 424D (*Complete Works*, 209, translation amended).
24 For the phrase "epistemic preparation," see Timothy Knepper, *Negating Negation: Against the Apophatic Abandonment of the Dionysian Corpus* (Eugene: Cascade, 2014), 99, whose interpretation of the Pseudo-Dionysius is generally consonant with that reflected in this chapter.
25 *The Mystical Theology*, 5, 1045D-1048B, (*Complete Works*, 141).
26 See Thomas Aquinas, *Summa Theologica*, I, 84, 6, 7, resp.
27 *The Celestial Hierarchy*, I, 3, 121C-D (*Complete Works*, 146).
28 Ibid., I, 2, 121B-C.
29 For the Ps-Dionysius, "symbol" and "analogy" are used synonymously. See, for example, *The Divine Names*, I, 592C (*Complete Works*, 53).
30 See *The Ecclesiastical Hierarchy*, III, 3, 429B (*Complete Works*, 219).
31 Paul Ricoeur: the symbol performs a "bond between man and what he considers sacred." *The Symbolism of Evil*, translated by Emerson Buchanan (Boston: Beacon Press, 1967), 5.
32 *The Ecclesiastical Hierarchy* I, 1, 372A (*Complete Works*, 195). See also, *The Celestial Hierarchy*, VII, 3, 209B-C.
33 See *The Celestial Hierarchy* X, 1, 272D-273A (*Complete Works*, 173).
34 See *The Mystical Theology* 1000D (*Complete Works*, 137).
35 See *The Ecclesiastical Hierarchy*, III, 3, 429A (*Complete Works*, 212).
36 Proclus, *Elements of Theology*, prop. 13. See Hans Urs von Balthasar's comments on the phrase in *The Glory of the Lord*, vol. 5, ed. John Riches (Edinburgh: T&T Clark, 1991), 618; *The Glory of the Lord*, vol. 6, ed. John Riches (Edinburgh: T&T Clark, 1991), 10.
37 For what follows, see ch. 1 of Jean-Luc Nancy, *Au fond des images* (Paris: Galilée, 2003).

38 As observed in a previous chapter, this is expressed in the following apothegm, derived from the hesychast controversies of fourteenth-century Byzantium, and used most recently in the onomatodoxy ("Name-worshiping") controversy of twentieth-century Greek and Russian theology, which has been established as an important influence on advances in the mathematical ideas of the infinite in the early Moscow School: "The energies/Name of God are God himself, but God is not his energies/Name."

39 Hans Urs von Balthasar, *Theo-Logic*, vol. 2, trans. Adrian J. Walker (San Francisco: Ignatius Press, 2004), 270–1. Supporting this thesis, that the embodiment of human rationality means that our speculative concepts are no less anthropomorphic than such images, see Louis Bouyer's article, "Anthropomorphism," in his *Dictionary of Theology*, trans. Charles Underhill Quinn (Tournai: Desclee, 1965), 30–1.

40 As "kiss," for example, or as "drunkenness." See *Enneads*, 3.8.10, 5.8.10, 6.7.35, etc.

41 *The Divine Names*, 645A (*Complete Works*, 63).

42 Ibid., 596C (*Complete Works*, 56).

43 *The Mystical Theology*, 1000D (*Complete Works*, 137).

44 Ibid., 1001A (*Complete Works*, 137).

45 Ibid.

46 Ibid., 1000D and 1048B (*Complete Works*, 137, 141).

47 Ibid., 1001A (*Complete Works*, 137).

48 See Letter IX, 1112B-C (*Complete Works*, 287).

49 *The Divine Names*, 649A (*Complete Works*, 66), quoting "Hierotheus," *Elements of Theology*.

50 *The Ecclesiastical Hierarchy*, 565B-C (*Complete Works*, 257).

51 *The Divine Names* 713B (*Complete Works*, 83), quoting "Hierotheus," *Hymns of Yearning*.

52 Ibid., 712B (*Complete Works*, 82).

53 *Chalice of God: A Systematic Theology in Outline* (Collegeville: Liturgical Press, 2012), 56.

Chapter 6

1 E. B. Pusey, *The Minor Prophets* (1860), 433.

2 1 Corinthians 15:28.

3 *La Connaissance Surnaturelle* (Paris: Gallimard, 1950), 305.

4 See, for example, the treatise, *Against the Anthropomorphites* of Cyril of Alexandria, as well as the tenth of Cassian's *Conferences* on prayer, discussed in the appendix to this essay.

5 See *Posterior Analytics*, 71b 33 and following and 78a 22 and following for Aristotle's original development of the distinction.

6 As Maritain taught us when we reflected on Bloy in the introduction, earlier.
7 For self-assertion (Selbstbehauptung), see Hans Blumenberg, *The Legitimacy of the Modern Age*, trans. Robert M. Walker (Cambridge, MA: MIT Press, 1985), part II, 125–277.
8 See Merold Westphal, *Suspicion and Faith: On the Religious Uses of Modern Atheism* (New York: Fordham University Press, 1999).
9 Lee Braver, "A Brief History of Continental Realism," *Continental Philosophy Review* 45 (2012): 261–89.
10 In this way French phenomenology marks what the late László Tengyeli has called a "third phase" in the history of phenomenology, of which the so-called theological turn is only an instance that exemplifies some of its key traits. See Tengyeli's article "New Phenomenology in France," *The Southern Journal of Philosophy* 50, no. 2 (2012): 295–303, as well as his developed articulation of the perspective in *Neue Phänomenologie in Frankreich* (Suhrkamp, 2012).
11 See Marion, *Certitudes négatives*.
12 Ibid., 255. He echoes, of course, Gilson's famous conception of a "metaphysics of Exodus," found, inter alia, in his *The Christian Philosophy of Saint Thomas Aquinas*, trans. L. K. Shook (South Bend: University of Notre Dame Press, 1994).
13 Jean-Luc Marion, "Débat avec Jean-Luc Nancy," in *Dieu-en-tant-que Dieu: La question philosophique*, ed. Philippe Capelle-Dumont (Paris: Cerf, 2012).
14 *Geschichte der Leben-Jesu-Forschung* (1906).
15 Jean Vioulac, *Apocalypse de la vérité: Méditations heideggériennes* (Paris: Ad Solem, 2014), translated into English as *Apocalypse of the Truth: Heideggerian Meditations*, trans. Matthew J. Peterson (Chicago: University of Chicago Press, 2021).
16 Interview with Tarek Dika and Chris Hackett in *The Quiet Power of the Possible: Interviews in Contemporary French Phenomenology* (New York: Fordham University Press, 2016). See the extended gloss on this definition that comprises my essay "The Love of Nothing and the Limits of Knowledge," in *Being Human: Groundwork for a Theological Anthropology in the 21st Century*, ed. David Kirchhoffer (Preston: Mosaic Press, 2013), 259–70.
17 *La Connaissance Surnaturelle*, 149.

Chapter 7

1 An early version of this chapter appeared in French as "Une façon de penser kénotique," *Revue catholique internationale : Communio* 242, no. 6 (2015): 83–96 and in English in Christiaan Jacobs-Vandegeer and Jean-Luc Marion (eds.), *The Enigma of Divine Revelation* (Cham, Switzerland: Springer Nature, 2020), 119–34.

2 Dom Gregory Dix, *The Shape of the Liturgy* (London: Adam and Charles Black, 1945), 276.
3 Bultmann, "Welchen Sinn hat es, von Gott zu reden?" 26–37.
4 In the following I make consistent use of two scholarly anthologies with commentary, which form the touchstones of contemporary theological study Cyril's thought in the English-speaking world: Norman Russell, *Cyril of Alexandria*. London: Routledge, 2000 and John Anthony McGuckin, *St. Cyril of Alexandria and the Christological Controversy* (Crestwood: St. Vladimir's Seminary Press, 2010).
5 *Commentary on John* 11.11, Patrologia Graeca (PG) 73, 556D-557D. See Marie-Odile Boulnois, "L'Eucharistie, mystère d'union chez Cyrille d'Alexandrie," *Revue des Sciences Religieuses* 74 (2000): 148.
6 PG 75, 1273B, 1325C-1328B. See also *On the Unity of Christ*, trans. John McGuckin (Crestwood: St. Vladimir's Seminary Press, 2015), 64, 105–6.
7 Laurence Welch, *Christology and Eucharist in the Early Thought of Cyril of Alexandria* (New York: International Scholars Press, 1993), 18.
8 See Bernard Meunier, *Le Christ de Cyrille d'Alexandrie: L'humanité, le salut et la question monophysite* (Paris: Beauchesne, 1997), part 1 ("Les deux Adam"), 27–100.
9 Third Letter of Cyril to Nestorius, PG 77, 113D (McGuckin, *St. Cyril of Alexandria and the Christological Controversy*, 270).
10 PG 77, 113B (McGuckin, *St. Cyril of Alexandria and the Christological Controversy*, 36).
11 Emphasis mine. This slogan, ultimately originated in the writings of Apollinaris. Cyril, in his day, wrongly understood it to be from Athanasius.
12 Russell, *Cyril of Alexandria*, 41. Cf. Job 1:14 and Phil. 2:6-11, respectively.
13 Tertullian, *De resurrectione carnis* 8.2 (PL 2, 852).
14 *The Third Letter of Cyril to Nestorius*, PG 77, 121D (McGuckin, *St. Cyril of Alexandria and the Christological Controversy*, 275). Emphasis mine.
15 McGuckin, *St. Cyril of Alexandria and the Christological Controversy*, 187.
16 *On the True Faith, to the Princesses Pulcheria and Eudokia*, 28, PG 76, 1369 B-C (see also E. Pusey, *Works of S. Cyril*, 7 vols [Oxford, 1868], 7.313). See Brian E. Daley, S.J. "'One Thing and Another': The Persons in God and the Person of Christ in Patristic Theology," *Pro Ecclesia* 15.1, 41 and Boulnois, "L'Eucharistie, mystère d'union chez Cyrille d'Alexandrie," 160.
17 McGuckin, *St. Cyril of Alexandria and the Christological Controversy*, 39.
18 See Ezra Gebremedhin, *Life-Giving Blessing: Inquiry into the Eucharistic Doctrine of Cyril of Alexandria* (Acta Universitatis Upsaliensis, 1977); Meunier, *Le Christ de Cyrille d'Alexandrie*, 179–94.
19 Cf. his third letter to Nestorius, paragraph 7, PG 77, 121A, quoted in McGuckin, *St. Cyril of Alexandria and the Christological Controversy*, 270.
20 See André de Halleux, "La distinction des natures du Christ 'par la seule pensée' au cinquième concile œcuménique," in *Mélanges D. Staniloae* (Sibiu, 1993), 311–19,

and "Le dyophysisme christologique de Cyrille d'Alexandrie," in *Logos. Festschrift für Luise Abramowski* (Berlin, 1993), 411–28.

21 *Sources Chrétiennes*, vol. 392 (PG 77, 568–72); St. Cyril of Alexandria, *Festal Letters 1–12*, ed. John J. O'Keefe (Washington, D.C.: Catholic University of America Press, 2009), 137–53. St. Cyril of Alexandria, *Commentary on John*, 2 vols., ed. Joel Elowsky (Downer's Grove: IVP Academic, 2013), vol. 1, 1.9, 96a, 4–74, Russell, *Cyril of Alexandria*, 106, and Boulnois, "L'Eucharistie, mystère d'union chez Cyrille d'Alexandrie," 166–7.

22 The same phenomenological distinction is made again in the First and Second Letters to Succensus, bishop of Dioceasarea, written after the Formula of Reunion, as well as in the Letter to Eulogius.

23 *De Carne Christi* V, 4.

24 This may be considered a principle in the Pseudo-Dionysius as well, as we have already seen.

25 Both his third letter to Nestorius, 7–9 and his *Scholia on the Incarnation*, 8 draw the Eucharistic unity and the incarnational unity together vis-à-vis this image. See M.-O. Boulnois, "Le modèle de l'union de l'âme et du corps dans les débats christologiques: les débuts de la controverse nestorienne," in *Annuaire. Résumé des conférences et travaux, École Pratique des Hautes Etudes*, tome 117 (2008–2009) (EPHE, 2010), 205–15; and "Le modèle de l'union de l'âme et du corps dans la controverse nestorienne sur l'union des deux natures dans le Christ," in *Annuaire. Résumé des conférences et travaux, École Pratique des Hautes Etudes*, tome 118 (2009–2010) (EPHE, 2011), 157–75.

26 Plotinus, *Enneads* 3.6.1–4.

27 Canon 10 of Constantinople II (553).

28 See Steven McKinion, *Words, Imagery and the Mystery of Christ: A Reconstruction of Cyril of Alexandria's Christology* (Boston: Brill, 2000).

29 For Apollinaris' use, cf. fr. 128 (H. Leitzmann (ed.), *Apollinaris von Laodicea und seine Schule. Texte und Unterschungen*, 1904); for Cyril's cf. his *Commentary on Luke*, 22 (PG 72, 909 B), 130–1.

30 *On the Unity of Christ*, 130–1 (PG 75, 1357C). Emphasis added.

31 *Against Nestorius*, II.33, PG 76, 61B (Russell, *Cyril of Alexandria*, 143). For a discussion, see McKinion, *Words, Imagery and the Mystery of Christ*, 207.

32 *Commentary on Isaiah*, 1.4, PG 70 181 C (Russell, *Cyril of Alexandria*, 77). *Commentary on Isaiah*, vol. 1, trans. Robert Charles Hill (Brookline: Holy Cross Orthodox Press, 2008), 25–6.

33 *Commentary on Isaiah*, 1.4 (PG 70 181 D); Russell, *Cyril of Alexandria*, 77. Cf. the *Commentary on the Gospel of John*, I. 14 (PG 73, 160 C).

34 Cyril develops this image further in his *Scholia on the Incarnation* (McGuckin, *St. Cyril of Alexandria and the Christological Controversy*, 301–2) and in *On the Unity of Christ*, 130–1, 132–3; *Sources Chrétiennes* 97, ed. M. Durand (Paris, 1964).

35 Aristotle, *Posterior Analytics* I 71b33–72a5.
36 Boulnois, *La Paradoxe Trinitaire*, 114.
37 2:5-7, NRSV.
38 On the term "theology" to name the new Pauline priority granted intellectual reflection on the disclosure (*apocalypsis*) of divine wisdom in the Cross in service to the *ekklesia*, see the argument undergirding N. T. Wright, *Paul and the Faithfulness of God*, 2 vols (New York: Fortress Press, 2013).
39 See H. Austryn Wolfson, *The Philosophy of the Church Fathers*, vol. 1, 3rd ed. (Cambridge, MA: Harvard University Press, 1971).
40 *On the Trinity* XIV.4.15, PG 76, 61B.
41 *On Divine Names* 640A, PG 73, 576D.
42 *Commentary on John*, 4.2, 360d (Russell, *Cyril of Alexandria*, 114).

Chapter 8

1 Hegel, *The Encyclopedia Logic*, trans. Klaus Brinkman and Daniel O. Dahlstrom (New York: Cambridge University Press, 2010), 198.
2 Schelling, *sämmtliche Werke*, ed. K. F. A. Schelling. Abteilung 2, XI *Philosophie der Mythologie*, 260.
3 Robert Spaemann, *Persons: The Difference Between Someone and Something*, trans. Oliver O'Donovan (Oxford: Oxford University Press, 2017), 95.
4 See his magisterial *The Expansion of Metaphysics*, trans. Hackett (*L'élargissement de la métaphysique* [Paris: Hermann, 2012]), as well as its companion volume, *Explorations métaphysiques* (Paris: Harmattan, 2012).
5 *Philosophical Fragments*, 55.
6 Braver, "A Brief History of Continental Realism," *Continental Philosophy Review* 45 (2012): 261–89. See discussion in previous chapter.
7 The locus classicus for this conception is his "The Saturated Phenomenon," in *Phenomenology and the 'Theological Turn': The French Debate*, Dominique Janicaud et al. (New York: Fordham, 2000). The concept was revised and expanded in his "The Banality of Saturation," *The Visible and Revealed* (New York: Fordham, 2008).
8 The *Glory of the Lord, vol. 1: Seeing the Form* (San Francisco: Ignatius Press, 1982).
9 See Husserl, *Ideas I* (1913), trans. F. Kersten (The Hague: Martinus Nijhoff, 1983), 63–9, §§ 33–4.
10 *Human Existence and Transcendence*, trans. William C. Hackett (South Bend: University of Notre Dame Press, 2016).
11 The "new" phenomenology of France, of which the "theological turn" is the inaugural and central movement, is marked by the recognition of the event

character of appearing from which the conditions for appearing can only be derived after the appearing of the phenomenon and a concomitant refiguring of subjectivity and the transcendental. See, again, Hans-Dieter Gondek and László Tengelyi, *Neue Phänomenologie in Frankreich* (Suhrkamp Verlag, 2011).

12 Chapter two of *"The Weight of Glory" and Other Essays* (Grand Rapids: Eerdmans, 1949), 16–29.
13 Jn 12:29.
14 Genesis 18.
15 Hans Urs von Balthasar, *Theo-Drama, vol. 3: Dramatis Personae: Persons in Christ*, trans. Graham Harrison (San Francisco: Ignatius Press, 1992), 530.
16 Rom 8:19.
17 4 Sent. D. 49, q. 2, a. 2.
18 *The Mystical Theology*, 1048B (*Complete Works*, 141).
19 *The Invisible Father* (Petersham: St Bede Publications, 1999), 161.
20 *The Mystical Theology*, 1040D (*Complete Works*, 140).
21 See the final lines of *The Mystical Theology*, 1048B (*Complete Works*, 141).
22 Ibid. What Rorem translates as "free of every limitation" (τῶν πάντων ἁπλῶς ἀπολελυμένου) is the sixth of seven final interwoven and partially overlapping phrases that resolve the text in silence. "Beyond every affirmation (θέσις)" and "beyond every denial (ἀφαίρεσις)" are the first and fourth.
23 *The Celestial Hierarchy*, 373B (*Complete Works*, 197).

Chapter 9

1 This is explored in constructive and programmatic fashion in *Eclipse of World* (in preparation). One may also consult my *Philosophy in Word and Name*.
2 Pavel Florensky, *Early Religious Writings: 1903-1909*, trans. Boris Jakim (Grand Rapids: Eerdmans, 2017).
3 Ibid., 29–30.
4 Ibid., 35.
5 Ibid., 53.
6 Ibid. See his essay "Reverse Perspective," in *Beyond Vision: Essays on Perception in Art*, ed. Nicoletta Misler (London: Reaktion, 2002), and his book, *Iconostasis*, trans. Donald Sheehan and Olga Andrejev (Crestwood: St. Vladimir's Seminary Press, 1996).
7 Ibid., 46–9.
8 Ibid., 50.
9 Ibid., 51.
10 Ibid., 55 and 25.

11 For the following, see ibid., 65–70.
12 Ibid., 66. Emphasis original.
13 Ibid.
14 Ibid., 67.
15 Ibid.
16 Ibid., 68–9.
17 Ibid., 69–70.
18 Ibid., 70.
19 1 Cor. 2:5.
20 Gal. 1:12; 1 Cor. 1:24 et al.
21 Rev. 21:5.
22 1 Cor. 3:22.
23 1 Cor. 2:16.
24 Vladimir Soloviev, *The Heart of Reality: Essays on Beauty, Love, and Ethics*, ed. Vladimir Wozniuk (South Bend: University of Notre Dame Press, 2003), 75.
25 It was largely rumination on Jean-Yves Lacoste's *Recherches sur la parole* (Louvain: Peeters, 2015) that permits this closing recapitulation of the apophatics of the sensible.

Appendix

1 John Cassian, *Conferences*, trans. Colm Luibheid and Owen Chadwick (Mahwah: Paulist Press, 1985), 28–9.
2 "The Image of the Invisible," Lumen Christi Institute, colloquium on the concept "image of God": http://vimeo.com/8030578.
3 Thomas Aquinas, *Summa Theologica*, trans. Fathers of the English Dominican Province (Notre Dame: Christian Classics, 1948), 415, col. 1.
4 Peter Kreeft, *Christianity for Modern Pagans* (San Francisco: Ignatius Press, 1993), 33–4.
5 NRSV.
6 References in *Early Greek Philosophy*, ed. Jonathan Barnes, 42–3.
7 Falque, *The Metamorphosis of Finitude*, 101, §23.

Bibliography

Aquinas, Thomas. *Summa Theologica*, trans. The Dominican Fathers of the English Province. New York: Christian Classics, 1945.

Aristotle. *Complete Works*, two vols., ed. Jonathan Barnes. Princeton: Princeton University Press, 1984.

Augustine, Saint. *City of God against the Pagans*. New York: Cambridge University Press, 1998.

Augustine, Saint. *The Literal Meaning of Genesis*, trans. Edmund Hill. Hyde Park: New City Press, 2013.

Balthasar, Hans Urs von. *Irenaeus' Against Heresies: Scandal of the Incarnation*, trans. John Saward. San Francisco: Ignatius Press, 1990.

Balthasar, Hans Urs von. *The Glory of the Lord*, vol. 5: *The Realm of Metaphysics in the Modern Age*, ed. John Riches. Edinburgh: T&T Clark, 1991.

Balthasar, Hans Urs von. *The Glory of the Lord*, vol. 6, *Theology: The Old Covenant*, ed. John Riches. Edinburgh: T&T Clark, 1991.

Balthasar, Hans Urs von. *Theo-Logic*, vol. 2, trans. Adrian J. Walker. San Francisco: Ignatius Press, 2004.

Barnes, Jonathan. *Early Greek Philosophy*. New York: Penguin, 2001.

Barthes, Roland. *Image-Music-Text*, trans. Stephen Heath. New York: Hill and Wang, 1978.

Bergson, Henri. *The Creative Mind*. New York: Dover, 1965.

Bernard, Saint. *On Loving God*, trans. Robert Walton, OSB. Collegeville: Cistercian Publications, 2009.

Bloy, Leon. *The Pilgrim of the Absolute*, ed. Raissa Maritain. Tacoma: Cluny Media, 2017.

Blumenberg, Hans. *The Legitimacy of the Modern Age*, trans. Robert M. Walker. Cambridge, MA: MIT Press, 1985.

Boethius. *Theological Tractates/ On the Consolation of Philosophy*, trans. H. F. Stewart et al., LCL 74. Cambridge, MA: Harvard University Press, 1973.

Borella, Jean. *Guenonian Esotericism and Christian Mystery*, trans. G. John Champoux. Hillsdale: Sophia Perennis, 2017.

Borella, Jean. *La crise du symbolisme religieux*. Lausanne: l'Age d'Homme, 1990.

Boulnois, Marie-Odile. "Le modèle de l'union de l'âme et du corps dans les débats christologiques: les débuts de la controverse nestorienne," in *Annuaire. Résumé des conférences et travaux, École Pratique des Hautes Etudes*, tome 117 (2008–2009), 205–15. EPHE, 2010.

Boulnois, Marie-Odile. "Le modèle de l'union de l'âme et du corps dans la controverse nestorienne sur l'union des deux natures dans le Christ," in *Annuaire. Résumé des conférences et travaux, École Pratique des Hautes Etudes*, tome 118 (2009–2010), 157–75. EPHE, 2011.

Boulnois, Marie-Odile. "L'Eucharistie, mystère d'union chez Cyrille d'Alexandrie," *Revue des Sciences Religieuses* 74 (2000): 147–72.

Bouyer, Louis. "Anthropomorphism," in *Dictionary of Theology*, trans. Charles Underhill Quinn, 30–1. Tournai, Belgium: Desclee, 1965.

Bouyer, Louis. *The Invisible Father*. Petersham: St Bede Publications, 1999.

Bouyer, Louis. *The Invisible Father*, trans. Hugh Gilbert, OSB. Petersham: St Bede Publications, 1998.

Brague, Rémi. *Du Dieu des chrétiens et d'un ou deux autres*. Paris: Flammarion, 2008.

Braver, Lee. "A Brief History of Continental Realism," *Continental Philosophy Review* 45 (2012): 261–89.

Breton, Stanislas. *The Word and the Cross*, trans. Jacquelyn Porter. New York: Fordham University Press, 1999.

Bulgakov, Sergius. *Icons and the Name of God*, trans. Boris Jakim. Grand Rapids: Eerdmans, 2012.

Bulgakov, Sergius. *The Lamb of God*, trans. Boris Jakim. Grand Rapids: Eerdmans, 2008.

Bultmann, Rudolph. "Welchen Sinn hat es, von Gott zu reden? (1925)," in *Glauben und Verstehen 1: Gesammelte Aufsätze*, 26–37. Tubingen: J. C. B. Mohr, 1933.

Capelle-Dumont, ed. *Dieu en tant que Dieu: La question philosophique*. Paris: Cerf, 2012.

Cassian, John. *Conferences*, trans. Colm Luibheid and Owen Chadwick. Mahwah: Paulist Press, 1985.

Cohen, Daniel. *Formes théologiques et symbolisme sacré*. Paris: Ousia, 2010.

Cyril of Alexandria, St. *Commentary on John*, 2 vols., ed. Joel Elowsky. Downer's Grove: IVP Academic, 2013.

Cyril of Alexandria, St. *Festal Letters 1-12*, ed. John J. O'Keefe, 137–53. Washington, DC: Catholic University of America Press, 2009.

Cyril of Alexandria, St. *On the Unity of Christ*, trans. John McGuckin. Crestwood: St. Vladimir's Seminary Press, 2015.

Daley, Brian, S.J. "'One Thing and Another': The Persons in God and the Person of Christ in Patristic Theology," *Pro Ecclesia* 15, no. 1 (2006): 17–46.

Damascius. *Traité des premiers principes, vol. 1, De l'Ineffable et d l'Un*, ed. Leendert Gerrit Westerink. Paris: Les Belles Lettres, 1966.

Dielz, H. and W. Kranz. *Die Fragmente der Vorsokratiker*, 10th ed. Berlin: Weidmann, 1952.

Dika, Tarek and Chris Hackett. *The Quiet Power of the Possible: Interviews in Contemporary French Phenomenology*. New York: Fordham University Press, 2016.

Dillon, John and Mark Edwards. *Oxford Handbook to Pseudo-Dionysius the Areopagite*, ed. Mark Edwards et al. New York: Oxford University Press, 2012.

Dix, Gregory. *The Shape of the Liturgy*. London: Adam and Charles Black, 1945.

Falque, Emmanuel. *Dieu, la chair et l'autre*. Paris: Presses Universitaires de Paris, 2008.

Falque, Emmanuel. *The Metamorphosis of Finitude*, trans. George Hughes. New York: Fordham University Press, 2012.

Florensky, Pavel. *Early Religious Writings: 1903–1909*, trans. Boris Jakim. Grand Rapids: Eerdmans, 2017.

Florensky, Pavel. *Iconostasis*, trans. Donald Sheehan and Olga Andrejev. Crestwood: St. Vladimir's Seminary Press, 1996.

Florensky, Pavel. "Reverse Perspective," in *Beyond Vision: Essays on Perception in Art*, ed. Nicoletta Misler. London: Reaktion, 2002.

Florensky, Pavel. *The Pillar and Ground of the Truth*, trans. Boris Jakim. Princeton: Princeton University Press, 1997.

Franke, William. *On What Cannot Be Said*, vol. 1. South Bend: Notre Dame Press, 2007.

Gebremedhin, Exra. *Life-Giving Blessing: Inquiry into the Eucharistic Doctrine of Cyril of Alexandria*. Acta Universitatis Upsaliensis. Almquist and Wiksell, 1977.

Gilson, Etienne. *The Christian Philosophy of Saint Thomas Aquinas*, trans. L. K. Shook. South Bend: University of Notre Dame Press, 1994.

Giulea, Dragos A. "The Divine Essence, that Inaccessible *Kabod* Enthroned in Heaven: Nazianzen's *Oratio* 28.3 and the Tradition of Apophatic Theology from Symbols to Philosophical Concepts," *Numen* 57 (2010): 1–29.

Graham, Laren and Jean-Michel Kantor. *Naming Infinity*. Cambridge, MA: Belknap Press, 2009.

Gregory of Nyssa, St. "On Not Three Gods: To Ablabius," in *Christology of the Later Fathers*, ed. Edward R. Hardy. Philadelphia: Westminster Press, 1954.

Hackett, William C. *Philosophy in Word and Name: Myth, Wisdom, Apocalypse*. New York: Angelico Press, 2021.

Hackett, William C. "The Love of Nothing and the Limits of Knowledge," in *Being Human: Groundwork for a Theological Anthropology in the 21st Century*, ed. David Kirchhoffer, 259–70. Preston: Mosaic Press, 2013.

Hackett, William C. "Une façon de penser kénotique," *Revue catholique internationale: Communio* 242, no. 6 (2015): 83–96.

Halleux, André de. "La distinction des natures du Christ 'par la seule pensée' au cinquième concile œcuménique," in *Mélanges D. Staniloae*, 311–19. Sibiu: Arhiepiscopia Ortodoxă Sibiu, 1993.

Halleux, André de. "Le dyophysisme christologique de Cyrille d'Alexandrie," in *Logos. Festschrift für Luise Abramowski*, 411–28. Berlin: De Gruyter, 1993.

Hamori, Esther J. *When Gods Were Men: The Embodied God in Biblical and Near Eastern Literature*. Berlin: Walter de Gruyter, 2008.

Hart, David Bentley. *You Are Gods*. South Bend: University of Notre Dame Press, 2022.

Hegel, G. W. F. *The Encyclopedia Logic*, trans. Klaus Brinkman and Daniel O. Dahlstrom. New York: Cambridge University Press, 2010.

Heidegger, Martin. *Mindfulness*, trans. Parvis Emad et al. New York: Bloomsbury Academic, 2016.

Heidegger, Martin. "On the Essence of Truth," in *Basic Writings*, ed. David Farrell Krell, 111–38. New York: Harper Perennial, 1993.

Heidegger, Martin. *On the Essence of the Truth: Plato's Parable of the Cave and the Theaetetus*. London: Continuum, 2009.

Heidegger, Martin. *Phenomenology of Religious Life*, trans. Matthias Fritsch and Jennifer Anna Gosetti-Ferencei. Indianapolis: Indiana University Press, 2010.

Heidegger, Martin. *Schelling's Treatise: On the Essence of Human Freedom*, trans. Joan Stambaugh. Athens: Ohio University Press, 1985.

Henry, Michel. *Barbarism*, trans. Scott Davidson. London: Continuum, 2012.

Husserl, Edmund. *Ideas I*, trans. F. Kersten. The Hague: Martinus Nijhoff, 1983.

Husserl, Edmund. *Logical Investigations*, vol. 1, trans. John Findlay. New York: Routledge, 2001.

Husserl, Edmund. *The Crisis of European Sciences and Transcendental Phenomenology*, trans. David Carr. Evanston: Northwestern University Press, 1970.

Irenaeus, St. *Libros quinquos adversus haereses*, IV, 20, 7, ed. W. Wigan Harvey. S. T. B. Cantabrigiae, 1857.

Jacobs-Vandegeer, Christiaan and Jean-Luc Marion (eds.). *The Enigma of Divine Revelation*. Cham, Switzerland: Springer Nature, 2020.

John of the Cross, St. *The Collected Works of Saint John of the Cross*, trans. Kieran Kavanaugh and Oscar Rodriguez. Washington, DC: Institute of Carmelite Studies, 1991.

Jones, Andrew Willard. *The Two Cities: A History of Christian Politics*. Steubenville: Emmaus Road, 2021.

Jüngel, Eberhard. "Metaphorical Truth," in *Theological Essays*, vol. 1. London: Bloomsbury, 2000.

Kant, Immanuel. *Anthropology from a Pragmatic Point of View*, trans. Victor Lyle Dowdell. Carbondale: Southern Illinois University Press, 1978.

Kant, Immanuel. *Prolegomena to Any Future Metaphysic*. New York: Cambridge University Press, 2004.

Kreeft, Peter. *Christianity for Modern Pagans*. San Francisco: Ignatius Press, 1993.

Lacoste, Jean-Yves. *Experience and the Absolute*, trans. Mark Raftery-Skehan. New York: Fordham University Press, 2004.

Lacoste, Jean-Yves. *From Theology to Theological Thinking*, trans. W. Chris Hackett. Charlottesville: University of Virginia Press, 2014.

Levinas, Emmanuel. "Meaning and Sense," in *Collected Philosophical Papers*, ed. Alphonso Lingis. Dordrecht, Netherlands: Martinus Nijhoff, 1987.

Levinas, Emmanuel. "Reality and Its Shadow," in *The Levinas Reader*. Oxford: Wiley Blackwell, 2001.

Lewis, C. S. "Transposition," in *'The Weight of Glory' and Other Essays*, 16–29. Grand Rapids: Eerdmans, 1949.
Mackinlay, Shane. *Interpreting Excess*. New York: Fordham, 2009.
Manoussakis, John. "Theophany and Indication: Reconciling Augustinian and Palamite Aesthetics," *Modern Theology* 26, no. 1 (2010): 76–89.
Marion, Jean-Luc. *Being Given*, trans. Jeffrey Kosky. Stanford: Stanford University Press, 2002.
Marion, Jean-Luc. *D'Ailleurs, La Revelation*. Paris: Grasseet, 2020.
Marion, Jean-Luc. *Negative Certainties*, trans. Stephen E. Lewis. Chicago: University of Chicago Press, 2015.
Marion, Jean-Luc. *The Erotic Phenomenon*, trans. Stephen E. Lewis. Chicago: University of Chicago Press, 2006.
Marion, Jean-Luc. "The Saturated Phenomenon," in *Phenomenology and the 'Theological Turn': The French Debate*, Dominique Janicaud et al. New York: Fordham, 2000.
Marty, Francois. *La connaissance de la métaphysique chez Kant: une étude sur la notion kantienne d'analogie*. Paris: Beauchesne, 1980.
McGuckin, John Anthony. *St. Cyril of Alexandria and the Christological Controversy*. Crestwood: St. Vladimir's Seminary Press, 2010.
McKinion, Steven. *Words, Imagery and the Mystery of Christ: A Reconstruction of Cyril of Alexandria's Christology*. Boston: Brill, 2000.
Merleau-Ponty. *The Visible and the Invisible*, trans. Claude Lefort et al. Evanston: Northwestern University Press, 1968.
Meunier, Bernard. *Le Christ de Cyrille d'Alexandrie: L'humanité, le salut et la question monophysite*. Paris: Beauchesne, 1997.
Morris, Thomas V. *The Logic of God Incarnate*. Ithaca: Cornell University Press, 1986.
Nancy, Jean-Luc. *Au fond des images*. Paris: Galilée, 2003.
Newman, John Henry. *Apologia pro vita sua*. New York: Dover, 2012.
Nichols, Aidan, OP. *Chalice of God: A Systematic Theology in Outline*. Collegeville: Liturgical Press, 2012.
Nietzsche, Friedrich. "On Truth and Lies in a Non-moral Sense," in *Basic Writings*, trans. Walter Kaufmann. New York: Modern Library, 2000.
Nietzsche, Friedrich. *Thus Spake Zarathustra*, trans. Thomas Common. New York: Random House, 1946.
Nietzsche, Friedrich. *Ueber Wahrheit und Lüge im aussermoralischen Sinne*, Digitale Kritische Gesamtausgabe. http://www.nietzschesource.org/eKGWB/WL/print.
Origen. *Contra Celsum*, ed. Henry Chadwick. New York: Cambridge University Press, 1953.
Percy, Walker. *Lost in the Cosmos: The Last Self-Help Book*. New York: Farrar, Straus and Giroux, 1983.
Pseudo-Dionysius the Areopagite. *The Complete Works*, trans. Colb Luibheid and Paul Rorem. Mahwah: Paulist Press, 1987.

Rahner, Karl. "Devotion to the Sacred Heart Today," in *Theological Investigations vol. 23: Final Writings*. New York: Darton, Longman and Todd, 1992.

Rahner, Karl. "Some Theses for a Theology of Devotion to the Sacred Heart," *Theological Investigations* 3 (1974): 321–30.

Rahner, Karl. "The Theological Meaning of the Veneration of the Sacred Heart," *Theological Investigations* 8 (1971): 217–28.

Ratzinger, Joseph. *Principles of Catholic Theology*. San Francisco: Ignatius Press, 2009.

Ratzinger, Joseph. *Truth and Tolerance*. San Francisco: Ignatius Press, 2004.

Ricoeur, Paul. *The Conflict of Interpretations: Essays in Hermeneutics*, ed. Dan Ihde. London: Continuum, 2000.

Rocca, Gregory. *Speaking the Incomprehensible God*. Washington, DC: Catholic University of America Press, 2002.

Russell, Norman. *Cyril of Alexandria*. London: Routledge, 2000.

Schelling, F. W. J. *Sämmtliche Werke*, Bd. 7, ed. K. F. A. Schelling. Stuttgart/Ausberg: J. G. Cotta, 1927.

Schleiermacher, Friedrich. *The Christian Faith*. London: T&T Clark, 2007.

Seaford, Richard. *The Origins of Philosophy in Ancient Greece and Ancient India*. New York: Cambridge University Press, 2020.

Soloviev, Vladimir. *The Heart of Reality: Essays on Beauty, Love, and Ethics*, ed. Vladimir Wozniuk, 75. South Bend: University of Notre Dame Press, 2003.

Soloviev, Vladimir. *The Justification of the Good*, trans. Boris Jakim. Grand Rapids: Eerdmans, 2005.

Spaemann, Robert. *Persons: The Difference between Someone and Something*, trans. Oliver O'Donovan. Oxford: Oxford University Press, 2017.

Tengyeli, Laszlo. *Neue Phänomenologie in Frankreich*. Berlin: Suhrkamp, 2012.

Tengyeli, Laszlo. "New Phenomenology in France," *The Southern Journal of Philosophy* 50, no. 2 (2012): 295–303.

Vetö, Miklos. *Explorations métaphysiques*. Paris: Harmattan, 2012.

Vetö, Miklos. *The Expansion of Metaphysics*, trans. William C. Hackett. Eugene: Wipf and Stock, 2018.

Vioulac, Jean. *Apocalypse de la vérité: Méditations heideggériennes*. Paris: Ad Solem, 2014.

Wahl, Jean. *Human Existence and Transcendence*, trans. William C. Hackett. South Bend: University of Notre Dame Press, 2016.

Weil, Simone. *La Connaissance Surnaturelle*. Paris: Gallimard, 1950.

Welch, Laurence. *Christology and Eucharist in the Early Thought of Cyril of Alexandria*. New York: International Scholars Press, 1993.

Wells, Adam. *Phenomenologies of Scripture*, ed. Adam Wells. New York: Fordham, 2017.

Westphal, Merold. *Suspicion and Faith: On the Religious Uses of Modern Atheism*. New York: Fordham University Press, 1999.

Whitehead, Alfred North. *Symbolism*. New York: Fordham University Press, 1985.

Williams, A. N. *The Divine Sense*. New York: Cambridge University Press, 2007.

Wolfson, Henry Austryn. *The Philosophy of the Church Fathers*, vol. 1, 3rd ed. Cambridge, MA: Harvard University Press, 1971.

Wolinski, Joseph. "Dieu," "II. Théologie patristique," in *Dictionnaire critique de théologie*, dir. Jean-Yves Lacoste, 3rd ed. Paris: Presses Universitaires de France, 2007.

Yannaras, Christos. *Elements of Faith: An Introduction to Orthodox Theology*, trans. Keith Schram. London: Continuum, 1991.

Index

Note: Page numbers followed by "n" refer to notes.

absolute 1–2, 42
  contingency 44
  freedom 18, 21
  idealism 178
  incomprehensibility of God 2
  incomprehensibility of humanity 2
  knowledge 23, 87–8
  pilgrim of the 2
  transcendence 27, 118, 125
  truth 22, 23, 25, 157, 179
absolutism of reality 77
abstraction 7, 46, 76, 78, 123, 158, 160, 181, 185, 186, 188, 201, 203, 205, 219, 227 n.4
  conceptual 27, 90, 102, 103, 119, 133
  epistemological 167
  formal 105
  intelligible 119
  rational 168
  reflective-interpretive 131
  speculative 135, 140
  spiritual procedure of 8
  theoretical 167
  way of 56, 62–3, 65, 66
agapē 93, 94
allegorēsis 141, 164, 168
allegorization 120, 124, 127, 128
"all unity" 48–9
amethektos metexetai 133
anachronism 79, 98, 179
anagogē (ἀναγωγή) 131
analogy
  of attribution 82
  of proportion 81, 82
analysis 87, 88
angelic modes of knowledge 29
angels and humans, distinction between 30–1
anthropic principle 29–51
anthropomorphism 8, viii, *see also individual entries*
  anthropic principle 29–51
  anthropocentric 78
  anthropocentrism-in-itself 79
  definition of 95, 146
  dogmatic 87
  foundational 155
  and modern thought 74–114
  naive 40
  poetic 26
  realism in 142–60
  of the second degree 156
  symbolic 80, 83, 87
  symbolical apophatics 117–141
"anthropomorphization" (*Vermenschlichung*) 94–5
anti-realism 150, 151, 154
apocalypsis (αποκάλυψις) 47, 48, 73, 129, 144–5, 157, 173, 223 n.2, 238 n.38
  apocalypsis tou Christou (ἀποκάλυψις τοῦ Χριστοῦ) 205
  apocalypsis tou mysteriou (revelation of the mystery) 3, 4
  apocalypsis tou theou (ἀποκάλυψις τοῦ θεοῦ) ("revelation of God") 157
apophasis 27–8, 50, 119, 121, 127, 129
  apophatic rationality 25
  symbolic 130, 141
apophatic theology 120
Aquinas, Thomas 24, 49, 64, 111, 112, 211, 215–16, 228 n.23
  on angels–humans distinction 30
  Commentary on the Sentences 81, 186
  conversio ad phantasmata 30, 33, 83, 188
  De Veritate 81
  on realism 150
  Summa Contra Gentiles 81
  Summa Theologiae 81
areoelastic fluttering 231 n.45

Index

Aristotle 66, 71, 107, 143
   on divinity 123
   epistēmē 45
   metaphor, definition of 100
   on "scientific" knowledge 146–7
ascetical apprenticeship viii
ascetical attitude viii
Athenian religiosity 62
Augustine, Saint 72, 119
   City of God 71, 185, 223 n.34, 232 n.8
   On the Trinity 174
Augustine of Hippo 66, vi, vii
   on fallenness 33–4
autonomy 23, 84, 94
   irrational 35
   relative 103
Avignon papacy 81

backtracking 9, 47, 78
Badiou, Alain 152
Balthasar, Hans Urs von 8
   essence (*ousia*)/energies (*energia*)
      distinction 16, 18
   The Glory of the Lord 179
   religious question 13–28
   Theo-Logic 134–5
   Theological Aesthetics 13–14
   Theo-Logic II 140–1
   on theophanic indication 15, 17–22,
      25, 29, 221 n.19
banality 3, 32
Barth, Karl 17, 57
Barthes, Roland 221 n.17
beatitude 3, 29, 30, 42, 44, 46, 71, 112,
   140, 186, 225–6 n.30
Begotteness 124
Being 46, 58, 153, 177, 178
Bergson, Henri 87–92, 188, 230 n.18
   critique of Kant 91
   on history of philosophy 87–8
Bernini
   "St Teresa in Ecstasy" 183
Blondel, M. 44
Bloy, Léon 1–7, 9
   on absolute 1–2
   on hyperbole 7
Boethius 43
Boulnois, M.-O. 172
Bouyer, L. 50, 186
Brague, Rémi 109

Braver, Lee 153
   A Thing of This World 150
Bulgakov, Sergius 1, 2, 75
Bultmann, Rudolph 6, 8, 163, 164, 176
   on speak of God 55–73

capable of the infinite (*finitum capax
      infiniti*) 41
Cassian, John 211–14
Catholicism 142
charity 93, 112, 216, 223 n.4
Christology, hypostatic union in 17
coactive knowing 93
Cohen, Daniel
   *Formes théologiques et symbolisme
      sacré* 120
coincidentia oppositorum 7
comprehension 225–6 n.30
comprehensor 42, 225–6 n.30
concepts 27, 88–92, 101–4, 118–19
Consolation 43
creatio 82
creaturehood 44, 177
critical self-consciousness 141
critique 34–6
   enactment of 34–5
   limitations of 35

Dante 9
Dasein 97, 98
death 18, 22
de la Cruzian, Juan 7
denouement 197
Descartes, Rene 147
dialectical reasoning 88, 110, 112
disconsolation 2, 5
divine
   divine-humanity 82, 97, 171
   essence 16, 17, 41, 121, 219, 225 n.29
   freedom 17
   intellectus 44
   intelligibility 27, 65
   possession 46
   presence 3, 15–16, 20–2, 25, 32, 50,
      71, 129, 212
   revelation 15, 18, 21, 41–3, 79, 109,
      120, 141, 144, 158, 168, 172
   self-possession 46, 47
   self-revelation 20
   self-seeing 46

speech 18, 65, 66, 123, 213, 221 n.19
transcendence 15, 27, 28, 80, 81, 104, 113, 122, 125, 128, 129, 176, 180, 186–7, 189
will 21, 30, 31
divine glory 2, 3, 5, 6, 8, 13, 17, 21, 25, 49, 121, 164, 173, 214
  anthropic mediation of 49
  self-revelation of 14
divinity
  divinity-as-seeing 46
  transgression of 75
division of labor 5
Docetism 103

Eastern Christianity
  theology of sacred images 16
Eliot, T. S. 9
emanatio 82
ennoia (ἔννοια), 119
ennoiai (ἔννοια) 131
Entgötterung (dedivinization) 97
epistemology 24, 32, 45–8, 79, 167, 170
  interpretation of revelation 45, 46
Ereignis (en-ownment) 97–8
eschatology 3, 4, 24, 29, 32, 35, 36, 38–42, 48–51, 55, 56, 68, 70–4, 77, 82, 84, 93, 99, 103, 105, 112, 119, 128, 133, 135, 140, 174, 185, 186, 211, 227 n.49, 232 n.8
  eschatological bliss 41
  "eschatologicity" of the Third 114
essence (*ousia*)/energies (*energia*) distinction 16, 18
eternity 3, 40, 41, 43, 49, 90
event 37
  phenomenality of the 41
expression (*Ausdrücke*) 14–15

faithfulness 48
fallenness 33–4
fatherhood 59
feeling 4–6, 17, 19, 88, 90, 91, 146, 218
  of disconsolation 2
fidelity 47, 48, 101, 102, 105, 154, 180, 187
finitude and infinitude, division between 42
Florensky, Pavel 1, 197–203
  Early Religious Writings: 1903– 1909 197–8

Foucault, Michel 79
freedom 2, 4, 34, 58–60, 78, 82, 83, 101, 153, 178, 179, 181, 187, 204
  absolute 18, 21, 23
  causal 44
  of contemplation 123
  divine 17
  human viii, 20, 23, 45, 94, 95, 98
  intellectual 103
  personal 31
  scientific 103
  sovereign 61, 185
  unconditional 24
free self-disclosure 109
free theurgy 48

Galileo 105, 147
Gelassenheit 99
geometry 199–200
German Idealism 179
Giulea, Dragos A.
  on Gregory Nazianzen 121
givenness 15, 37, 225 n.23, 225 n.24
  and appearing, distinction between 38
  divine 42
  language of 40
  and manifestation, distinction between 109
  phenomenological 41
gnōsis 93
greatness 4, 80, 132
Gregory of Nyssa 64–6, 72, 135
  critique of Eunomian rational 124

haecceitas 188
Hegel, G. W. F. 7, 178–9, 188
  on absolute idealism 178
  phenomenology of Spirit 92–3
  on transcendence 177
hegemonic rationality 154
Heidegger, Martin 37, 55, 94, 95, 99, 100, 105, 157, 158
  critique of anthropomorphism 100
  on fallenness 34
  Gestell 79
  on humanity 96
  Mindfulness 95, 97
  on mindfulness of enownment of Being 97–8
  on nihilism 157

on ontological difference   153, 181
on transcendence   180
Hellenism   122, 124, 127, 129
Henōsis (ἕνωσις)   129, 131, 165–7, 171
Herr-lichkeit ("Lordliness" or "Lordly glory")   22
Homer   78
"hominization" of beings   96
human-divinity   82
humanity   1, 4, 14, 17, 19, 25, 37, 48, 49, 58–60, 67, 72, 73, 75, 78, 84, 85, 93, 94, 104, 106, 111–13, 124, 129, 132, 143, 144, 147, 150–2, 154–7, 159, 165, 166, 172, 179, 186–9, 197, 198, 213
  absolute incomprehensibility of   2
  alienation of   5
  divine-humanity   82, 97, 171
  and divinity, union of   6
  epistemic capacity   80
  rational character of   227 n.4
  religious and cultural evolution of   47
  self-destructive mastery of   95
  topology of   99
  vice-regental   26
human speech   48, 61, 65, 69, 86, 125
huparchis (ὑπάρχις)   188
hupostasis (ὑπόστασις,)   188
Husserl, Edmund   17, 46, 71, 105, 180, 203
  on feeling   19
  Logical Investigations   14–15
  on transcendence   179–80
hyperbole   7–8, 24, 72
hyper-intelligible reality   33
hypostasis   16, 17, 74, 134, 213
Hypostatic Union   2

Iberian Scholasticism   37, 135
idolatry   36, 63, 101–3, 106, 148, 158–9, 212
  transcendental   79
images   89, 100, 102, 163–75
immortality   44, 46, 143
impossibility
  practical   41–2
  strict   41, 42
incarnation   1, 16, 32, 67, 77, 79, 112, 118, 125, 128, 131–4, 145, 164–8, 179, 184, 206, 213, 218, 219, 231 n.47, 237 n.25
indication (*Anzeichen*)   14–15
  sensory   23
  theophanic   15, 17–22, 25, 29, 221 n.19
infinite   124
injustice   3–5
intelligence   1, 4, 19, 67, 107, 170–3, 186, 197, 200
  angelic   119
  created   41, 42
  creative   118
  human   5, 80, 120, 164
  marginal   106
  morality of   80
  mythic   204
  narrative   48, 143, 203
  pure   30
  religious   vii
  theoretical   143, 145
  of things   97
intelligibility   vii, 19, 25–7, 34, 61, 62, 64, 65, 71, 83, 96, 105, 106, 108, 114, 120, 140, 148, 152–7, 159, 160, 164, 181, 182, 184, 189, 198, 204, 221 n.11
intuition   25–6, 78, 87–9, 110–12
  finite   42
  religious   26
Irenaeus, St.   93

jouissance   183
Judaism   108

kabod-Yahweh   14, 17, 21, 25
  theophanies of   16
Kant, Immanuel   1, 38, 62, 78–85, 100, 103, 109, 111, 112, 142, 158, 182
  on analogy   81
  Bergson's critique on   91
  critique of reason   83–4
  dogmatic *versus* symbolic anthropomorphism   87
  Lumèire   179
  on metaphysics   104, 105
  "noumenal" realm from philosophical inquiry   151
  Prologue to Any Future Metaphysic   80

on realism 150
on transcendental idealism 178
on transgressive realism 155
on truth 85
kenōsis (κένωσις) 39, 109, 165, 166, 168, 172
Kierkegaard, Soren 156, 178
    intellectual model 179
    on transgressive realism 152, 154
knowing-as-seeing (noēsis noēseōs) 46
knowing-awareness 97

Lacoste, Jean-Yves 30, 40–2, 68, 70, 99
    "De la donation comme promesse" 40
    on division between finitude and infinitude 42
    La phénoménalité de Dieu 40
Leitourgia (λειτουργία) 132
Levinas, Emmanuel 153, 154, 156
    "face," phenomenology of 17
Lewis, C. S.
    "Transposition" 182–5
light of glory (*lumen glorae*) 41
logos vom mythos 107, 108, 111
love 23

McGuckin, A. 166–7
manifestation
    and givenness, distinction between 109
    of God's absolute alterity 18
    of the *kabod* 18
    of the presence of God 18
    self-manifestation 16, 23, 39, 46
    sensory 14, 15, 17–19, 221 n.19
    of theophany 17
Manoussakis, John 14, 15, 221 n.14
Marion, Jean-Luc 30, 37, 38, 40, 44–6, 79, 179, 226 n.39
    D'Ailleurs, La Revelation 156
    on negative certitude 231 n.42
    on realism 153–6
Maritain, Jacques 2
Maritain, Raisa 2, 5–6
materiality 29, 33, 39, 77, 90, 104, 112, 114, 125, 134, 167, 185
mathematics 199–201
Maximus the Confessor

Ambigua 13
mediation 88, 101, 150, 213, 216s
    anthropic, of divine glory 49
    hierarchical 132
    immaterial 119
    incarnate 166
    of the light of glory (*lumen glorae*) 41
    of material body 33, 167
    self-mediation 26
    of sensible reality 16, 134
    spiritual 119
Merleau-Ponty, Maurice 15
metamorphosis 50, 86, 206, 217
    eschatological 72
meta-philosophy 107
metaphor 3, 5, 6, 24, 25, 48, 84–6, 98–101, 103–5, 108, 112, 127, 132, 140, 146, 160, 172, 185, 188, 213
    definition of 100
metaphoricity 87, 98–101, 103
metaphysics 4–6, 24, 27, 31–3, 37, 40, 45, 56, 84, 87–9, 94, 95, 97, 105, 123, 125, 145, 152, 155, 155, 179, 181, 188, 222 n.30, 230 n.19, 231 n.47, 235 n.12
    metaphysical banality 32
    metaphysical density 169
    metaphysical desire 112
    metaphysical intuition 92
    metaphysical knowledge 104
    metaphysical modernity 85
    metaphysical presupposition 91, 101, 147
    metaphysical skepticism 151
methexis 44
mindfulness 97–8
monotheism 46
moral responsibility 80
mystical theology 135
myth, definition of 204

Nancy, Jean-Luc
    Au fond des images 133–4
narratives 100, 107, 112
negative certitude 231 n.42
negative theology 6, 8, 64, 71, 124, 130, 132, 135, 142, 144, 159, 163, 186, 188, 184, 197, 205

Neoplatonic causality   24, 26, 82
Neoplatonic system   113
Neoplatonism   90
Newman, John Henry
    Apologia   43
Nicholas of Cusa   135
Nietzsche, Friedrich   84, 105, 149, 157, 159, 182
    Lebensverachtung   77, 79
    metaphysical modernity   85
    on transposition   182
    on truth   84–6
nihilism   1, 37, 157–9
noesis and *noema*, correlation
        between   180
Nous (Νοῦς)   125

onomatodoxy ("name-worshiping")   16, 221 n.11, 234 n.38
ontological difference   21, 153, 181
Origen   169
    Against Celsus   123

paganism   108, 219
paradoxical presence of the Third   113, 114
participatio   82
Patristic theology   127, 163
Pauline mysterion   32
Paul of Tarsus   217–19
Percy, Walker
    Lost in the Cosmos   17
perfect immediacy   22
personality   145, 152, 156, 159, 187
    marginalization of   158
phenomenology   46, 50, 55, 59, 60, 79, 150, 153, 154, 235 n.10, 237 n.22, 238–9 n.11
    of "face"   17
    of faith   167
    phenomenological apparatus   45
    phenomenological consciousness   180
    phenomenological desideratum   44
    phenomenological givenness   41
    phenomenological intelligibility   156, 157
    phenomenological intuition   222 n.25
    of revelation   29, 36–41
    of Spirit   93, 177

    of transcendence   176, 180–2, 225 n.24
    of transgression   155
Philo of Alexandria   128
philosophy, as human endeavor   187–9
pistis   48
Plato   46, 47, 63, 94–5, 108, 143
    On the Essence of the Truth   94
Platonism   186
Plotinus   46, 99, 143, 169
Porphyry
    Against the Christians   124
post-structuralism   150, 151
presence-as-absence   62
presence-as-presence-as-absence   62
Presocratics   32
presupposition   152
    metaphysical   91, 101, 147
    theological   55
    undialogical   19
primal phenomenon of potency   16, 17
Proclus   186
    allegorical manner of approach   120
    Commentary on the Parmenide   63
Protagaras
    epistemological subjectivism   79
prothesis   48
Pseudo-Dionysius the Areopagite   6, 7, 9, 78, 89, 105, 106, 108, 113, 142, 144, 186
    The Ecclesiastical Hierarchies   67, 186
    The Mystical Theology   130
    negative theology   163
    symbolical apophatics   117–41
pure objectivity   22
pure subjectivity   22
purification   6, 24, 27, 111, 112, 120, 123, 127, 130, 189, 200

radical democratization   113
radical hierarchization   113
Rahner, Karl
    The Trinity?   29
Rancière, Jacques   27
rationalism   224 n.11
rationality   9, 37, 64, 65, 79, 86, 103, 111, 152, 163, 164, 170, 172, 200, 203, 224 n.11
    abstractive   204

apophatic 25
conceptual 61, 153, 197
Greek 25
hegemonic 154
human 84, 96, 156, 168, 234 n.39
hyperbolic 25
intrinsic 124
of revelation 38
rational worship 173
realism 142–60
    anti-realism 150, 151, 154
    speculative 151
    transgressive 151–7
reason 154
    human 37, 58, 79, 80, 84, 96, 104, 107, 109, 110, 111, 144, 153, 155, 156, 158, 168, 171
recollection 178
redemption 75, 167, 174
reification 90
relative autonomy 103
religious fidelity 47
religious question 13–28
representedness 97
ressourcement 44
resurrection 3, 30, 31, 39, 40, 50, 71, 72, 77, 102, 103, 112, 120, 128, 133, 140, 165, 175, 185, 198, 217–19
revelation
    divine 15, 18, 21, 41–3, 79, 109, 120, 141, 144, 158, 168, 172
    epistemological interpretation of 45, 46
    of the holiness of God 21
    as incarnate thought 112
    paradoxical structure of 21–2
    phenomenology of 29, 36–40
    revelation of the mystery (*apocalypsis tou mysteriou*) 3, 4
    self-revelation 14, 20, 23, 178
    supernatural 84
    of theophanic indication 22
    "total phenomenon" of 18
    transcendental accounts of 40
ritual vii, 26, 32, 47, 68, 70, 75, 77, 91, 92, 131, 200, 201

sacra doctrina 64
sacred images, theology of 16

sacrifice 7, 14, 26, 49, 127, 135, 162–8, 171–3
St. Bernard Clairvaux 22–3
St. Cyril of Alexandria 6, 8
    Commentary on Isaiah 171
    Commentary on the Gospel of John 164
    image in Christology, priority of 163–75
    On the Unity of Christ 169
St. John of the Cross 7, 59, 71, 109, 111, 112
    The Living Flame of Love 71
Schelling, F. W. J. 95, 145, 177–9, 202
    On the Essence of Human Freedom 94
Schleiermacher, Friedrich 2
Schweitzer, Albert
    Quest for the Historical Jesus 156
"scientific" knowledge (*epistêmê*) 146–7
"scientific validity" about God 58
Scotus, Duns 30, 31
secularism 223–4 n.7
self 23–4
    self-destruction 199
    self-diminution 109
    self-disclosure 21, 109
    self-eclipse 71
    self-emptying 109, 164, 172
    self-excessivity 25
    self-experience 60, 183
    self-expression 135
    self-giving 49, 50, 109
    self-manifestation 16, 23, 39, 46
    self-mediation 26
    self-presencing 29, 55, 134, 204
    self-preservation 85
    self-referring 65
    self-sufficiency 84, 103, 128
    self-transcendence 25, 114
    self-transgression 25
    self-transparency 147
semitic-symbolic apophaticism 122
sensory manifestation 14, 15, 17–19, 221 n.19
serenity 62, 95, 99
sign 70, 197–206, *see also* symbols
    unity-in-difference of 56–7
sin 44
Socrates 148

Soloviev
  "The Universal Meaning of Art"   206
sonship   59
sophianicity   75
Spaemann, Robert   178
speculative realism   151
speech "about" God   55–73
Suarez, Francisco   84
  Metaphysical Disputations   147
suffering   3, 94, 169, 170
super-goodness   106
symbols   26–7, 32, 69–70, 83, 88, 92, 100, 102, 112, 118–20, 198, vii, *see also* sign
  definition of   201
  of morality   111
  symbolical apophatics   117–41
  symbolic anthropomorphism   80, 83, 87
  symbolic apophasis   27–8

tautology   149
thanksgiving (*eucharistia*)   68, 69, 75, 165
theological aesthetics   14
theological turn   235 n.10, 238–9 n.11
theophany   16–20, 22, 26, 122, 171
  divine   129
  sensory   15, 16
  theophanic indication   15, 17–22, 25, 29, 221 n.19
transcendence   7–9, 34, 51, 72, 111, 125, 176–89, 224 n.9
  absolute   27, 118, 125
  of death   46
  divine   15, 27, 28, 80, 81, 104, 113, 122, 125, 128, 129, 176, 180, 186–7, 189
  irreducibility of   176–82
  personal   24
  phenomenology of   176, 180–2, 224 n.24
  self-transcendence   25
transcendental idealism   178
transcendental idolatry   79
transcendentalism   38, 84, 151
transdescendence   224 n.9
transgression   26, 45, 159, 170, 179, 181, 199

  of divinity   75
  self-transgression   25
  transgressive realism   151–2
"transposition" (*epiphora*)   99, 182–6
Trinity   23, 49, 64, 68, 69, 169, 227 n.50
Triune Nature   2
truth   84–6
  absolute   22, 23, 25, 157, 179
  anthropomorphization of   94–5
  as apocalyptic disclosive manifestation   46
  definition of   86
  as noetic   46

unanticipatability   176
Unbegotteness   124
un-concealing (*a-letheia*)   95
uniqueness of things, principle of   105
"Unknown God"   62, 65, 66

Vergötterung (divinization)   97
"Vermenschung" of being   96–7
Vetö, Miklos   179
viator   42
Vioulac, Jean
  Apocalypse de la verité   156
vision   112

Wahl, Jean   224 n.9
  Existence humaine et transcendance   181
  Traité de métaphysique   181
  on transcendence   181
way of abstraction   56, 62–3, 65, 66
"way of excess"   186
Weil, Simone
  La Connaissance Surnaturelle   145–6, 160
Welch, L.   165
William of Ockham
  political and economic controversy   81
Wirkungsgeschichte   35

Xenophanes   26

Yannaras, Christos   105
  Elements of Faith   viii

www.ingramcontent.com/pod-product-compliance
Lightning Source LLC
Chambersburg PA
CBHW071819300426
44116CB00009B/1373